Re-imagining Government

Re-imagining Government

Public Leadership and Management in Challenging Times

Barry Quirk

palgrave
macmillan

First published 2011 by
PALGRAVE MACMILLAN

Palgrave Macmillan in the UK is an imprint of Macmillan Publishers Limited, registered in England, company number 785998, of Houndmills, Basingstoke, Hampshire RG21 6XS

Palgrave Macmillan in the US is a division of St Martin's Press LLC, 175 Fifth Avenue, New York, NY 10010.

Palgrave Macmillan is the global academic imprint of the above companies and has companies and representatives throughout the world.

Palgrave® and Macmillan® are registered trademarks in the United States, the United Kingdom, Europe and other countries.

ISBN–13: 978–0–230–31441–2 hardback
ISBN–13: 978–0–230–31442–9 paperback

This book is printed on paper suitable for recycling and made from fully managed and sustained forest sources. Logging, pulping and manufacturing processes are expected to conform to the environmental regulations of the country of origin.

A catalogue record for this book is available from the British Library.

A catalog record for this book is available from the Library of Congress.

10 9 8 7 6 5 4 3 2 1
20 19 18 17 16 15 14 13 12 11

Printed and bound in Great Britain by
CPI Antony Rowe, Chippenham and Eastbourne

Contents

List of Figures

Preface

The book is intended for anyone who is curious about the workings of government and the public realm of government action. It should be useful for enquiring citizens who are baffled about the opacity of government; for elected politicians who have to navigate the labyrinths of formal power; and for those who work in and for the public sector; as well as for students of politics, public policy and public management. Through rich stories and even richer ideas I aim to provide useful insights into how government and public services can be improved.

If democratic governments fail or if they provide poor and ineffectual public services, the long-term impact on society is great. The impact is on taxpayers, on those who need and use public services and on the wider community of citizens. More narrowly, it matters keenly to those working in and for government.

My personal fascination with government and public services started when, as a community activist in the 1970s, I became deeply involved in environmental issues and in social housing movements. From there I got myself elected into local government and I spent an intense four years grappling with the niceties (and the not so niceties) of urban politics. After this experience and after establishing a mission-driven social enterprise, I became a salaried public servant and for the past 17 years I have been a chief executive in local government in London. In addition to my practical experience in London, I have had the privilege of holding a number of key roles in the UK's public service including being a national efficiency champion to the government; spending four years as a non-executive director on the board of HM Revenue and Customs; and leading for UK local government on a range of policy and management issues.

As a Londoner, I am blessed with living and working in one of the most brilliant cities in the world. Its heritage is awesome and the scale of its future opportunities is vast given that its global connections are unmatched by other cities. But its community needs are pressing and they combine with a complex but fertile capital city politics. In a sense, London is my personal laboratory but for this book I have also drawn upon a very wide range of experiments from across the globe. This is largely because my managerial pursuit of excellence has led me to seek out best international experience – across Europe, in the US, in Australia and elsewhere.

To this end, I have researched far and wide for evidence of what works best. I have focused on what forms of government are the most effective; what styles of politics really connect with citizens; what sorts of strategies are the most cost-effective; and what types of management action deliver best public value. My own learning came less from reading than it did from visiting places and studying governments and their public agencies. I firmly believe that first order learning is best acquired through the soles of your feet and through personal experience. Second order learning occurs when you try to make sense of the patterns you discover through the application of theory and insight.

This book is not a dry account of the effectiveness of public institutions. Neither is it a juicy jaunt through the comings and goings of a group of powerful politicians. In very many liberal democracies, governments face serious questions about the scale and the scope of the state. Their taxpayers and the users of public services wrestle over the rights and responsibilities they respectively have as citizens in the same state. These fundamental questions require serious enquiry and substantial answers. This book is an attempt to get beneath the veneer of 'the public' and answer deeper questions than 'how does public agency A compare to public agency B?' or 'how do a small group of people attain political power and keep it for as long as is feasible?' These are important and interesting questions but I am not addressing them here.

Practical public problems dominate the real world in which all governments operate. And these problems become more complex as societies change and develop. My argument is that if we are to solve these problems in ways that meet the incredible demands of the 21st century, we need to re-examine the foundations of democratic principles and democratic practices. It is no good just being practical and approaching each new problem afresh. We need to rework the theories, ideas and concepts that first energized democratic approaches so that we can begin to re-imagine government itself.

Most books contain one powerful idea, which the author illustrates and expands over a few hundred pages. By contrast, this book is about very many ideas and how together they can help us approach practical public problems and assist us to re-imagine the fundamental purposes of democratic government. After setting out the framework for democratic governments in the world today, in the following chapters I selectively explore the art of politics and public policy as well as the craft of public management. In this way my aim is to tease out the moral, political, and managerial issues involved in improving the overall quality of life within a community or across a nation.

The book deals with the question of how democracies determine the 'public interest', how they build 'public value', and how they respond to the demands of 'public reason'. It also deals in some depth with how public decisions are made, as well as with how common cause is discovered and developed in communities. The way in which different places and different geographies impact upon government is also examined, as is the challenge to governments in reducing risks and hazards, and finally, in reducing the overall cost of government itself.

These knotty issues and complex problems have intensely occupied me for over thirty years. And I suspect they will continue to challenge public policymakers for decades to come. Throughout this book I draw upon my experience as a practitioner to give colour and life to the foreground of these problems, but I draw as much upon theories and ideas to give depth and relief to the background to these problems. Books that are analytical break things down into their constituent parts. My aim instead is to integrate, to synthesize, and to draw strands together. To make modern a quote from the 16th-century essayist Michel de Montaigne, in this book I have collected a bouquet of other people's flowers, only the ribbon that ties them is my own.

In the meandering journey I have made to collect the information and compile the insights for this book, I have been greatly assisted by very many people. In particular I have learnt so much more from my colleagues in Lewisham in south London. These include Sir Steve Bullock, an exemplar local urban mayor for the modern age. And while I draw upon my experience in Lewisham and London, I have written this book entirely in a personal capacity.

It was John Nalbandian of Kansas University who first prompted me to consider writing a book. While Gerry Stoker, of Southampton University; Geoff Mulgan; and the patient and careful coaxing of my publisher, Steven Kennedy, each gave me encouragement to complete the journey. In addition, I have greatly benefited from a challenging but marvellously supportive community of management peers. These include Derek Myers, Geoff Alltimes, Rob Whiteman, John O'Brien, Mike Bennett, John Nicholson and John Foster. Each of these colleagues made me feel that my private musings merited public airing. Their promptings mean that my four children, Verity, Linus, Zach and Elliot, at last have a chance of perusing, or shelving, their father's peculiar preoccupations about public service and public policy. None of these urgings would have led me to complete this book were it not for Katherine Kerswell. Her inspiration is the reason why I felt capable of writing this book; her tolerance is the reason why I have been able to finish it.

London, February 2011

Chapter 1

Introduction

Liberal democratic governments are exploding from within. The demands of taxpayers for a lower cost state, the desires of service users for more relevant and reliable public services, and the designs of citizens for a more dynamically responsive and accountable politics have democratic government bursting at the seams.

The challenges that face liberal democratic governments over the next two decades are fiscal, political and social. The fiscal constraints on these governments, following the 2008 Crash and its widespread impact on public revenues, arise not just from the scale of their debts but also from the substantial structural deficits that infect their national accounts. For when a good deal of current spending is financed from borrowing, it is not surprising that countries as diverse as the US, Japan, Britain, France, Spain, Germany, Italy and the Netherlands were each considering large-scale deficit reduction measures, once they judged that their fiscal stimulus policies achieved their aims.

The internal political pressures on these governments stem from public and media demands for ever greater transparency and accountability. These demands for transparency themselves arise from what appears to be a corroding confidence in public ethics and government decision-making. At its heart is a cynical suspicion about the motives of those who stand for election and those who occupy public leadership roles. The social challenges to these governments include the impact of an ageing population, a growing concern about the failure to achieve fair outcomes across societies, and the increasing connectedness of all societies through web-enabled social networks. Together these challenges are testing liberal democratic governments to their limits.

Nonetheless, it remains the case that democracy is the most peaceful way for large groups of people to settle their arguments and make decisions in the overall public interest. But democracy works best when power centres are plural; when political institutions, including political parties, are relevant and resilient; when tolerance of ethnic and religious differences combines with political cultures that encourage freedom of

1

2 *Re-imagining Government*

expression and assembly; and when growing numbers of citizens demand as much from their government as they do from their markets. These conditions are broadly present in much of Europe, in North America and in Australasia as well as in a dozen or so other nations. But most of what counts as democracy, even in these nations, falls far short of these ideals.

At the beginning of the 21st century, the demands of democratic discussion are intensifying, at the same time that the character of public dialogue seems to be coarsening. When adversarial politics combines with cynical polemics it reduces the quality of public debate. And when a critically enquiring media move into more aggressive forms of journalism that seek to cast political practice in the worst possible light, the workings of democratic governments seem tawdry.[1] And yet those who live in the most liberal democracies in the world rightly cherish the open nature of their governments. They enjoy the personal freedom and material benefits that their open democracies afford them. And from this relatively prosperous and open vantage point, they often look askance at nations with weaker democratic traditions. For in these nations their people appear to live their lives within the tighter confines of tradition and custom.

As a result, those living in liberal democracies often critique the poor opportunities for self-expression that these other nations afford their citizens. And in the most extreme cases these criticisms can lead to public sentiment to 'intervene' – either to offer support to emerging democratic threads within a nation or, in extremis, to invade and overthrow 'tyrants'. But liberal democratic governments need to act with caution and care. The developed West needs to reflect with more humility about the historically thin nature of its own models of democracy. For in the so-called homes of liberal democracy, universal suffrage is in reality only three generations deep. In Britain, a nation that often lays claim to its four hundred years of parliamentary experience, it is rarely mentioned that before the 1832 Reform Act fewer than one in fifty adults were allowed to vote; and that women have only been entitled to vote for the past 80 years. And Britain's democracy is fairly thick – many liberal democracies have even thinner veneers of democratic practice.

The changing kaleidoscope of democracies

The world's nations comprise very many different types of democratic forms. Each form changes because of the pressures upon each nation, but each change also has an impact on other nations – its neighbours, its allies and its opponents. In this way the kaleidoscope of the world's democracies changes in an interactive and dynamic fashion. The largest nations in the world are themselves an odd mixture, reflecting their particular historical paths. China's gradualist approach to political openness follows on from its economic modernization at a painfully slow pace. India's once secular and tolerant mass democracy appears to have declined into a slightly dangerous form of competitive populism. And Russia's headlong race into democracy in the 1990s, in the absence of established political institutions and the rise of economic banditry, risks slipping one of Europe's most important nations into a form of elective autocracy.[2]

But more generally, liberal democracies have been successful – being internally competitive and being open to change has enabled their economies to grow and their peoples to flourish.[3] Thus by the end of the 20th century over 80 nations could claim to have some form of democratic government. However, very many of these governments are not as effective as they should be. Some are too strong (exercising power without much legitimacy and accountability – let's say, illiberally) and others are simply too weak – unable to engage their citizens in any meaningful way in the challenges that their nations face. But powerful economic, social and technological forces threaten to shake the very foundations of these democratic governments. Their purposes may have been first imagined over two thousand years ago but they need to be revised, reviewed and refashioned if they are to be relevant for the 21st century.

An appreciation of these first imaginings is critical to any understanding of the challenges to today's democracies. It was the Ancient Greeks who first introduced the notion of people's assemblies – where a community could govern itself. From that time the word 'democracy' became used as a descriptive term for this pioneering regime of self-government. As a result, Athens is said to be the cradle of democracy. However, the Romans introduced a set of ideas that were just as powerful in shaping first order approaches to government. For it was the Romans who realized that those who govern should have limits to their powers. It was the Romans who claimed their Republic to be a 'public possession' (*res publica*). And it was the Romans who devised the concept of the rule of law. Together these ideas, of self-government through elected representation and equality before the law, are the foundations of democratic government. But for over two thousand years the word 'democracy' remained as a narrow descriptive noun designating a system of rule.

It took until the great period of reform and revolution in the late 18th century for the word democracy to be used as a term of agency (a *democrat*), then as an adjective (*democratic*), and finally as a verb (to *democ-*

ratize).⁴ The idea of democracy as a way to govern did not really feature until the late 18th century. Before that point, 'liberty' had been the key political idea. For the central political concern, across the globe, had been with how people could free themselves from the exercise of arbitrary authority of their kings, emperors or religious leaders. Despite the varied traditions and customs across the globe, most people were expected to display fealty and loyalty to their king, their prince, their local overlord and/or their religion.

In England, this was given shape and structure in the Civil War in the mid-17th century when Royalists insisted that the power of the King was a God-given possession, while the Parliamentarian Henry Parker argued to the contrary that the people were 'the fountain and the efficient cause' of secular power.⁵ This powerful idea, that free people combine together to create a sovereign state that is then able to enact their collective will, flowered in England in the mid-17th century and blossomed in the US and in France over a century later. The struggle for liberty of speech, of assembly, of action as well as of belief preceded the struggle for democracy by several hundred years. And in fact it took until the late 20th century for the twin ideas of liberty and democracy to find genuine and sustained confluence in the West.

However, the key features of modern democratic government were honed in the late 18th century across Europe and in the United States of America. The design of government, the mechanics of its operation and the principle features of public institutions were forged during this amazingly fertile period. In so doing, the very idea of 'democracy' was converted from a flat description of a regime form to a forcefully dynamic political movement. This is why all democratic governments need to return to the powerful constitutional ideas developed by these late 18th-century reformers and revolutionaries. The core principles of elected representative government developed then have strong echoes in today's world. That said, there are limits to the lessons that can be drawn. These reformers and revolutionaries reshaped their governments in very different circumstances from those we face in the 21st century. Their late 18th-century societies were so much smaller in scale, their social fabric was simpler and less socially diverse, and the pace of change they experienced was far slower than that which pervades the globe now.

At the beginning of the 21st century, those liberal democratic governments that are deep in deficit reduction plans are grappling with the very purposes of government itself. They may be scaling back government activities, but they are also reviewing the very purpose of such activities – their effectiveness as well as their efficiency. How can present day democratic government be more relevant and useful? How can the cost of government be lowered? These simple questions dominate current concerns about government, politics, and the role and scale of public spending in Western liberal democracies. In very many instances citizens can't quite believe the cumbersome character of their governments and the scale of the public services they orchestrate. As consumers, they have learnt how to get what they can afford. But as citizens, they struggle to make sense of the differing layers of their governments – be they at local, city-wide, regional, state, federal or national level.

In Western liberal democracies citizens tend to view the private realm as the arena for accomplishment. By contrast, the public realm seems somewhat devoid of achievement. What's more, as potential users of public services, citizens harbour serious doubts as to the ability of many public organizations to deliver timely, reliable and quality services. Added to which their governments are depicted, through a media-soaked environment, as little more than a theatrical drama in which the citizen's role is as passive spectator to the comings and goings of those whom they periodically elect. Against this backcloth it is not a surprise that citizen interest in government is energized as much by a sense of outrage over reported instances of incompetence, corruption, abuse of power and lack of accountability, as by a positive spirit of engagement for the common good.

We might conclude that together these factors ought to dampen citizens' enthusiasm for democratic engagement and finding common cause. And we would not be wrong. Indeed there are many accounts of deep disaffection with democracy and disenchantment with democratic institutions. And these are not confined to the strongly libertarian (almost anti-governmental) political movements across the US. They include grass-roots 'taxpayer' style movements that seek to limit the scope and scale of government through tax limitation strategies; and they also include more academic accounts of declining public sentiment and rising disaffection with government. These latter polls tend to focus on the corroding confidence in government and the declining levels of trust in elected politicians and appointed public officials.[6] However, the real picture of citizens' attitudes towards their governments is more complex and textured than it appears from opinion poll headlines. The trust that citizens place in their government depends upon the quality, cost-effectiveness and reliability of public services; the extent of popular influence on government; and the extent to which they believe the politicians they elect and the public institutions that serve them act in a trustworthy manner.

But before we get overly pessimistic, it is worth remembering that people have not completely withdrawn from public life; nor have they wholly abandoned the public realm in the communities in which they live. All local communities have hundreds of active people engaged in common or public pursuits enlivening and energizing the life of their localities. And in all countries, people want to have some degree of involvement in those public issues that directly affect their lives. Are their public utilities (water, energy, roads and public transport) cost-effective? Are the streets in which they live clean and safe? Do their local schools educate their children well? Do their local health services prevent ill health? Do local agencies give sufficient care and dignity to vulnerable elderly people? And do their police forces prevent crime and catch enough criminals? In this way we can see that public issues are critical to both the quality of citizens' lives and the quality of their life-chances. But citizen involvement in public issues or public services does not of itself generate trust in government.[7] More tellingly, citizens want to be assured that those who govern (and those who advise them) are free from corruption and act reasonably selflessly with the power and resources at their disposal.

In the West, we regularly hear that corrupt and fraudulent practice holds back many governments in developing nations and undermines their progress towards a more open and liberal democracy. But concern about corruption is not restricted to developing nations. In a public opinion survey about the behaviours considered 'extremely important for public office holders' in the UK, 61 per cent of respondents said that it was important that public office holders were competent at doing their job. However, the following factors scored higher among respondents: not taking bribes (85 per cent); telling the truth (76 per cent); making sure that public money is used wisely (74 per cent); not using their power for their own gain (73 per cent); and being dedicated to doing a good job for the public (66 per cent). In short, citizens want to be assured that people in power do not abuse the authority that election to office affords them more than they want to be assured that they are competently doing the right things.[8]

But this mistrust of public office holders and disaffection with democratic government exist in parallel with a desire by very many citizens to find new and accessible avenues to connect with their governments and with the public services they provide. For just as people want to have an influence on public issues that affect their lives, they also want to engage in fulfilling social movements that have the potential to enrich their lives. For despite the widespread scepticism in which citizens hold their governments, they also suspect that the biggest of society's problems can only be solved through democratic discussion and some form of collective choice.

The origins and changing nature of public leadership

Many of the public problems that governments set out to solve have roots in economic and social causes that occur within their boundaries. But government is not just about resolving internally generated domestic problems. It is also about delineating the difference between 'them' and 'us' – between communities and between nation states. For government powers civic and national identity as much as it resolves internal disputes. And a sense of fealty to nation is most usually developed through the collective act of protecting territory or, in extremis, of waging war against others. Throughout history, those states that could raise the most revenues and conscript the biggest armies could most usually wage the more effective wars. And those who fought wars more effectively tended to survive the longest. Thus across the generations, just as war has provided the starting point for very many states, so war has been the origin of much of public leadership: leadership that launched wars or leadership that prevented wars.

That is why long before economic policy and social policy became the dominant tools of the state, governments were engaged in geopolitical policy. They had to deal with the politics of disputed territories through the threat of 'hard power' or the craft of diplomacy. In this way, military strategy preceded other forms of government strategy by several hundred years. Thus, long before administrative competence and media management were tools of the trade of effective public leaders, military leadership skills were a founding stone for public leadership.[9] Hence the first lessons of leadership stem from military experience at war and from the competing claims on the battlefield of strategic planning and strategic insight.[10]

These battlefield lessons of planning and preparedness, of resilience and agility, and of marshalling resources and summoning motivation have strong applicability in respect of the leadership of schools, of hospitals, of police commands and of political parties. And they apply with equal force to the leadership of larger public agencies, of cities and of government more generally. One general lesson has been learnt – the overall quality of political, professional and managerial leadership is central to the success of government at all levels. Leadership matters.

those who seek elected public office do so for many diverse reasons and motives. In theory they bring their convictions and their reason to bear on current public problems. In practice they are fuelled by an array of personal motives and ambitions. They profess to want to govern so as to make their nation or their community a better place in which to live. But often the ambitions they have for themselves are those they wish to project more widely. And those who seek appointment to public office do so for as equally diverse a set of reasons and motives. They may be dispassionate policy analysts who seek to be close to those in power so that they can advise them; or they may be passionate managerial leaders who seek to effect organizational change in the public sector. They may have found a personal vocation in the confines of a profession or a policy domain; or they may more simply be public employees carving out a career in the intricate labyrinths of the state. For those working in government, what is usually termed a 'life of public service' is in practice the conduct of elected public leadership, the vocation of a public profession or the craft of public management.

Politicians, their advisors and the managers they employ to deliver public services spend a lot of time trying to develop new approaches to solving public problems. But most public problems are knotty and stubborn. They are not easily solved by the adoption of a new smart policy or by more focused efforts on the part of public professionals. Many public problems have persisted for generations – and they often come in the shape of dilemmas, predicaments, quandaries and puzzles. And as such, the adverse unintended consequences of any proposed solution may well outweigh its positive intended consequences. Indeed, action by government, by the state, may be the very thing that triggers further problems.

Instead, real solutions to public problems may be best found among the people who share the problem rather than from those working for government. In recognition of this truth many of the most effective public leaders today (whether they are elected or appointed) are those that avoid traditional 'programmes' and instead act as social innovators and civic entrepreneurs working alongside citizens. These public officials are not simply harnessing tax revenues and user fees for better effect to solve problems from without; they are also trying to mobilize the resources that are already within the community, igniting community spirit and stimulating social action to help solve these public problems from within.[11]

At their most effective, public leaders set the goals to be achieved; they set managerial accountabilities in place; they marshal the resources available to them; they choose the right functional and operating strategies; and they attempt to inspire and motivate their people to do of their best. Effective public leaders know also that the way in which public service agencies are organized has a significant bearing on their effectiveness and their efficiency. For while committed people can make poorly organized systems work moderately well, they will work better if they are well organized. But being 'organized' does not imply adopting tight systems of 'command and control'. Organization is not the same as rule-based bureaucratic hierarchy. This is because in the social reality within which public agencies operate in the 21st century, power is diffuse, knowledge is dispersed and sources of innovation are diverse. New approaches to disclosure and transparency are needed alongside new systems of managerial coordination, if the rising demands of public accountability are to be met. And while public agencies need to adopt new styles of organizing to achieve better results, so too must their governments. They will need to exercise strategic control over public agencies but this will occur as much through cultural means and cues as through classic command and inspectoral oversight.[12] In this way the requirements of public leadership have moved from its origins in the landscape of military conflict to the softer landscape of shaping cultural objectives for communities and for the public institutions that serve them.

Digital era governance

The ubiquity of information and communication technologies will also contribute significantly to the success or failure of democratic government in this century. These technologies will influence the character of government, public organizations and public services as much as they impact upon the character of private sector service delivery. And they will produce new pressures and demands on the exercise of public leadership. In a sense, we are at the beginning of a new form of 'digital era governance' where a good deal of the practice of politics and the change and innovation in public services stems from how technology is used to deliver service to the public. The explosion of connectedness between people across the globe flows directly from web-enabled technologies and it accelerates political connectedness and changes to social networks.[13]

Active, critical citizens will not be blocked by government inertia, they will use web-enabled tools to find routes around the blocks and identify the information they need, and use it as they see fit. And by combining and recombining ideas and information, web-enabled service users will imagine new public services and set up new ways to begin to deliver them themselves. But technology enables more than service – it is a tool of enquiry and transparency. In 2010, the website WikiLeaks revealed huge numbers of hitherto confidential documents on the US approach to the wars in Iraq and Afghanistan and its overall diplomatic effort. Enforced disclosure of official secrets altered the climate of diplomatic effort – what once were private musings became very public knowledge.

Taken together these digital era changes will alter the very nature of how public work is organized. But this has contrary consequences. At all levels, governments not only have large databases about their citizens and the services they use, they also have powerful software tools to mine these databases. This means that across public organizations, the strength of computerized networks enables tighter and more centralized monitoring and control of organizational activity – producing a centralizing effect. And it also means that the distributed nature of data and the cheap availability of software tools empower the front-line professionals that are employed to serve the public – producing a countervailing network effect.[14]

The dominant design template for governing, erected in the imagination of the reformers and revolutionaries of the late 18th century, was developed in the shadow of revolutionary wars. These templates are now about nine generations old. It is time for them to be re-imagined. The principles they set out yesterday still have value and import today but they need reworking if they are to serve tomorrow's needs. The challenges to government have grown with the increasing scale and complexity of modern societies, with the accelerating pace of change of modern life and with the interconnected character of the global economy. Following the global recession of 2008, very many democratic governments are pursuing substantial deficit reduction strategies to lower the overall cost of welfare benefits and lower the cost of public service delivery. These aggressive adjustments in government spending are intended to limit the exposure of their economies to further shocks and disruption.

In this context it has become an urgent task to re-imagine the purposes of government and renew the nature of government for the 21st century. But we are not starting afresh. We simply need to re-imagine government in the new circumstances in which we find ourselves – examining the relevance and salience of yesterday's principles for governing so that we can renew approaches to delivering better public value to tomorrow's citizens.

The nature of this book

In modern democracies, governing well requires an open, healthy and challenging political culture; it requires effective policies and strategies that are directed to solve people's social problems; and it requires efficient approaches to designing and delivering public services. The fabric of effective government is made by weaving together the threads of good politics, good policy and good management. However, politics, policy and management draw on three different traditions of enquiry and use three different ways of thinking and operating. Politicians use the world of semantics – they craft meaning with words (usually spoken). Policy advisors use the world of schematics – they design strategies and draw diagrams to represent how reality can be changed. By contrast, managers use the real world of practice – they deliver results through people and organizations. To be successful, all governments and public agencies need to blend these three traditions together. But they do so by recognizing the distinctive capabilities that politicians, policy advisors and managers bring to the art of good governance. One cannot substitute for the other. Success in one domain is no guarantee of success in the other. To borrow a metaphor from Jerome Kagan, successful politicians, policy analysts and managers are like tigers, hawks and sharks. Each may be incredibly potent in their own territory but impotent in the territory of the other.[15]

Perhaps this is why most books on government stem from one or other tradition. Open a book on government and it can be one of three things. It can be a book about politics – either a technical account of the politics of governing or a canvass of the dark arts of politics and the shifting fortunes of the dramatis personae of the unfolding national political scene.[16] It can be a book about public policy – either about how decisions can be reframed so as to optimize the public good or about how policies need to be reshaped to achieve better public outcomes. More rarely it can be a book about how public institutions can be better organized so as to be fit for purpose or how the management of public institutions can be improved so as to secure better services at lower cost to the taxpayer. And yet the politics of governing, the art of choosing strategy and the managerial craft of executing and implementing are all intertwined. In this book I shall draw upon all three traditions – I shall attempt to show how good government requires the best from its tigers, hawks and sharks.

In politics and studies of public policy there is a tradition of intellectual enquiry that rests on a form of high minded cynicism. In this tradition, politicians are depicted as being engaged in elaborate 'rent-seeking' behaviour to gain and sustain themselves in public office (occupying office and charging a 'rent' to their citizens). Politics is described simply as a competitive power game. What's more, this tradition depicts public managers and public service professionals as self-interested agents engaged in empire building and career-enhancing routines.[17] But there is also a perfectly respectable idealist tradition of enquiry which suggests that politicians and public managers are fuelled by a cooperative spirit of service in the achievement of purposive social results and noble public goals. I am not by disposition a cynic although I do see some merit in a perspective that encourages a general scepticism about the actions of those engaged in governing and managing. But while scepticism may be a useful resting place it is no place for permanent settlement.[18] Hence I try to mix practical realism with ideas and ideals. This is because I believe that public progress is driven by people who are passionate about public goals and who want to achieve betterment in their communities and nations. Of course, people are often mistaken in their pursuit of policy and, what's more, progress can often occur through happenstance. But more often it occurs when good people do good things and they do them well.

Good governance requires the triad of good politics, good policy and good management. Well-intentioned politicians can receive the best advice, use the right decision process and yet choose the wrong strategy. But even good intentions and great strategy do not protect against failure if public institutions are poorly organized and resourced and if management has insufficient competence, capability and confidence to deliver. Therefore, while I shall draw heavily on the literature of politics, policy and management, I shall not limit myself to them. To govern well and to deliver ever better and ever more cost-effective public services requires an appreciation of practical moral reasoning, practical decision-making, and practical managerial economics. Governing involves choosing between different options, different priorities, and different paths. It is at heart a moral pursuit about the public good even though its practice requires a fair degree of egoism and sometimes the cruel exercise of dark arts.

Books on government inevitably draw on concepts, ideas and theory for insight. And general insights can be incredibly useful for those politicians, policy advisors and public managers who face practical problems or real-life dilemmas. However, theoretical answers to theoretical questions offer little solace to those politicians, advisors and managers trying to solve real problems. They are searching for practical answers to real-life problems. That is why in this book I shall use 'ideas in practice' as an aid to those who are keen to grapple with the goals of government.

In re-imagining government I shall pay particular attention to a number of interrelated factors. These are in respect of how the public interest is determined; how public decisions are made; how common cause for the public good is built; how geography and locality bring unique challenges to governing; how effective and ethically based public leadership is critical for the success of government; how government is involved in helping everyone cope with risk and uncertainty; and finally, how the 2008 Crash and the recession that followed have created a new urgency for action across democratic nations to lower public sector costs.

In the complex world of government, getting good things done requires an ability to examine what constitutes the public interest in any one practical circumstance. It also requires a capacity to engage with many stakeholders and with civil society to discuss openly the dilemmas and conundrums involved in shaping public value, finding common cause and explaining the reasons why any given course of public action is in the public interest. Explained like this, the tasks may seem overly dry and dark. To give life and light to the explanations, I shall set out these issues in terms of actual stories – real-life problems, issues and cases.

The fish is in the sea and the sea is in the fish

The stories in this book are of personal and social problems in the real world. One story is about Kevin Hines, a San Franciscan who jumped off Golden Gate Bridge in the year 2000 but who survived and who subsequently challenged the authorities to build a safety net under the bridge. A community centre in Sheffield in England acts as the starting point for a story that explains how, against the odds, it is possible to build community and common cause. Another story is of the decision dilemmas that faced the mayor of a local authority in London as to whether to demolish or rebuild a Victorian swimming pool. A further story is about the uniqueness of a place called *No Place* in the north-east of England, showing its blended connections with other places and how geographical variety challenges the presumptions of uniformity in governing. Three public managers delivering different projects and services serve as the centrepiece for another story; this time about the critical nature of value-driven and ethically based leadership in public institutions. This is followed by the real story of how Mayor Vazquez in Perote, near Mexico City, alerted the world to the threat of swine flu and how the unfolding drama of 'the pandemic that wasn't' threads together arguments about how much the role of government is concerned with minimizing risks, threats and harms. And finally, I recount the sad tale of the collapse of the 800 Wool-worths stores in the UK in December 2008 – revealing what it shows us about the 2008 Crash, the recession and the public sector retrenchment that followed.

Mostly I draw on real people's stories, although in a few cases I have used fictional identities. I use these and other stories to illuminate wider issues about government, public decision-making, public policy and finance, as well as public management. I don't claim that these stories encapsulate the governance, public policy and public management issues in their totality; however, they do act as a useful starting point for exploring these wider issues more generally. Stories can tell small interesting tales and at the same time they can also illustrate large and important narratives. When Arthur Miller was asked whether his play *The Death of a Salesman* was a tale about one man's journey or a broader tale about the Depression, he responded that 'the fish is in the sea, and the sea is in the fish'.

The challenges to democratic governments include global warming, international terrorism, social dislocation and crime, an ageing and dependent population, and a critically informed and demanding citizenry, as well as dealing with the most severe economic instability for three generations. The impact on public finances of the global economic recession raises another serious challenge – the downward and aggressive adjustment to state spending. Given this array of challenges, we should not be surprised that a variety of perspectives are needed to illuminate the way forward for government. The variety of these challenges to government demands requisite variety in the perspectives for government in meeting these challenges.[19] For no single perspective can help us to re-imagine our government and renew our public services. That is why in this book I shall investigate practical problems through several different perspectives.

Making life better

The core purpose of any government is to build a better nation or a better community so that its citizens are more easily able to improve their own lives. Democracy is judged not just by fair and inclusive process but by better life outcomes for citizens. But how do governmental decisions and actions make life better for everyone? And if not for everyone equally, how do governments create favourable conditions for those citizens who are least capable of improving their own lives? To start to address the question it is crucial to have some appreciation of how well-being varies across nations and communities.

There have been a number of national and international attempts to assess well-being. One European study placed Denmark as the nation with the population with the highest overall level of well-being in Europe, with Ukraine as the nation with the lowest levels. In this study, overall well-being was viewed as comprising three components: personal well-being; social well-being; and well-being at work.[20] Many nations are now looking at how best to assess the overall well-being of their citizens. But moving from an assessment of well-being to adopting policies that enable well-being to flourish involves heroic assumptions about the efficacy of government policies. However, there is some evidence that such assumptions are worth pursuing.

Over a 26-year period to 2007, some 360,000 people in 52 countries were subjects of several different waves of representative surveys about their personal feelings of life satisfaction, subjective well-being and happiness. A recent canvas of all this research by Ronald Ingelhart of the University of Michigan highlights two key findings. First, it shows that while reported levels of 'happiness' rose in 87 per cent of the 52 countries for which reliable time series data was available, reported levels of 'subjective well-being' rose in 77 per cent of the countries and reported levels of 'life satisfaction' rose in just 63 per cent. One reason Ingelhart suggests why reported happiness levels have risen greater than reported levels of life satisfaction is that the latter is more sensitive to economic conditions than happiness and that in many ex-communist countries the political and social liberation of the past two decades has been accompanied by economic collapse. In particular, reported levels of life satisfaction in Russia plummeted in line with worsening economic conditions.[21]

Second, it shows that there are a number of contextual factors influencing reported levels of subjective well-being. Economic growth is an important contributory factor to rising levels of subjective well-being. But it is not as important as the combined effects of social liberalization and democratization. Moreover, these factors together create a sense of freedom and control which then amplifies the impact on people's sense of subjective well-being. Put simply, Ingelhart's analysis shows that a more open political culture based on democracy has a bearing on people's sense of freedom and well-being but only when accompanied by wider social liberalism and a thriving economy.

But a concentration on democracy, liberty and freedom is not enough. Improvements to life expectancy and to broader human capabilities are the core of any progressive goals for liberal democratic governments.

But in democracies, politicians who seek elected office often make the same mistake. They convince themselves that electors are bound to respond to shinier promises for better government programmes. In truth, electors are unimpressed by grand policy promises and major programmes of reform. For more often than not, the most successful politicians are those that avoid the dry language of programmes and policy instruments and instead tap the wellsprings of electors' sympathies and hopes, offering an emotional agenda for their nation or their community.[22] In this way the practice of so much of democratic politics is an attempt to turn a widespread sense of resignation into a sense of hopeful change. But hope is more than wishful thinking and it is also more than holding a strong conviction that things will turn out well.[23]

Being optimistic can help. Having an optimistic stance may be essential in helping us to maintain our mental health while also trying to achieve positive results in the world. By contrast, a pessimistic stance may help us deal with the inevitable setbacks in life and help us cope with the apparent falsity of human progress.[24] Optimism certainly encourages a positive and open outlook towards the future. And crucially, an optimistic stance can be acquired or even learnt.[25] But it remains a stance. Having a stance towards something is not the same as creating something. For example, my optimistic stance about the effectiveness of any particular government may be as valid and reliable as my optimistic stance towards whether it will be sunny on my birthday next year. The key point is that my optimism does not make the government any more effective and it does not alter the chances of it raining on my birthday. My optimistic stance will affect neither outcome.

Public leadership that tries to make things better seeks to impose itself on the future so as to influence it. It may take an optimistic stance towards future events but it will only make things better by active leadership and management. The tradition shared by politicians and public managers alike can be described as progressive pragmatism – a philosophy of practical action to improve the quality of life and life-chances in a nation or a community. Pessimists and optimists are observers. Their expectations, respectively, are for things to get worse or better. Pessimists tend to look through rose-tinted spectacles at the past, while optimists tend to look through rose-tinted spectacles at the future. Progressive pragmatists, by contrast, plant roses and then they nurture them.

Throughout this book I offer concepts and ideas that are intended to be useful to people involved in governing or managing public services. Facts and evidence are an essential basis for governing but they are seldom transferable from one problem to another. What is transferable is an approach, a perspective, an idea. By interweaving stories with deeper ideas I have tried to make reading this book a fruitful experience. My aim is to provide not only food for thought but ideas for action. Ideas can help us understand the world better but they are also a crucial precursor for changing things for the better. In government, practical ideas are truly useful only when they generate better practice for better public service. It was Abraham Lincoln who wanted his legacy to be practical betterment: 'I want it said by those who knew me best that I always plucked a thistle and planted a flower where I thought a flower would grow.'

For my part, this form of hopeful progressive pragmatism offers the best path to good government. And good government is needed – not strong government, nor weak government. At its simplest, bad governments restrict and limit the potential of their citizens – by contrast, good governments centre their concerns on improving the life and capabilities of their citizens. My argument is that to improve their effectiveness, they need to re-imagine their core purposes. They need to re-imagine how collective challenges are best addressed. They need to re-imagine how public interest questions are defined and determined. They need to re-imagine how their citizens can best discover common cause for themselves. And they need to re-imagine the very purpose and scope of welfare systems and public services.

The next chapter starts with the story of how one of the Founding Fathers of the American Revolution, James Madison, dealt with the vexed issue of escalating public debt and the controversial issue of how to design effective government. The challenges he faced in the late 18th century have some striking similarities to those faced by liberal democratic governments throughout the world today.

Chapter 2

If Men Were Angels

Re-imagining government

'But what is government itself, but the greatest of all reflections on human nature? If men were angels, no government would be necessary.'[1] So wrote one of the Founding Fathers of the American Revolution, James Madison, who wrestled with two key public problems in the period between 1788 and 1790 – how best to handle the problem of public debt and how best to redesign government? Both of these challenges have extraordinarily loud echoes across the world nine generations later.

At the time of the American Revolution there were fewer than four million people in the newly created United States (although notably some 700,000 of these were black slaves). However, the US economy laboured under an enormous burden of debt built up largely as a legacy of war. The then overall debt was some $77m. Of this $11.7m was owed to foreign governments (mainly the French); $40.4m was domestic debt, mostly from the Revolution; and $25m was state debts owed to Americans who had sold food, horses and supplies to the revolutionary forces. Some, mainly Southern, states had paid off their wartime debts while others still had large debts. At that time it was thought that until foreign debts were paid and credit restored, mainly with the Dutch bankers in Amsterdam, the United States would not be treated seriously in Europe.

The fiscal plan to reduce this debt was crafted by George Washington's secretary of treasury, Alexander Hamilton. Hamilton had been a long-term friend and collaborator with James Madison. However, Hamilton's fiscal plan for his 1790 budget included the 'assumption' of all state debts by the federal government. James Madison strongly opposed this assumption as his home state of Virginia had already paid off its wartime debts and, in effect, would be saddled with paying the dues of other states. Moreover, many of these debts were in the form of securities that had been paid to soldiers for their service in the war. These soldiers had then sold them on to speculators at a fraction of their original value. This incensed Madison who felt that unscrupulous bankers were cheating battle-worn veterans. To his mind, those who had been loyal to their country were in danger of losing out to those whose loyalty was simply to the profit motive.

James Madison was a small, frail and fragile man. He was known for being painfully shy: according to one of his biographers, he was someone who instinctively sought out the corners of rooms. However, as a politician he was a convincing debater who completely disarmed his opponents through mixing a diffident personal style with a studious approach to mastering technical detail. In political debate Madison relied not on the force of his personality but on the force of his argument. And remarkably for such a shy man, his arguments usually won out. That is why initially he managed to frustrate Hamilton's fiscal plans. He mobilized opposition to the assumption of state debts such that the House was gridlocked for several months. There was no solution to the national debt problem with James Madison blocking the way.

It took the strategic cunning of Thomas Jefferson to grease the gridlock. Jefferson was an inscrutable enigma but he was also James Madison's long-term mentor and inspiration.[2] And in that year, he was also George Washington's secretary of state. In the middle of June 1790 he met Alexander Hamilton while waiting outside the President's office. Jefferson was surprised at Hamilton's demeanour. He was not his usual confident self; he was sombre, haggard and dejected – he appeared a beaten man. Hamilton told Jefferson that his entire fiscal plan was trapped in congressional gridlock because of Southern congressmen led by James Madison. Jefferson had strong Virginian connections with Madison and he decided to invite both Hamilton and Madison to a private dinner at his home in New York City on Sunday 20 June. His aim was to help the main protagonists ease their differences on the matter.

Jefferson's account of the dinner suggested that Madison agreed to acquiesce to Hamilton's plan to consolidate the debt on the basis that the new seat of government was to be located on the Potomac River. In Jefferson's words, 'as the pill would be a bitter one to the Southern states, something should be done to soothe them and the removal of the seat of government to the Patowmac was a just measure'. In this way a private deal over how best to handle public debt led to Washington DC becoming the capital of the United States (thereby separating the seat of American government from the centre of American finance). On July 9 the House passed the Residence Bill to transfer the national capital from Philadelphia to the Potomac by 32 votes to 29. Two weeks later Hamilton's Assumption Bill was passed by a near identical vote – 34 to 28; but only as James Madison stayed silent after opposing the plan several months earlier.[3]

The interplay between national politics and public debt can be seen throughout history. But no more than now, for public debt casts an incredibly long shadow over early 21st-century politics – a shadow that is longer and darker than it was in James Madison's days. The scale of the problem may be greater but the prevailing mood is similar. For now as then, the close embrace between governments and banks is characterized not by mutual admiration but by mutual suspicion. Banks need governments to regulate markets generally but they also need them to step in when financial markets begin to fail. And governments need banks: to lubricate the wheels of the economy and also to buy their sovereign debt so that they can finance urgent and important government activities.

The credit crunch of 2008 and the recession that followed halted the global economy and produced severe deficits in the public finances of very many nations. Many governments began to struggle to adjust their fiscal policies. Very many governments became involved in major efforts to reduce the level of their public (or government) debts and also to reduce their reliance on borrowing to finance expenditure – the deficits they have in their annual spending plans. Plans to reduce debt levels and deficit levels are linked but they are not the same. Those governments that entered the recession with relatively high debt levels faced the biggest challenges. Throughout advanced economies, the stimulus measures adopted by these governments pushed overall fiscal deficits to about 9 per cent of their GDP. This means that 'debt-to-GDP' ratios in these economies are expected to exceed 100 per cent by 2014, some 35 percentage points of GDP higher than before the global crash.[4]

Most democratic governments in advanced economies are struggling to reduce the level of their public indebtedness and reduce the deficits in their revenue accounts in the backwash of the most severe recession in generations. Unfortunately none of them can settle the matter by relocating their capital to somewhere near the Potomac River. The pill of fiscal consolidation is far larger and bitter than that which James Madison had to swallow in 1790. And in the incredibly crowded and transparent world of the early 21st century, it is far more difficult to discover new ways to sweeten the pill (or to 'soothe' the electorate; to use Jefferson's term) that meet the tests of ethics, equity and accountability. Fresh political imagination is needed to find new ways of soothing the short-term pain of major public spending retrenchment if the longer term gain of prosperous economic growth is to be realized. Faced with substantial retrenchment of public service provision and welfare entitlements, many politicians will feel duty bound to do as James Madison and oppose the prevailing fiscal plan. The political challenge that needs to be grasped is that which seeks to build new opportunities for social and community growth from the new realities that this retrenchment brings.

But Madison was not solely preoccupied with the nature of debt and its impact on the national economy. For several years, he had been consumed by the issue of how best to design effective government. In this he had acted as the liberal foil to Hamilton's centralizing tendencies in their joint authorship of the *Federalist Papers*. In particular he was determined to make sure that the then growing power of government did not limit the liberty of the individual. In *Federalist No. 51* he had written about the importance of establishing a structure of 'checks and balances between the different departments' of the government and as a result constrain government's tendency to oppress the public. In making his argument, Madison wrote the following:

> Ambition must be made to counteract ambition. The interest of the man must be connected with the constitutional rights of the place. It may be a reflection on human nature, that such devices should be necessary to control the abuses of government. But what is government itself, but the greatest of all reflections on human nature? If men were angels, no government would be necessary. If angels were to govern men, neither external nor internal controls on government would be necessary. In framing a government which is to be administered by men over men, the great difficulty lies in this: you must first enable the government to control the governed; and in the next place oblige it to control itself.[5]

In this, the most cogently drafted paragraph on the quandaries of governing, James Madison puts his finger on the key problem for those searching to build ideal government – the passions and flaws of mankind. If men were angels, recessions would not occur as there would not be the excessive confidence, hubris, mania, panic and 'animal spirits' that fuel financial and economic crises.[6] If men were angels, public debt would not become a problem as public revenues would match public spending; development across the globe would be even and consistent; equality of life-chances would be observable and evident; and all public servants would be noble, selfless pursuers of the common good. If men were angels, we would not need government to help us resolve our disagreements, to choose between competing claims, nor to offer us moral leadership. But neither men nor women are angels. And so following Madison, we need to govern ourselves with as much humility and moral reasoning as we can muster. Madison favoured active government ('to enable the government to control the governed') but he was also wary of over-zealous government (so that it is obliged 'to control itself'). Government needs to deal with the necessities of the moment, to build our common welfare and also to protect our liberties.

Core purposes: necessity, welfare and the common good

Most people, most of the time, solve most of their own problems. When they are unable to do so, they tend to get together with other people like themselves with similar problems so that they might solve their problems together. When people are unable to solve problems themselves or solve them through social action together, they look to government to attempt to solve these problems collectively through public decision, public action and some form of taxpayer funded or subsidized service provision. The problem with many modern governments is that they too readily assume that their primary purpose is to enable these collective solutions to problems. They too readily forget their critical role in protecting people's liberties and in helping people help themselves. And they also forget their vital role in stimulating mutual action among people to solve their problems socially. This is not because governments get carried away with the allure of collectivism. All governments, whether national or local, are intrinsically driven to identify public problems in order to solve them. Instead, they need to make sure that their drive to solve public problems does not divert them from their fundamental purpose of fostering a self-reliant, resourceful and cooperative citizenry.

The search for practical solutions to real-life public problems has been the purpose of government for millennia. No matter that the problem is whether or not to invade a neighbouring country or whether it is to tax people more so as to spend the available revenues on the needs of a few. Circumstances can render both choices necessary. And while the character of government has changed dramatically over centuries, the three essential purposes have remained. The first is to achieve public action in the context of disagreements between people as to 'what should be done' about public or shared problems. The second involves expanding the welfare or the well-being of people generally. And third is the drive to establish a common ground or a common good among all people regardless of their differing customs and traditions. All three of these purposes have ancient roots. The first two were clearly explained two thousand years ago by the classical Roman political theorist, Cicero. For Cicero, governing involved the necessity of deciding between competing claims and contrary interests and resolving them by decisive action. Cicero was the arch realist – someone who stressed the pragmatism, the expedients, the necessities of governing. The rhetoric of politics often lays claim to high principle but the practice of politics, as Cicero recognized, is more often characterized by expedient necessities to get things done.

But Cicero also established that the overall welfare or well-being of the people is a primary purpose of government. The idea is best expressed in his famous Latin motto '*salus populi suprema lex esto*' or in English, the 'welfare of the people above all.'[7] The *salus populi* motto, and its focus on overall welfare, was used by John Locke in his *Second Treatise on Government* in 1690. Stated generally, the motto argues for overall welfare as the highest goal of government. John Locke used the expression in arguing against King Charles's rotten boroughs – electoral districts that continued to have seats in Parliament despite the fact that they were grossly depopulated. As a result, the handful of voters in these districts were wide open to King Charles's bribery so that they would elect his cronies as their MPs. Locke was wrestling with the problem of legitimacy. In particular, who has the legitimacy to redraw electoral procedures for Parliament?

This may seem an abstract problem – but it is real. Legitimacy was the besetting problem faced by the US and British governments' 'sponsoring' of democracy in Iraq and Afghanistan. The means of deciding on the nature of the democratic process in Iraq and Afghanistan cannot itself be democratic. That is why democracy cannot be its own legitimacy. A democratic process must ultimately acquire legitimacy from something other than the democratic process itself. Legitimacy cannot follow simply from a process but must instead derive from some substantive norm. For Locke, this norm was not the will of the people (which could only be ascertained by a process of gaining consent) but rather the good of the people.[8]

John Locke argued that the good of the people involved the 'preservation of mankind'. It did not involve any 'injury or oppression of the people'. And it specifically sought to avoid 'unequal subjection'. The *salus populi* ethic of John Locke therefore underscores a core purpose of government as being concerned with its citizens' overall life expectancy, their quality of life and their quality of life-chances. The motto itself has been adopted by the State of Missouri and by several local governments across the globe.[9] While ancient in origin the *salus populi* or welfare purpose has been substantially revived in the past decade with the rise of outcomes-focused public services and with the acceptance that economic growth hasn't produced widespread happiness and that, in consequence, governments need to focus a little less on the sustaining service activities that have limited impact and rather more on improving the overall well-being of their population.[10]

The third purpose of government – to connect people with the 'common good' – also has ancient roots. It can be sourced from Plato's original concern that separate social groups would tend to seek laws that served their own interests and that to combat this tendency, 'citizen laws' should be developed that served everyone's interests. The modern use of the phrase 'the common good' has more recent origins. It can be found in the debates held among the 18th-century British reformers and their American revolutionary cousins. Despite their differences, these reformers and revolutionaries all placed individual citizens at the heart of their emerging democracies. However, they were also acutely aware of the competing claims of conscience and religion on individuals' fealties. They therefore developed the notion of 'the common good' so that the claims of religion could be acknowledged while people were also offered an option to claim fealty to the commonwealth or common realm of all people. These 18th-century debates, in England and the US, about religion and the common good offer rich and fertile territory for resolving many of the contemporary dilemmas about the competing claims of nationhood, citizenship, and ethnic, cultural and religious fealty.

While all these three purposes of government (necessity, welfare and the common good) are interlinked, the constitutional reformers of the 18th century realized that they also serve slightly different interests. In a history of the development of ideas about the common good in 18th-century Britain, Peter Miller argued that:

> The revolutionary ideas of representation and federation redefined the very understanding of community that had guided the early statesmen. 'Necessity', 'salus populi' and 'common good' remain part of the language of politics but they serve a different master.[11]

The rise of the responsive state and contemporary challenges

Governments have many purposes but they all centre on the changing needs of their people. Early governments sought to provide security against external threats or internal hazards – they developed the 'protective state'. Throughout history, people surrendered certain aspects of their liberty to a coercive state in exchange for that state offering them protection in a world full of hostile threats. Modern governments have moved on from this minimalist Hobbesian approach based on 'hard power' and coercion. Instead they have adopted approaches that seek to attract and persuade people through the exercise of 'soft power'.[12] In addition to assuring protection and security, they also sought to assure the rule of law as well as deliver improvements in the overall quality of life and quality of life-chances for their citizens – they developed the 'contractual state' and then they built the 'welfare state'.

The contractual state ensured that commercial obligations were backed by the force of the law. And the welfare state ensured that a safety net provided for those for whom the market failed. Low wage economies sometimes led to the creation of 'low income' benefits being developed on a means-tested basis; and likewise low employment economies sometimes led to the development of 'out of work' benefits, usually for a time-limited period. Some governments, mainly in northern Europe, developed strong safety nets that placed high burdens on their taxpayers, while other governments (notably in the US) built looser safety nets with correspondingly lower taxpayer burdens. The failure to adopt universal healthcare insurance in America lowered the scale of the welfare state in the US although it led to a rapid rise in overall healthcare costs. However, if spending on public education is included, the overall scale of America's welfare state throughout the late 20th century was similar to that in Europe.[13] These welfare state economies are further hampered because their populations are ageing fast and the numbers of people in work who are able to support those out of work (that is, those who have retired, are too young to work or who are workless) are also dropping. The working age populations of the US, Canada, Australia and the UK are forecast to grow relatively slowly over the next 40 years. In other large nations (such as China, Russia, Japan, Germany and Italy) the working age population is substantially declining; while India, Pakistan and Nigeria have the largest forecast increases in their working age populations (increasing by 76 million, 51 million and 52 million people respectively by 2050).[14]

In the 21st century, democratic governments need to go beyond this contractualism and this welfarism. There is a danger that politics in the recession-ravaged West will become embroiled in a sterile debate about the size of government. Big governments have done virtuous things and irresponsible things; and small governments have done likewise. As David Brooks of the *New York Times* argues, 'the best way to measure government is not by volume, but by what you might call the Achievement Test. Does a given policy arouse energy, foster skills, spur social mobility and help people transform their lives?'[15] In this way, the quality of government is more important than its quantity.

Governments need to help their economies reshape to meet the challenges of a fiercely competitive world economy, while also assuring their citizens that they are dynamically responsive to changing public sentiment – in short, they need to build the 'responsive state'. The responsive state is concerned with more than just assuring the security of its citizenry; more than enforcing citizens' and companies' legal obligations upon each other; more than securing collective social insurance; and more than the delivery of core public services (such as clean water, energy supplies, good education and quality healthcare). The responsive state has to remain relevant to changing demands and needs and stay in tune with the quickly shifting sentiments of its citizens and the fluid character of their social and cultural life.[16]

The grinding poverty and hardship of previous generations contrast sharply with the problems of relative affluence and poverty of the early 21st century. Consider the prosaic issue of eating food. It has taken about five generations for the role of the state in the developed world to move from a concern to prevent famine, to a concern with how best to prevent the health consequences of obesity epidemics.[17] The focus of government action in this example has shifted from an approach that attempted, through incentives and subsidies, to alter the behaviour of farmers to one that attempts, through social marketing and behavioural 'nudges', to alter the behaviour of those who eat the food that the farmers produce.[18]

But this tale of increasing affluence is not universally true. In James Madison's time the world's population was less than one billion in total: by 2010 over one billion people lived in extreme poverty on less than the equivalent of $1.25 per day.[19] In absolute terms therefore, more of humanity is poorer than it has ever been before. And very many of the world's poorest people live in democracies – either in India or in the African continent. In the early 21st century, the world is made up of many nations with many different types of governments operating at very different stages of development. Moreover, the development of all states is highly variable. Some states with democratic governments seem to be engaged in very different stages of development at once. Consider the case of South Africa. In 2010, its government was extending basic water supplies to its township communities, tackling persistent violent crime and building urban infrastructure while also hosting the football World Cup. This rapidly developing nation, a vitally important member of the British Commonwealth, was governing on at least three different levels at once.

And yet since 1989, with the collapse of the bi-polar 'old world' order, a good deal of attention has been paid to the risks and uncertainties in a new multi-polar world. In this world, some people suggest that one of the most intractable problems is the character of weak and failing states whose governments are not subject to open competition nor capable of being removed from office by their citizens.[20] In this way the absence of democracy is presented as a failure. For these weak and failing non-democratic states are often the site and source of some of the world's most dangerous problems – particularly international terrorism. But attempts to import democratic regime styles into some non-democratic countries (such as Iraq or Afghanistan) have proven extraordinarily difficult, if not forlorn, because of the resistant strength of established customs and cultures.

The governments of emerging economies with large and growing populations (such as in Brazil, Russian, India or China) are governing in the context of considerable urbanization and/or economic growth. By comparison the challenges that confront most mature democracies seem relatively easy. The febrile atmosphere in which domestic politics is conducted in these democracies may lead us to think otherwise but the challenges they face are fairly straightforward. How best to revamp their economies so that they can compete better in the world? How best to reshape their public services so that they cost less and empower people more? And how best to restore trustworthiness in politics and government so that those elected can connect better with those who elect them?

Democracy in flux

In 1950 there were 20 democracies in the world. Of these, 12 were Westminster-style parliamentary democracies, the remainder involved forms of direct election of presidents. By 2005 there were 81 democracies in the world of which 28 were parliamentary style, 24 were presidential and 29 were 'semi-presidential' (a democratic regime type that includes both a directly elected president and a separately elected parliament with a prime minister). This means that parliamentary systems are now in a minority with two-thirds of democracies having a system that involves some form of popular direct election. And in plural societies, differing democratic regime types have developed to take account of the degree of segmentation within those societies.[21] Importantly, differing democratic regime types vary not only in how power is formally distributed but in how political cultures function and, specifically, how political parties operate. James Madison did not anticipate the rise of mass political parties – for him power had to be checked between 'factions'; and factions arose from highly localized and particular interests not from nationally organized political parties.

Over 100 years after Madison was drafting the *Federalist* papers, Max Weber was writing in Europe during the height of industrialization and the rapid growth of mass political parties. He is perhaps most famous for suggesting that governments uniquely develop a monopoly on the legitimate use of force (through the powers of 'the state') and that they also develop highly rational and legalistic structures of authority that is then exercised through a hierarchically organized civil service.[22] However, he also suggested that political parties could not be trusted with power as intra-party competition became more important in channelling ambition than inter-party competition. He therefore favoured presidential systems over parliamentary systems – to keep parties in check. Since Weber's time, with the development of differing democratic regime types it has become clear that the form of government has a bearing not only upon who gets to make public interest decisions but on how they get to make them. This is because the behaviour of political parties in selecting candidates for office, in holding them to account once they are elected, and then in how they function once they have attained power in government, depends critically on the constitutional form of government in place.[23]

It has become commonplace to hear of widespread citizen apathy towards government and politics as well as a declining citizen interest in politics itself. This may have occurred for deep cultural reasons in mature democracies; and it may also be because the gap between the governed and those who govern has simply widened. Some social anthropologists suggest that there is an inherent biological tendency for people to be wary of those in power. They argue that it is common in human societies for social groups to avoid selecting strongly dominant characters to positions of power and instead to select people with average characteristics – thereby avoiding the prospect of tyranny and fostering egalitarian group dynamics.[24] More conventionally, modern political scientists have sought to describe the elitism of political practice in mature democracies that appear to have become overly confined to 'a mixed, but small cadre of elected politicians, unaccountable officials, specialist lobbyists, narrowly focused experts and professional protesters'.[25]

Whatever the nature of the powerful, and the character of those that surround them, the key issue is the extent to which ordinary citizens are empowered to act in public and to engage with each other for common cause. In mature democracies, citizens now have more strands and streams of social, cultural and political activity to choose from to be engaged in public life. Active membership of mainstream political parties or mainstream political movements may not give them the sense of connections that they seek. Moreover, as electors, when it comes to party alignment, a more educated citizenry has undoubtedly moved from 'agencies of loyalty, toward agencies of choice'.[26]

Furthermore, the election of democratic governments from among the competing political parties does not happen in empty space. Elections occur in a heavily media-rich environment. Electors obtain political information directly but they also obtain it as a by-product of their personal media preferences. The source of electors' political information has changed considerably over time. In 1935, they were informed about politics by attending a mass meeting or by watching a newsreel that accompanied the movies they watched at the cinema. In 1970, they were informed through their membership of mass associations (such as in trade unions and so on), by the political news on mass-consumer TV or through their purchase of mass-circulation newspapers. In 2010, electors become informed about politics through mass televised debates, a bewildering array of niche TV channels, a myriad of offerings via the internet and personalized communications, through social media networks and via their mobile phones.[27]

Throughout the world, the post-modern mix of broadcast and narrowcast media is creating democracies in flux. At one level, the growth of self-generated media content is lowering the barrier to entry into politics. For example, new forms of 'crowd sourced' politics can arise from viral campaigns launched at the periphery of political life by a handful of committed media-savvy individuals and which within days can enter the political mainstream. At another level, the very existence of networks of political activists can itself spawn emergent and self-organizing approaches to political campaigns around clusters of hot political topics either nationally or locally. And at a further level, these highly complex 24/7 demands place considerable pressures on elected politicians to keep ahead of the emerging political debate.

To succeed in politics, what is needed is not only a mastery of high pressure, mass televised debates but also a mastery of networked, niche and narrowcast communications to a bewilderingly diverse citizenry. Moreover, mature democracies appear to operate in a sort of 'faux confessional' age where political leaders are expected to reveal themselves as individuals as well as reveal their politics and their policies. The intellectual challenges of leadership are thereby matched by its invasive emotional demands.[28] Added to these pressures, the 'new media democracy' is itself an immense challenge to democratic governments. It challenges not only the responsiveness of democracies but also their representativeness.

The growth of new media requires elected representatives to be hyper-responsive to citizen demands – as it ratchets up the direct demands upon them to respond personally to emails, blogs and twitters as well as to more conventional phone calls and letters. And new media also stretch the nature of representation by offering new opportunities for people to engage with their elected representatives other than simply through their locality. For example, citizens of a particular religious faith may, on a particular issue pertinent to them, lobby all representatives who share their religious faith rather than simply lobby their local representative. For while party-based electoral systems are the fundamental element of representative democracy in the West, they capture but one element of what may be wanted in a genuinely representative system.[29]

The test of a healthy democracy therefore lies in both the representative character of its electoral system and the responsive nature of its government. Representativeness is usually gauged through the electoral system. And all electoral systems balance a variety of political objectives – such as mathematical fairness in representation, geographical accountability through local representation, decisiveness in electoral outcome, and stability in the government that is elected. Importantly, there is a vital 'negative power' to consider in relation to electoral systems: namely, the ease by which electors can eject an unpopular government.[30] More usually, commentators focus on the degree and extent of its representativeness – of which party alignment is an important, but not sole, dimension.

But what also matters is that democratic governments are dynamically responsive to the changing public sentiment of their electors. Being responsive is as important as being representative. In their appraisal of responsiveness in government, Stuart Soroka and Christopher Wlezian argue that what matters is that governments are dynamically responsive to changing public sentiment and that, when making new policy, they need to reflect these shifting preferences.[31] The authors suggest that the electorate and those they elect need to be dynamically attuned to one another. In their words, 'a responsive public behaves much like a thermostat. It adjusts its preferences for "more" or "less" policy in response to what policy makers do.' Following this line of reasoning, the test of a successfully responsive government is that it is highly adaptive and that it not only keeps a close connection with its citizens but it also keeps an even closer connection with their changing views and values.

Open democratic societies are always evolving and as they evolve so too do their governments. Good government does not result directly from wisely drafted constitutions nor does it spring from the minds of wise politicians and their wise advisors. In a canvass of the sources of good and bad power, Geoff Mulgan has written that, 'good government results from the alignment of the many vital forces that reward the good and punish the bad, including laws and constitutions, the personal ethics of politicians and officials, the vigour of the media and critics, and the moral voice of the outside world.'[32]

A connected world, a freer world

By 2010, the media site Facebook would have been the fourth largest country in the world if its members were citizens. Its users were then posting 55 million updates each day onto the site and sharing more than 3.5 billion pieces of content with one another each week.[33] At the end of 2010, *Time* magazine chose Mark Zuckerberg, the 26-year-old founder of Facebook, as their 'person of the year'. The social networking site he founded was then closing in on 600 million users and at the turn of the year secured investment from Goldman Sachs and a Russian investor that valued the company at $50bn (£32bn). *Time* pointed to the incredible changes that social networking was making to global human communication by referring back to Virginia Woolf's comment that, 'on or about December 1910, human character changed.' As Richard Stengel, the editor of *Time,* argued:

> she was exaggerating – but only a little. Woolf saw a fundamental shift in human relations taking place at the beginning of the 20th century 'between masters and servants, husbands and wives, parents and children.' Those changes, she predicted, would bring about transformations in every sphere of life, from religion to politics to human behavior. Few would say she got it wrong. A century later, we are living through another transition. The way we connect with one another and with the institutions in our lives is evolving. There is an erosion of trust in authority, a decentralizing of power and at the same time, perhaps, a greater faith in one another. Our sense of identity is more variable, while our sense of privacy is expanding. What was once considered intimate is now shared among millions with a keystroke.[34]

The complex and recursive character of global connections plainly affects the personal world and the social fabric in which personal life is conducted. But it also affects politics very substantively. The biggest political changes occur at times when generational changes combine with technological transitions.

At the turn of the first decade of the 21st century, two separate but linked events happened in the Arab world (in Tunisia and in Egypt). In Tunisia, a 26-year-old street trader, Mohamed Bouazizi, committed self-immolation after being humiliated by a municipal inspector. Protests about his death spread through Facebook and Twitter, and his parents' claims of corruption touched a chord with a Tunisian populous sick of bribery. Just 18 days after Bouazizi set fire to himself, the 23-year dictatorship of President Ben Ali collapsed in the famous Tunisian Jasmine Revolution.

In less than one month, a similar internally generated revolution occurred in Egypt. For in February 2011, Cairo appeared to be the centre of democracy's global force. At the epicentre was 30-year-old Wael Ghonim, a Google marketing executive who had been moderating the Facebook pages for those Egyptians who were demanding that the President for the past 30 years, Hosni Mubarak, stood down. Wael Ghonim had been detained and blindfolded by government forces for 12 days – upon his release his powerful call for continued democratic change arguably became the spark that ignited the final push for Mubarak's downfall.

The experience in these two countries (with a combined population of some 94 million people) of popular and non-violent uprising against longstanding dictatorships shows that liberty from the oppressive power of dictatorship is a powerful force. Of course, only time will tell whether these nations develop the democratic governments that their popular uprising demanded. But it certainly shows that Karl Popper's call for an 'open society' of some 60 years ago is as relevant as it was in the period just after the Second World War, and that it has probably been given added impetus by the connectedness of the 21st century:

> the longing of uncounted, unknown men to free themselves and their minds from the tutelage of authority and prejudice. It is their attempt to build up an open society which rejects the absolute authority of the merely established and the merely traditional while trying to preserve, to develop, and to establish traditions, old and new, that measure up to their standards of freedom, of humanness, and of rational criticism.[35]

Perhaps we should be a little wary of depicting the overall impact of internet-based social media on politics as benign. Those who are optimistic even suggest that the ubiquity of the internet inherently fosters openness in democracies. Perhaps they are right. Certainly the revolutions in Tunisia and Egypt suggest that by fostering openness it enables knowledge to become communal and for popular action to be concerted. But it may also be a case of wishful thinking. The capacity of humans to use technology for good or ill is too casually overlooked. True in June 2009 thousands of young Iranians poured onto the streets of Tehran using social media to protest at what they believed was a fraudulent election. This was the first global evidence of a twitter-inspired political movement and many in the West thought that it showed how technology was a potentially powerful tool for a new generation of Middle Eastern democrats. However, over the following months (once Iran's Green movement had lost its energies) the Iranian police used social media technologies to identify the protests' ringleaders so they could be more easily arrested. An internet policy analyst from Belarus, Evgeny Morozov, has studied the responses of governments from Tehran, Moscow, Beijing, Canberra, London and elsewhere to argue, perhaps pessimistically, that the internet can be used to target dissenters and stifle dissent as much as it can be used as a tool to foster open democratic dialogue.[36]

The deeper truth is that the power and potential of social networks are only beginning to be understood as millions of people are realizing their benefits and harnessing the opportunities they offer. Self-generated content increasingly fills the web and the networked nature of connectivity creates the positive conditions for self-organizing mechanisms to occur. But it may be that this explosion of social media is greatly empowering those who are already connected.

Thirty years ago the American sociologist Mark Granovetter showed how people with few close friends but lots of acquaintances used their social networks to become more socially mobile than people with fewer acquaintances but with a closer knit group of friends.[37] He called this effect 'the strength of weak ties'. The social media age is amplifying the import of Granovetter's findings because the social media network amplifies the power of connections, greatly empowering those who are connected. It offers new opportunities to those connected and it presents profoundly different challenges to governments in how they govern. In the face of this and other challenges, it is no good simply for government to undergo a change of degree (doing a bit more of this or, as seems more likely, a bit less of that), instead it has to undergo a dramatic change of kind.

Growing good government

Good government is the product of design and desire. That is because government needs organization and architecture but it also needs energizing by will and intent. Good government blends the concerns for equality with the realities of egoism. It finds expression in the principles that those in government use to describe their actions but it is illuminated more by the moral sense and deeper feelings that fuel these same actions.[38] That said, we know that the people in government and in public service share the same human potential and the same human flaws as everyone else. And if we accept James Madison's inference that men are not angels, it requires us not only to build robust constitutional codes for our governments but also to develop an affirming, encouraging and forgiving political culture. For if I have a right of transparent enquiry into your conduct as a public official, I should also have a corresponding duty to consider exercising forgiveness when you wrongly and inevitably transgress.

Citizens need change, taxpayers demand change. And as a result, politicians invoke change. Whether this change involves public sector retrenchment or public service reform, it is up to front-line public managers and professionals to generate and then implement the necessary changes. And when the change involves altering the boundary between the state and the citizen, it is vital that the agencies of civil society are fully involved. But we tend not to associate public action with dramatic, radical and transformative change. Too often it is the private realm that is depicted as the arena for accomplishment and for the display of that accomplishment. By contrast, public agencies are depicted as slow and timid. And what's more, much of what constitutes the practice of public life appears to have atrophied – to have wasted to the imagination.[39] But this need not be so.

The neglect and decline of the public can be halted and public life can be revived in ways to meet the rhythm and pulse of the current age. The debate in the 'public square' may have changed its location (from town square to blogosphere, from factions to parties and so on) but public debate is crucial if we are to re-imagine government and renew public service. New web-based technologies enable crowd-sourced discussions and emergent pressures for change from networked digital activists. Of course not all digital activism is benign – but it is open and transparent and encourages dialogue and not simply defensive debates. And of course, small changes of degree in the direction of the state can sometimes be left to professional politicians and their advisors. But the large shift of direction that is required to meet the fiscal challenge of reducing public deficits among many of the world's mature democracies requires public debate not private deals.

For if profound change is to happen across government and the public sector, we need to combine the shifts in people's values, aspirations and behaviours with the shifts in organizations, strategies and practices.[40] In the public sector, too many approaches to reform are like the search for the 'best mousetrap' – looking for the most ideal solution on welfare reform, on public service design and on public service delivery – to then apply everywhere. The gist of my argument is that the scale of the challenge our democratic governments face is so vast, its variety across our communities so diverse, that single, 'best mousetrap' solutions won't work. While planning is important to the achievement of goals, strategic planning has its limits. Those responsible for governing and leading public agencies need to recognize that emergence characterizes the world in which they operate and that to succeed they need to adopt a disciplined and intuitive approach to innovation and not simply rely on well-oiled strategic plans.[41]

In an increasingly liquid world we need to be fluid in our approach to governing and organizing public services. And we need to blend the best of public leadership with the best of public management. Over the next decade, if politics is to be the art of the possible, then public management needs to be the art of the soluble.[42] To solve complex public problems it is important that all public executives recognize that they operate amid 'interlaced webs of tension in which control is loose, power diffuse and centres of decision are plural'.[43] They need to unleash the energy of citizens and communities so that they can better solve their own problems. And they need to work more effectively with citizens and communities to tackle those genuinely urgent and costly public problems that need solving now.

The following chapters investigate how these urgent and costly public problems are best addressed by using practical problems and then suggesting how deeper ideas and concepts can be brought to bear upon them. The next chapter deals with the story of Kevin at the Golden Gate Bridge in San Francisco. It shows how ideas about the public interest are best illustrated; how the demands of public reason are best met; and how the requirements for building public value are achieved in practical circumstances.

Chapter 3

Jumping to Conclusions

Public interest, public value and public reason

Kevin stood next to the four-foot high barrier on the Golden Gate Bridge. His palms were sweating, his throat dry and his mind was racing. Seventy-five metres down, just under five seconds if he jumped, was the cold, green water of the San Francisco Bay. Despite the tears streaming down his face, a German tourist approached him and asked if he would take a picture of her on the bridge with the glory of San Francisco vista behind her. After he clicked the camera shutter something clicked in his mind. She had not even noticed his state of personal distress – clearly no one cared; not even a stranger. He had been wrestling with his conscience for forty minutes before that incident. A stream of consciousness laced with despair pumped adrenaline through his veins – he ran three paces, vaulted the barrier and started his plunge into the water.

Just one second after he let go of the rail he realized he had made a mistake. What appeared to be certainly right became, in an instant, definitely wrong. He had changed his mind but was hurtling downwards at almost 90 miles per hour. The distorted reality that had haunted him for years, as a sufferer of bipolar disorder, became reframed during those few seconds. He had wanted to die: but now falling fast, he chose to live. Braced for impact feet first, he closed his eyes tight and prayed.

Incredibly, he survived the impact. He plunged to a depth of ten metres and now was swimming ferociously upwards through the depths of the bay to reach the surface – to breathe again. Less than an hour later, exhausted from treading water, he was fished out by the Coast Guard. He was freezing cold, with his lungs partly clogged with the salt water of the bay. He had two splintered vertebrae and one sprained ankle. But he was alive.

Kevin is one of just 30 people to have survived the jump off the most popular suicide spot in world.[1] People travel across the globe to jump off the bridge. Kevin was from San Francisco but most jumpers are not. They travel from far and wide, contemplating their mission over days of travelling and planning. Most people jump from the bridge while facing the city. They plunge to their death looking at one of the most beautiful views in the world. About 30 people jump off Golden Gate Bridge each year – over time it is estimated that over 1500 have jumped – and 98 per cent die. In 2006, amid much controversy, the filmmaker Eric Steel produced *The Bridge*, a film that captured from several vantage points a number of suicide jumps as well as a handful of thwarted attempts. The film also contained interviews with surviving family members of those who jumped; interviews with witnesses; and, in one segment, an interview with Kevin.

This film evocatively presented the despair and isolation of the jumpers. It prompted psychiatric professionals and some bereaved families to begin a campaign to erect a safety net. Some twenty years earlier, Richard Seiden of the University of California, Berkeley, concluded from his extensive longitudinal research of 515 people who had been prevented from jumping off the Golden Gate Bridge that, after a period of over 25 years, 94 per cent were still alive or had died of natural causes. In other words, the despair which had led them to want to take their own lives was temporary, and that the vast majority of people who had wanted to jump to their deaths subsequently went on to lead normal lives after they had been prevented from jumping. The appalling loss of human life at the Golden Gate Bridge is of course an aggregate of many private tragedies. But more than that it saddens our sense of humanity as physically healthy people are plunging into the ocean to their near-certain deaths because of their temporary mental instability. Most people who jump are like Kevin: they are undergoing an intense mental ill health episode – what they plan to do seems right to them at that precise time.

That is why Kevin subsequently became one of the fiercest advocates for a safety net under the Golden Gate Bridge – a measure intended to prevent people with mental health problems like himself from jumping to their death. Kevin's campaign was focused and targeted. In the wake of Eric Steel's film, he conducted a first class lobby campaign using the media to best effect. By presenting the policy problem of suicides from Golden Gate Bridge through his own story, he was able to personalize the issue and gain emotional connection with the wider public. The regional TV media and the *San Francisco Chronicle*, among others, covered the public debate over many months.

Kevin's campaign was directed at the Golden Gate Bridge Highway and Transportation District (GGBHTD), a public body charged with the overall management of the bridge and the development of transit and ferry services in the Bay Area. This agency is not a private company but a special purpose public sector organization which raises finance from tolls and other fares and which has control and oversight of the bridge's maintenance and operations. The GGBHTD could not jump to conclusions as to what should be done about the numbers of jumpers from the bridge. They had to consider carefully how best to balance the narrow public interest in preventing people jumping with the specific public interest in preserving the heritage of the bridge. They had to consider the value to the public of the bridge and the value lost through the action of the jumpers. And finally, they had to deliberate and decide on the basis of reason, exercised in the glare of public attention.

The GGBHTD is governed by a 19-member board of directors supported by a general manager, Celia Kupersmith, and a group of senior public officials. As an organization, GGBHTD is unique: it was formed under the authority of the Golden Gate Bridge and Highway Act of 1923 and incorporated on December 4, 1928, to include within its boundaries the City and County of San Francisco, the counties of Marin, Sonoma and Del Norte, as well as most of Napa and part of Mendocino counties. In 1969, the California State Legislature authorized the GGBHTD to use bridge tolls to develop transit service in the US Highway 101 Golden Gate Corridor as a means of managing traffic congestion and avoiding costly highway expansion. The result has been a bus and ferry transit system that affords convenience and economy across the Bay Area. In the summer of 1970, the GGBHTD inaugurated a ferry service between Sausalito and San Francisco. In the winter of 1970, the bus service commenced with a few local shuttle routes and expanded its service with transbay routes in 1972.

In her annual statement in September 2008, Celia Kupersmith set out the 2009–10 budget of the GGBHTD and the challenging projects underway to improve safety on the bridge and enhance transit across the District more widely. While the overall budget of GGBHTD is $223m, the annual costs of the bridge itself total $94m; comprising some $66m of annual operating costs and a further $28m of annual capital works to the bridge. And with the rise in general toll fees to $6 for a single crossing and the overall number of crossings expected at some 40 million, the bridge was estimated to gross nearly $100m in income in 2009–10. This is just $6m more than the total annual running and maintenance costs for the bridge – a sensible operating surplus but not enough, on its own, to finance the cost of a permanent safety net under the bridge.

The Golden Gate Bridge and the public realm

These facts about the bridge, its governance and management, are understandably overlooked in the visitor's sense of awe at the sight of the bridge and its sweeping beauty. The physical and financial realities of the bridge pale beside its architectural, iconic and cultural status. But for the bridge to function and to deliver public value for the residents of the area, it is plain that those who are responsible for its management and maintenance must attend to the wider public benefits of the bridge as well as to its operating requirements. They need to pay special and particular attention to the deep requirements of public accountability. They need to assure public accountability for what is being delivered now and for what is being designed for the future. They need to be responsible for the safe operation of the bridge – for those crossing in cars, cycles and on foot. And they need to consider the safety to the wider general public, including preventing suicide attempts from the bridge. In doing this they need to balance their responsibilities for the operational management of the bridge, with the need to preserve its architectural wonder and ensure the sustainability of its finances into the future.

The Golden Gate Bridge is a public bridge and its board is plainly a public sector body. It is not a separately elected body but its governance is woven from the fabric of the elected governance of the area. The board is made up of a mix of elected and non-elected representatives from each of the six counties of the Bay Area as well as representation from the mayor of San Francisco. The 19 directors are nominated by the mayor of San Francisco, local mayors and local Boards of Supervisors. Nine directors are from the city and county of San Francisco, four from Marin County, three from Sonoma County and one director comes from each of the three counties of Napa, Mendocino and Del Norte. Together with the officials they employ, these directors need to ensure that GGBHTD acts as a public agency and that it operates within the disciplines of public accountability. As a public body, its considerations need to be conducted with reference to the public good and in the public interest.

And the essence of being accountable to the public is openness in decision-making. Openness itself is a combination of disclosure and transparency. For example, the Board of Directors meets on the second and fourth Fridays of each month. Present and past Committee and Board agendas as well as associated staff reports can be found for each meeting. Any public hearing or special workshop meetings are noted on a publicly available calendar. The Board of Directors has five standing committees that regularly meet in public. Agendas and associated staff reports can be found for each committee. Moreover, all public hearings are called by the Board of Directors to consider public comment on a variety of matters, including implementing a toll adjustment, considering a new fare, raising an existing fare, or implementing a major reduction in service. And finally, as part of its community outreach work, the District periodically hosts special workshops in public to provide additional information or education on potential impacts to services.[2]

Between 2006 and 2008, the GGBHTD considered various engineering options to provide a suicide safety barrier. The generic design concepts agreed produced the following three options for an engineering and environmental study: the construction of (1) a net under the bridge; (2) a fence structure added to the existing railing; and (3) the replacement of the existing railing with a new structure. The GGBTHD directed $250,000 of its own resources to this study on the understanding that a further $1.75m would come from non-District sources.

In 2008, the Board of Directors spent several months considering measures to improve safety on the bridge so as to prevent suicides. In July and August 2008, they invited public comments and observations on the need for safety measures and the form that these safety measures should take. They received many thousands of submissions from the public and interested parties as part of their consultation exercise about the options for making the bridge safer. Public agencies also commented. Opportunity for comment was afforded in public meetings, online and through formal written submissions.

As might be expected, views as to the proposals varied widely. Many people passionately objected to any alteration to the appearance of the bridge, although some accepted that alterations to historic landmarks could be made sensitively if they safeguarded life. Many people argued passionately for some form of suicide prevention mechanisms. Professional arguments between architects, historians, psychiatrists, economists and bereaved family members were ventilated for months. Written submissions combined analysis, aesthetics and emotion in almost equal measure – and the emotion was not confined to bereaved family members; some of the most emotion-laden submissions came from professionals and professional lobby groups. But this was not a referendum, not an exercise in direct democracy. The decision to be made was a public decision not a decision for the public to make. Consultation was an exercise to inform the Board who had to take the decision.

And on 10 October 2008, and to Kevin's considerable delight, the Golden Gate Bridge Board of Directors voted 15 to 1 to install a plastic-covered stainless-steel net below the bridge as a suicide deterrent. This option was known as the 'locally preferred alternative' (LPA). The selection of the net option provided for additional directions covering: the preparation of written responses to comments; the negotiation and execution of a memorandum of agreement to mitigate the adverse effects the net might have on the historic property of the bridge; and, finally, the preparation of any additional required studies such as an assessment of the increased potential for bird collisions. Once all this work was complete, it was then incorporated into two final documents: a FEIR (final environmental impact report) and a FONSI (findings of no significant impact) – both of which were submitted in May 2009 when the Board finalized the memorandum of agreement for the construction of the net. When completed, the net will extend 18 feet on either side of the bridge and is expected to cost up to $50m to construct.

What these jumpers plan to do (and what most of them succeed in doing) is the most private of acts; stopping them doing it raises some of the most public of questions. But why? First, why should the users of the bridge who pay the tolls pay for the costs of stopping people jumping? Or if the bridge makes an operational deficit in its accounts to finance the $50m cost of the safety net, why should the general taxpayers in the San Francisco Bay Area meet these costs (after all most of the jumpers come from outside the area)? Put differently – under what conditions should taxpayers' money be used to prevent private actions? Second, how is it possible to compare on a single benchmark the private cost of individual lives lost with the public value of the bridge? If we presume responsible citizens pay their taxes for reasonable public purposes, should not we also expect commensurate levels of responsibility on those people walking across bridges? Third, the Golden Gate Bridge is an architectural icon of the US let alone San Francisco: its aesthetic quality and its acknowledged position as a heritage site give it a revered status in American life. Altering its appearance because of the private actions of a relatively few people may reduce its iconic value to the public at large. Does the obvious benefit to a small number of individuals merit the cost in money and loss of amenity to the millions who use and view the bridge?

Fourth, many people are killed in San Francisco each year for any number of other reasons – for example, in the same year that Kevin jumped from the bridge, 61 people were murdered in San Francisco (the lowest number for a decade) and 50 people died in road traffic accidents in the city. If $50m is available to prevent deaths then some might argue that it should be spent trying to prevent some of these murders and/or reduce some of these accidents rather than on measures that try to prevent the intentional deaths of the jumpers from the Golden Gate Bridge. Fifth, if this was a bridge in private ownership on private land, the issue would almost certainly be a private matter for the landowner and bridge owner. But when it comes to any proposal to make significant changes to a public facility, the public may have a legitimate expectation for a comprehensive public consultation and deliberation of the issues before any public body arrives at a decision. And even then any public decision may also be subject to a process of judicial questioning or review. This requirement for public issues to be subject to reasoned debate and deliberation is the foundation of good government. For at bottom, politics and policymaking are mostly a matter of persuasion – policymakers cannot simply issue edicts.

Kevin's quest to get a safety net placed under the Golden Gate Bridge provides a powerful lens to approach questions of public policy and the changing role of government. It presents in microcosm the dilemmas of deciding issues in the public interest, searching for ways to expand public value, while engaging the public themselves in a reasoned debate about what should be done in the name of governing for the greater good. These three interlocking issues frame what we mean by 'the public' and what we mean by public action. They define the contours of government: the boundaries, the outlines, between our private lives and our civic lives as citizens. On what basis do we decide when some public action, usually financed from general taxation, is in the public interest? How do we ensure that public money is used to further public value? And how do we ensure that the public themselves are engaged in a reasoned discussion about how public action is pursued? Governing well requires reasoned discussion among members of a community. Governing well also requires collective choices to be made in the public interest. These principles explain the foundations of good government. But applying them involves questions of practice and not of theory.

Answering specific questions about particular cases (such as that involving the Golden Gate Bridge) involves practical considerations about tangible examples. Answers to 'whether', 'why' and 'how' are usually practical responses to knotty problems in the real world. The main problem with accounts about public policy and government is that they too often fail to help us address the real, everyday and practical issues we face. Whether a suicide deterrent scheme is needed for the Golden Gate Bridge is a practical question: as is whether it would work; how much it would cost; and who should pay for it. To answer these questions through the lens of a simple cost–benefit analysis is to attempt to reduce human life to an opportunity cost and/or to attempt to calculate the beauty of the Golden Gate Bridge. Instead, we need to discover answers to these questions through the lens of debating, discussing and choosing. The Board of Directors chose in the public interest. Their choice was informed by the best available evidence and by a comprehensive attempt to capture the kaleidoscope of public and professional opinion on the issue. They tried to choose wisely and sensitively. But what does their choice tell us more generally about governing in the modern world?

Claims making: the social construction of public problems

In truth, each and every day, in each and every country, we can find attempts to answer questions like that posed by the jumpers at the Golden Gate Bridge. In so doing, we find public officials first identifying what social problems need fixing; and then identifying ways of fixing them. The question posed by the jumpers is in the form of a serious social problem – suicide. But that is just one serious social problem among very many. How is it that this problem was identified for possible solution rather than other problems? Why are some social questions posed and not others? Usually, social problems are defined as conditions that are harmful to society – as though they are external objects. This approach is called 'objectivist'; it couches social problems as though they undermine the well-being of wider society from somewhere outside of society itself. In this sense 'crime' is a social problem, but so too are 'racism' and 'global warming'. Simply listing social problems tells us nothing. Think of the problem of obesity. If it is viewed 'objectively', it may be described in social problem terms because fat people are discriminated against (as is believed in the US by the National Association to Advance Fat Acceptance which was founded in 1969 as a civil rights organization dedicated to ending size discrimination in all its forms) or because fat people are, over time, a drain on scarce healthcare resources. Both views are objective but both stem from very different approaches to defining the problem.

An account of social problems that centres on a more subjective approach would attempt to describe them as 'topics of concern'. When this approach is adopted, we realize that people will disagree about defining the nature of the problem, let alone how the problem is best addressed. The sociologist Joel Best argues that social problems are built by 'claims makers'.[3] These are people who try to persuade others that something is wrong and needs fixing. Claims makers identify 'troubling conditions' that need attention and usually require public resources to fix. Joel Best writes of the 'natural history of a social problem'. The natural history has six stages.

First, people make claims that there is a problem with certain characteristics and causes. Sometimes these people also suggest certain solutions to these problems. Second, the media report on these claims makers so that news of their claims reaches a wider audience. Third, public opinion shapes itself on the problem identified by the claims makers. Opinion polls may be carried in the media about 'what people think about this issue' and so on. These reports then have an effect on other people's opinions (those who weren't surveyed by the pollsters). Fourth, lawmakers and policymakers create new ways of addressing the problem identified. Fifth, public agencies and their professional staff implement the new policies, and in so doing they discover new aspects of the problem through the detailed practice of solving the problem. And finally, if the approach adopted is even just modestly effective, the problem is solved or is transformed in character somehow. This natural history of social problems is entirely observable in relation to the case of the Golden Gate Bridge and it demonstrates the intertwined nature of claims making, media coverage and the nature of professional problem solving by public agencies.

Single purpose agencies collaborate to solve problems

When an identified social problem does not sit easily within one public agency's remit, several agencies that have a stake in the issue tend to try to solve the problem through some form of collaborative working. Even in the case of the problem at the Golden Gate Bridge, which was clearly a matter for the GGBHTD, $1.75m of the $2m that went into their complex suicide deterrent study came from other local and regional public agencies. The problem of jumpers from the bridge was not simply an operational topic of concern for the GGBHTD, it had far wider significance for San Francisco and the wider Bay Area.

Collaborative working between public agencies increases the multidisciplinary perspectives that are focused on tackling the problem. And, as knotty persistent social problems will have several aspects or dimensions to them, it is all the more useful for them to be solved through the perspectives of many professional disciplines. For the risk taker, collaborative working leverages the prospects of success for each agency involved (after all, the $0.25m from GGBHTD leveraged a further $1.75m – just as a starter). For the cautious, collaborative working may serve to spread the risk of not succeeding in solving the problem. More realistically, it broadens the base for solving the problem. In their book *Leadership for the Common Good*, John Bryson and Barbara Crosby wrote:

> We live in a world where no one is 'in charge'. No one organization or institution has the legitimacy, power, authority, or intelligence to act alone on important public issues and still make substantial headway against the problems that threaten us all … Many organizations or instit-

utions are involved, affected or have a partial responsibility to act, and the information necessary to address public issues is incomplete and unevenly distributed among the involved organizations. As a result, we live in a 'shared power' world, a world in which organizations and institutions must share objectives, activities, resources, power or authority in order to achieve collective gains or minimize losses.[4]

Single purpose public agencies, like the GGBHTD, understandably struggle to solve problems outside their immediate domain. They maintain bridges and ferry people across the harbour; they are not expert in dealing with people who have mental health problems. In this way we can see why the police struggle to reduce crime. They may be able to solve crimes (they seek to answer 'who did it?' questions) but they cannot solve the problem of crime ('why are they doing it?' questions). Employment agencies struggle to reduce unemployment: they may be able to get some people jobs but they cannot create jobs for everyone.

And yet across the world governments have continued to establish single purpose public sector agencies in the belief that this would narrow their focus and sharpen their attention on deliverable goals. However, this approach flies in the face of developments in social planning which have identified the interconnected nature of social problems (the so called 'wicked problems')[5] and the need therefore for public agencies to adopt shared solutions across organizational boundaries to help solve these problems. Hence, in order to be successful in meeting the real and tricky challenges in their operating environment, single purpose agencies have tended to widen their sphere of influence and broaden their network of stakeholders. The GGBHTD has specific functions and it performs a narrow set of activities, but it does so within the wider network of governance that exists in San Francisco. This means that when it had to address an issue outside its normal sphere of specialism it could call upon other public agencies to advise, to get involved, and to help fix the problem.

Solutions to public problems tend to be discovered collaboratively in pursuit of a practical solution to some locally occurring problem. We may look to national governments to solve public problems. But this is often futile. Of course some problems are resolved by prescriptive national policy innovations – but this is the exception rather than the rule. (Governments would not issue an edict that all bridges had safety nets erected beneath them!) What's more, there is ample evidence that successful innovation in problem solving occurs at the intersection between apparently distinct specialisms or ways of thinking.[6] And while professionals will naturally seek to collaborate with others who work with the same client group or in the same location as themselves, the more fruitful collaborations may occur across apparently unconnected specialisms. This means that successful collaborations will not always occur spontaneously – they need to be orchestrated.

Those who collaborate include public service entrepreneurs, whether elected or appointed, public service users themselves, private sector businesses working for public service contracts, and voluntary and community associations working to fulfil some not-for-profit social mission. The questions these collaborators seek to answer are often knotty, seemingly intractable and stubbornly persistent. They may also involve genuine dilemmas, quandaries, conundrums, paradoxes or trade-offs. After all, public policy is trying to achieve very many purposes. Sometimes these purposes are aligned, sometimes they are contrary, sometimes they are in conflict.

Bridges, however, are very simple instruments of public policy – they link places together to ease transport and grease the wheels of local and regional economies. But they can also present, as in the case of the Golden Gate Bridge, many other public policy issues: of heritage, culture, environment and safety. Other instruments of public policy can produce even more vexed questions to which elected politicians and their advisors need to find practical answers.

A systems approach to solving public problems

If we are to accept a systems approach to problem solving, we need to acknowledge two factors. First, that many problems once solved create further unintended problems to address; and second, that the actors in the policy process (whether elected or appointed) are not neutral, detached observers. It is therefore crucial that the private and personal interests of those advising and deciding on public choices are made explicit to the public so that inevitable biases can be minimized. In an account of the interconnected nature of problem solving in public policy, Robert Goodin described it as follows:

> Policy analysts use the imperfect tools of their trade not only to assist legitimately elected officials in implementing their democratic mandates, but also to empower some groups rather than others. Furthermore, policy is never permanent, made once and for all time. Puzzles get transformed into actionable problems, and policies get made on that basis. But that gives rise to further puzzlement, and the quest for ways of acting on these new problems. The persuasive task of policy making

and analysis alike lodges in these dynamics of deciding wh
to solve, what counts as a solution, and whose interests to s∈

But policymakers don't function in a hermetically sealed box sepa-
rated from the real world. They operate in a hyper-informed media-based
networked world. This is a world where the information gap between
public service experts (on bridge safety, for example) and citizens generally is narrower than ever before. For every expert with five years of
specialist training and ten years of experience, there are many thousands
of graduate level educated citizens with time on their hands to question,
query and debate the advice of the expert.

In all democracies, the legitimacy of elected politicians to take public
decisions appears lower than ever before – and not simply because of the
public's declining view of the general trustworthiness of elected politicians and appointed public servants. For despite the democratic mandate
of any politician, electoral systems are always flawed and public sentiment and opinion change at a far faster rate than electoral cycles. What's
more, 24-hour rolling news channels have their impact in setting a tone
for what topical issues merit public attention, and elected politicians
often feel the need to respond with urgency to the 'stories of the day'.
Many public agencies try to deal with the demand for disclosure and
transparency by broadcasting all their meetings and discussions online
for citizens to view directly, but in the daily blizzard of bewildering
information, most people want edited chunks of information that fit their
diverse interests and plural preferences – in short, they crave 'narrow-
casting' not broadcasting.

In this way, the demands of public accountability on public agencies
are immense. In the most general terms, the task is 'do more and do better
with less taxpayers' money, while being accountable to a socially diverse
public with differing views about what should be done, for 360 degrees
and for 24 hours each day'. To meet the needs of the 21st century, public
agencies need to be disciplined in how they approach public problems;
they need to be practical in their approach to solving these problems; and
they need to be mindful of why the problem they are solving is a public
problem in the first place.

So what deeper issues does the story of the Golden Gate illustrate?
Plainly, it is a practical example of public policymaking that shows how
those governing the issue not only need to weigh various factors they
also need to examine these factors from different angles. Figure 3.1
shows how each practical issue or social problem has to be viewed from
each of three different angles. First, what is the nature of the public

interest in the issue being tackled? Second, how is it feasible to expand public value in the issue being addressed? Finally, when the public are deliberating issues and/or when public officials are determining issues, they need to approach them on a reasoned basis.

It is not sufficient for public officials (whether elected or appointed) to express their 'opinions'. They have to explain the reasons why they hold that opinion. And in particular, they need to be able to explain how they arrived at the public decision they made. The expression may be that, 'everyone is entitled to their opinion', but it does not apply to public officials. They may hold strong political or personal convictions about issues. And these convictions will hold sway with their general opinions. But public officials are rightly expected to give reasoned expression to their decisions. They need to be able to explain the basis for their views – the ideas and the evidence that enabled them to come to the conclusions that they have. The public would not accept a public decision that was based on an irrational or unreasonable basis. In this way, reason and the public discussion of reason are crucial to determining any public interest issue.

Figure 3.1 is intended as a straightforward schema to be useful in considering how best to approach knotty and complex social problems.

Figure 3.1 *The public triangle*

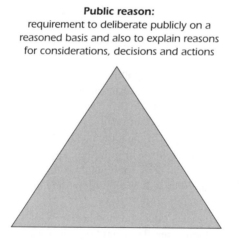

Public reason:
requirement to deliberate publicly on a
reasoned basis and also to explain reasons
for considerations, decisions and actions

Public interest:
identifying, articulating,
disclosing and choosing
actions in the public interest

Public value:
seeking to expand civic and
public value in contrast to the
capture of private or social value

Public interest

At its simplest, the market economy is the arena for the pursuit of personal and private interests, while the public economy is the place where the common, combined or collective interests of the public are paramount. What constitutes 'private' or 'public' interests differs across societies and across time. Indeed, people may well argue that the very concept of the public interest is fragile under examination. However, the term has both colloquial and legal currency. Although the roots of the concept of 'the public interest' can be found in ancient history, perhaps the gradual enclosure of farmland in England produced the simplest explanation of the underlying issues. For hundreds of years throughout England (between the 15th and the late 18th centuries) the competing interests of commonwealth and enclosure were hotly debated in terms of the respective rights of tenants and landlords to graze sheep and farm previously common land.

Those arguing against enclosure suggested that any protection afforded to private interests on land needed to be accompanied by similar protections for public interests. Of course in practice, the very definition of what constitutes the public interest is contingent and dependent upon circumstances. Consider the modern case of a football club wanting to relocate to a better and more convenient location. At what point do public interest considerations come to the fore? Does it depend upon whether its fan base is local or regional? Does it depend upon the existence of any local multiplier effect on the local economy from its stadium relocation? Or does it depend upon the cultural role the club plays in the overall life of the community? Football fans will have passionate views about these subjects; other people who may have no interest in football whatsoever may hold equally passionate views; while many people may be wholly indifferent. The key is to attempt to set out clearly what are the public interest issues in the problem that needs fixing. Is it a public interest problem or is it instead a private, sectional or social interest dressed up as a public interest problem?

In many countries, the development of a legally enforceable 'public interest test' has occurred in respect of competition policy, in some regulated utility markets and in the withholding of official information or state secrets. Hence, proposed actions across many sectors of the economy and some enquiries across many sections of the government may be legally stopped if these actions or enquiries can be shown to restrict, reduce or jeopardize the public interest. However, in each case it is up to the public agency to argue that an action (say, a merger between two regulated companies) or the provision of specific information (say, the emails of the secretary of state for security or defence) is contrary to the public interest.

This is not to say that private, social or public interests are so easily and rigorously definable. Indeed, they often bleed into each other. After all, the pursuit of personal wealth and advantage is a driving force in the world; with competitive self-interest acting as the fuel for much of what passes for public progress. And throughout history, people have combined their interests to pursue a shared agenda (through voluntary associations, guilds, companies and other organizational forms) and thereby have delivered considerable civic and public good. More usually, it is in the pure realm of politics and civics that people invoke 'the public interest'. And, as ever, the issue of what comprises the public interest is contingent on the problem being addressed and the issue being pursued.

Public value

The idea of 'public value' is associated with the work of Mark Moore of the Kennedy School of Government at Harvard University. Mark Moore spent many years studying how entrepreneurial management is fostered in government.[8] In his work on public value, he has illustrated how successful public service managers, mainly in the US, seek to build a 'licence to operate' so as to deliver enhanced social results and service outcomes to their public. Using widely drawn examples of public managers such as librarians, environmental protection staff, police commissioners and housing officials, Moore demonstrates how public service managers use both operational management techniques and service strategies to generate improved outcomes for service users and for citizens more widely. He also extended his analysis to include how elected politicians mobilize support for particular programmes in US cities and how they adopt specific advocacy and negotiation techniques to ensure they succeed in implementation.

Mark Moore's public value approach was initially overlooked as it was published just after *Reinventing Government* by David Osborne and Ted Gaebler.[9] In their popular and successful book, they offered a more accessible, and assertive, 'how to' guide to changing public agencies. Their account remains powerful and useful but Moore's more conceptual public value idea has proved more enduring because it enables any issue to be appraised, evaluated and measured in terms of its public value. So while Moore's work appears to be more theoretical than the approach of *Reinventing Government*, it has proved to have more practical applications. It is essentially concerned with maximizing service effectiveness and efficiency through better management. It incorporates the redesign of services, the engagement of service users in their design and delivery, and the management of operational process improvements. At its most practical, the search for public value involves a combination of two sorts of metrics: of cost-effectiveness and of service outcomes.[10] In short, it stresses 'how' things get done in a public sector or governmental context.

A paper prepared by the British government's 'strategy unit' in 2002 suggested that 'public value refers to the value created by government through services, laws, regulation and other actions.'[11] This paper adopted a governmental rather than a managerial perspective on the idea of public value. While value is determined by citizens' preferences, expressed through a variety of means, the strategy unit paper argued that, 'the value *added* by government is the difference between these benefits and the resources and powers which citizens decide to give to their government.' Put simply, public value is the public sector equivalent of shareholder value. If public servants design services poorly or implement services ineffectively and inefficiently, the public will not receive value from the services their taxes finance. Hence the practical attraction of Moore's emphasis on getting public servants focused on the relentless pursuit of ever better public value.

Before the 1990s, public service management was largely described as 'public administration'. And the role of public officials was seen as assuring impartiality in policy advice, balancing equity with efficiency in programme management and ensuring the smooth functioning of public bureaux. Over the past two decades there has been a growth of public value research in the both the US and the UK, focused mainly on the management education of public service officials.[12] The overall impact of this trend has been to promote a 'can do' and entrepreneurial ethic among public servants by stressing their managerial leadership role in discovering and expanding public value through reshaping services and focusing on social results and service outcomes. By building 'a licence to operate', successful public managers may well deliver progress in public policy but they are best advised to do so by making the values they are advancing explicit rather than pretending their actions are merely pragmatic and entirely value neutral.

Public reason

If governing involves discussing and choosing, there are two layers for considering the demands of public reason. First, people's views differ about what should be done to enhance the overall public good. Therefore a prime task of any government is the creation of 'safe havens' for reasoned discussions among people with different views. In any community, disagreeing peacefully is a prerequisite for building the ground for possible agreements. Second, those politicians who are elected as representatives of the wider citizenry need to discover ways of informing themselves so that they can arrive at reasonably based decisions that affect the public.[13] And they also need to make sure that the decisions they make are open to reasonable enquiry and that they are explained reasonably to their public.

In making public decisions, citizens expect their elected politicians to call upon their basic beliefs and their general political outlook, but they also expect them to call upon sound ideas and reliable evidence. When it comes to political decisions, we seem to sway between wanting politicians who stay true to their beliefs and wanting politicians who respect the evidence or the facts – even as 'the facts' inevitably change. In this way we are tempted by conviction politicians who try to bend the facts to meet their prior belief while at the same time we are seduced by pragmatic politicians who adapt their approach to meet the changing tide of facts. But this is not new – debates about whether reason should precede belief or whether belief is a necessary preliminary to reason have endured for centuries. Indeed, a 19th-century British polymath, William Clifford, wrote a classic essay on the 'Ethics of Belief'. In his essay, Clifford argued that there is a duty to believe carefully, in the light of reason alone. He began his essay with a story:

> A shipowner was about to send to sea an emigrant ship. He knew that she was old, and not overwell built at first; that she had seen many seas and climes, and often needed repairs. Doubts had been suggested to him that she possibly was not seaworthy. These doubts preyed upon his mind, and made him unhappy; he thought that perhaps he ought to have her thoroughly overhauled and refitted, even though this should put him at great expense. Before the ship sailed, however, he succeeded in overcoming these melancholy reflections. He said to himself that she had gone safely through so many voyages and weathered so many storms that it was idle to suppose she would not come safely home from this trip also. He would put his trust in Providence, which could hardly fail to protect all these unhappy families that were leaving their fatherland to seek for better times elsewhere. He would dismiss from his mind all ungenerous suspicions about the honesty of builders and contractors. In such ways he acquired a sincere and comfortable

conviction that his vessel was thoroughly safe and seaworthy; he watched her departure with light heart, and benevolent wishes for the success in their strange new home that was to be; and he got the insurance money when she went down in mid-ocean and told no tales.[14]

Surely William Clifford was right when he argued that the shipowner was negligent and should receive our censure. After all, his 'faith' in his ship was acquired without reason. Clifford is careful not to be drawn in by the sincerity of the shipowner's beliefs – they are irrelevant to the truth. For as he says in two crushing sentences: 'the sincerity of his conviction can in no wise help him: because he had no right to believe on such evidence as was before him. He had acquired his belief not by honestly earning it in patient investigation, but by stifling his doubts.'

William Clifford's brilliant essay brought a radical answer from the American philosopher William James in his own essay 'The Will to Believe'.[15] James sees belief as a choice between options – 'our passional nature not only lawfully may, but must, decide between propositions ... "do not decide, but leave the question open", is itself a passional decision – just like deciding yes or no – and is attended with the same risk of losing the truth.' But James is wrong when he argues that refusal to believe something is a kind of faith. In a recent summary of the debate between Clifford and James, the British philosopher Simon Blackburn suggests that, 'you may believe that feng shui really works. I refuse to believe it. I do not necessarily believe that it does not work, I may refuse to come down either way. I may not think it worth thinking about ... the more faiths you absorb, the more risks you fail to pay off ... your disrespect for caution, for evidence, for plausibility may lead anywhere. "Those who can make you believe absurdities", said Voltaire, "can make you commit atrocities." By contrast my caution cannot do any such thing.'[16]

And so, just as we are tempted to admire those politicians with a strong will to believe, we are also more likely to trust and respect those politicians who temper their will to believe with a more reasoned and cautious view of issues. In some extreme instances, stifling one's doubts is the best way forward when pursuing public politics (think of Churchill during the Second World War); but it can also be the most reckless way to deal with the public challenges that beset governments.

Citizens expect their political representatives to be sensitive to custom and tradition and to preserve the best of current circumstances; but they also expect them to make public decisions on a reasoned basis and to explain the reasons for their decisions. Full disclosure and explanation is the essence of public accountability. Some suggest that public consent matters most. And gaining public consent is undoubtedly extremely important. Public authorities that act without consent follow a perilous path. However, consent is no guarantee of public virtue. History is littered with examples where people were able to convince themselves of the good sense of something that subsequently proved to be completely wrong-headed and even wicked. It is amazing what people can convince themselves is true if enough other people seem also to believe it! For example, some 100 years before James Madison was contemplating how best to design government, the courts in Salem, Massachusetts were condemning dozens of women, and some men, to death on grounds of witchcraft.[17] Public consent on an issue is important – it is simply not the same as arriving at the truth on an issue.

People will differ as to what is the right problem to tackle and they will differ as to the right way to tackle it. Everyone views the world through strong cultural lenses that bias our perception, our judgement, and flavour our reasoning. Over 350 years ago, the British political philosopher Thomas Hobbes wrote in *De Cive* (The Citizen) of the competition between people with different desires. People disagreed, according to Hobbes, not simply because of competition over resources but more because the human condition would result in disagreement:

> The desires of men are different as men differ among themselves in temperament, custom and opinion. What one person praises another will condemn and call evil. Indeed, often the same man at different times will praise and blame the same thing. As long as this is the case there will necessarily arise discord and conflict.

From this we could be tempted to despair and conclude that agreement on complex public problems is infeasible. But the right conclusion to draw is that we should avoid the pursuit of ideal goals; and we should avoid heroic attempts at consensual agreements that are all encompassing and embrace everyone. In solving public problems we are trying to make things better, not ideal. In so much of public policy, the perennial searching for the ideal acts as the enemy of the urgent implementation of the good. The test of reasonably based public discussion in a plural and open world is more about how dissenting voices are afforded their say; how decisions about public problems can be made; and how public action can be achieved which neither tyrannizes minorities nor ignores their voices.[18]

Amartya Sen, the Nobel Prize-winning economist and social thinker, argues in his book *The Idea of Justice*[19] for a practically reasoned approach to enhancing justice and removing injustice. He argues against idealized approaches that serve simply to pursue 'perfect justice'. He stresses how reasoned discussions about public issues can help policy-makers accommodate plural and divergent views about what should be done in real and practical circumstances. While he recognizes that public action involves public agreement on a general way forward, he suggests that in some circumstances it may not be feasible to combine all views into one agreed way forward. As he argues:

> reasoned discussion can accommodate conflicting positions that may appear to others to be 'unreasoned prejudice', without this being quite the case. There is no compulsion, as is sometimes assumed, to elim-inate every reasoned alternative except exactly one … prejudices typically ride on the back of some kind of reasoning – weak and arbi-trary though it may be … unreason is mostly not the practice of doing without reasoning altogether, but of relying on very primitive and very defective reasoning. There is hope in this, since bad reasoning can be confronted by better reasoning.

The demands of public reason are real and can be exhausting. It is difficult to create safe havens for the public discussion about issues when you know these issues are hotly contested by different sections of the public. It is difficult to marshal all the reasoned bases (in concepts and evidence) that pertain to any one topic of public concern. And it is diffi-cult to be open to public enquiry about the reasons for decisions made in the public's name. But each of these difficulties needs to be overcome if the public are properly served and their problems genuinely solved.

Summary

An unintended consequence of building the most iconic and beautiful bridge in the world is that, since its construction, some 1500 people have committed suicide by jumping off it into the cold deep waters of the San Francisco Bay. Longitudinal research has shown that those jumpers who were prevented from leaping off the bridge went on to live full lives once their mental ill health episodes were over. And while greater numbers of people are murdered in San Francisco each year and/or die in fatal road traffic accidents than die jumping off the bridge, the nature of their deaths is different. People who are murdered are most usually killed by their 'intimates', such as family members, or by acquaintances (gang members or other 'prominent nominals' known to the police). Few murders involve random attacks from strangers. Strategies for preventing murders are therefore more complex than strategies for preventing suicides. And preventing traffic accidents is equally complex. The hazards of traffic accidents have led to substantial improvements in car safety and in enhancements to the design of highways and the associated highway furniture so as to reduce the impact of accidents. But the point of this chapter is not to highlight the efficacy of different strategies for preventing deaths by different causes in San Francisco. The case of the jumpers from the Golden Gate Bridge demonstrates the multiple aspects of governing in the 21st century.

Whether or not $50m should be spent on suicide prevention on the Golden Gate Bridge is a matter for those charged with the responsibility of operating the bridge for the benefit of the public. They were subject to well-organized 'claims makers' who argued that the jumpers were a topic of public concern that required a more adequate public response than was available hitherto. Those responsible for the governance of these issues in this part of California decided to consider all available options and then to narrow the options to three. They were subject to lobbies and campaigners from every angle, arguing every case (to name just four: the safety of pedestrians, the cost to the taxpayer, the preservation of historic architecture, and the potential problem of bird collisions). The Board of Directors and senior managers of the GGBHTD conducted a reasoned debate among themselves and, as importantly, they orchestrated a reasoned debate among the public. In so doing, they discovered ways of achieving better public value and they also built a 'licence to operate' to implement the finally agreed safety net proposal. At the conclusion of the process, an environmental impact report was accompanied by a FONSI report – which outlined the 'findings of no significant impact'. Conventional media and social media all played their part as did the impact of formal political lobbying. The case shows the extraordinary demands of public accountability at the beginning of the 21st century and the urgent and complex challenges to public agencies to do right and to do right well.

The absence of an ideal solution did not mean that no solution was possible. As Amartya Sen evocatively argues, 'If we are trying to choose between a Picasso and a Dali, it is of no help to invoke a diagnosis (even if such a transcendental diagnosis exists) that the ideal picture in the world is the Mona Lisa.'[20] The case of the Golden Gate Bridge shows that governing requires an appreciation of the public interest, a drive to generate better public value, and an ethic that involves public reason in discussing problems and choosing the best and most practical way forward that delivers the public good.

Chapter 4

Finding a Common Cause

Cooperation, community and the commons

A two-storey Victorian school in the Hillsborough area of the city of Sheffield in England is no longer used for teaching young children; it houses the Burton Street Foundation. The Foundation is an independent, mission driven organization that serves a number of social and community purposes. It specializes in hosting services for adults and older children with learning difficulties and with physical disabilities. But it also offers a range of other services to the local community in that part of the city of Sheffield. It offers dance classes for younger children and for older people. It offers music sessions for songwriters and musicians alongside drama sessions and art opportunities as well as gym and health sessions. And it houses a training and employment service that provides personally tailored sessions to people to help them back into employment. The Foundation is not a service provider – it is a 'community anchor' or a 'community hub'. It exists because Sheffield City Council had the foresight to transfer the building (at a price beneath market value) to a local community group rather than sell the land to the highest bidder or knock it down and redevelop the area for housing or office space.

Every day of the week the Burton Street Foundation is teeming with people of all ages and abilities. They thrive in the safe and assuring spaces of this rambling building. They are not usually doing things alone. Rather they dance, sing, craft and learn together in small social groups. The Burton Street Foundation lies at the centre of a strong network of social and community life in Sheffield. While it is home to these activities, it doesn't run them. It is not, however, a neutral landlord taking rent from the most promising tenants. It is a mission driven organization that wants to serve local community interests by providing a thriving place for much needed and highly valued community activities. It survives on a cocktail of funding from public, private and third sector organizations that provide the financial lifeblood to the organizations that operate from within the building.

The Burton Street Foundation is a great example of active community-based work. By being a community hub it offers space to emerging

57

community groups. In this way it helps community to develop. It enables common cause to be discovered among different types of social and community groups. The users of the building are not there because the building exists; they are there because it houses a social or creative activity that they wish to take part in. They learn life skills; they build a sense of personal accomplishment through their acquisition of craft skills; they engage with each other in activities that centre on work, heritage and place; and in so doing they help embroider the fabric of community locally. The building is successful because it blends together an array of complementary local uses that is socially useful and financially sustainable.

There are buildings just like this in many urban centres in many countries. Once important centres of the urban landscape, many of them are now underused or unused. Many of them are crying out for refurbishment, renewal and revitalization. Mostly they are prized but decaying assets that stir strong sentiments in people locally. Everyone wants them to be saved, to be sustained, to be brought back into a socially purposeful use, but few people can imagine how they can be enlivened so as to meet modern needs. And that is why the most usual outcome is wholesale redevelopment which sees them bulldozed and rebuilt for a single use: for housing, for retail space or for office space.

The economics of redevelopment means that the cost of financing the investment needed to bring old buildings back into use requires a sustainable stream of rental income from someone. And this is where it often falls down – few local community groups can develop the business model that makes their proposed use viable. And often local buildings become the site for squabbles between competing claims from different community groups who each want to use the building for their exclusive use. The Burton Street Foundation shows how this problem can be solved if the public authorities locally and the community groups themselves possess sufficient imagination and entrepreneurship. But the reason why this doesn't often happen is because it is often highly complex and difficult for different community groups to move beyond competing claims to finding common cause together.

In Britain, local governments are encouraged to consider the potential for transferring underused or unused public assets to community groups so that they can run these buildings for themselves. The idea of this policy is for each locality to identify the practical potential to enliven their communities through active 'public asset transfer' to existing community groups. But this is not a simple or straightforward policy to pursue. Some assets are, in fact, liabilities; some community groups are only interested in exclusive use; and some proposed uses are simply non-viable. But the Burton Street Foundation shows that it can be done. Community anchors and community hubs can spring up in the most unlikely settings. And complementary community uses can be devised which draw communities together and which ensure financial viability.[1] Of itself, asset transfer is a modest proposal but it represents one thread of a complex weave of public policies designed to alter the relationship between citizens and the state. In moderate form, these policies promote a modern type of community development; in radical form, they promote a change in the model to a more 'ownership state' where public facilities and assets could somehow be owned jointly by the service users and also by the employees who provide the services.[2]

One reason why these types of solutions are not commonplace is that public institutions have strong incentives to raise money by simply selling their unwanted assets in the marketplace and reinvesting the receipts gained in other public purposes locally. What's more, most public agencies are required to obtain 'best consideration' in their sale of their assets – seeking the maximum possible receipt from the sale. This acts to prevent fraud and corruption as well as guaranteeing that the public get the most money back for an asset that was, originally, developed out of public funds. However, many local governments can take wider community benefit considerations into account when selling assets – they can sell below market value if some alternative use can evidence wider community benefit. This is what Sheffield City Council did when they sold the school in Burton Street to a community organization at a price far below the market value.

But often community-based solutions to local problems fail not because public agencies hoard public assets but because the ideals of community leaders cannot be put into practice. The community groups themselves may not possess the capabilities to take on the responsibility of managing and running an asset. What's more, local community groups may contain too many personal rivalries to establish common cause among themselves. The ideals of common cause, in communities as much as in organizations, are often undermined by the egoism of individual action.

The call for social or collective action can seem naively idealistic amid the day-by-day clamour for personal or sectional advantage. Competitive individualism appears as the more realistic model – and one that is easier to achieve. If you have an asset you want to sell, it may be so much simpler and easier for you to put it on the market and accept the highest bidder than welcome offers from groups of people who propose to share their use of it somehow. Competitive individualism that is predicated on self-interest seems so sensible whereas cooperative action based on common cause seems so much harder to achieve. Why is this? Why does it seem so hard to find common cause? This chapter investigates the main arguments against cooperation and suggests that, in large part, they are based on conceptually impressive but, nonetheless, imagined barriers. There are real stumbling blocks on the path to finding common cause but by identifying them it is entirely feasible to find routes around them. Re-imagining the route to finding common cause is the central purpose of this chapter.

The roots of cooperation for the common good

In the liberal democracies of the modern world, we can mostly do what our natural inclination suggests to us. We can pursue any goal we choose and we can live our lives as we see fit. Of course, some of us grow up in conditions of more social or cultural restraint than others; some of us experience greater hardships than others; and some of us will set ourselves more stretching personal goals than others will – but in the context in which we live our lives, the choices we make are ours to make. What's more, most governments tend to view the actions of their citizens as though they are entirely fuelled by self-interest. That is because the model of citizens as rational actors in pursuit of their self-interests has bled across from classical economics to infect most of public policy.

However, our individual drive to do well is not simply about what we can get. It is also about what we can give. We live among others, and the demands of society require us to be for others and not just for ourselves. Of course we start with a concern for our immediate family. Indeed, the meaning of the word 'kindness' stems from concern with the well-being of our 'kinship', although its meaning has stretched over time to encompass more generalized sentiments such as sympathy, generosity, compassion and empathy – as well as words that have more ancient roots, notably *philanthropia* (love of mankind) and *caritas* (brotherly love).[3] As social beings we naturally feel with and for others – something that renders us simultaneously self-regarding and other-regarding. In fact our sympathetic attachments to other people help us to stay mentally sound and healthy: the absence of sympathy and empathy is characteristic of sociopathic personality disorder. The balanced individual needs feedback from others – we continually seek the affirming recognition and respect of others, not for what we have, nor for what we have done, but for who are and for what we contribute by being ourselves.

In a deep sense, our drive for personal fulfilment co-exists with our desire to get on well with others and fulfil the sense of obligation that we have to the community in which we live. And we balance this with our drive to action, to doing things, and to achieving things. We know that we must act, but we also know that the prospect of failure looms over our proposed actions. How, in the context of all these doubts, can we act with conviction and urgency? How can we act for personal fulfilment while also acting for the common good? How can we find common cause with others – pursuing common goals and making choices together? If we find that making choices for ourselves is hard, how much harder is it to make social or collective choices – choices for a group of people or choices for everyone?

Most classical economists would have us believe that rational self-interest and egoism fuel human progress. But we should harbour serious doubts about this assertion. After all, it was in Adam Smith's first book, *The Theory of Moral Sentiments*, that he examined the sources of human virtue and where he attributed much of human conduct to sympathy.[4] Smith's conclusions have found strong support from the past fifty years of research in evolutionary biology, where 'sympathy based cooperation' has been shown to have deep roots in our evolutionary path. While the modern human psyche reflects these strong tendencies towards cooperative behaviour, the precise evolutionary root of cooperative behaviour is hotly contested. Its most likely origin was kin-based group selection and the generational transfer of culture, custom and tradition.[5]

These evolutionary theories have been supported by recent brain science which has shown that we are most probably hard wired to be sympathetic to the feelings of others.[6] Just as are also probably hard wired to thrive in moderately sized groups of 150 or so people – groups small enough that we can feel close to everyone but not large enough for us to get lost in the crowd.[7] What's more, and unlike all other animals, we also seem to be hard wired to exercise retribution and punishment to those who fail to cooperate. For the punishment of cheaters appears to be a full blown feature of what it is to be human.[8] Whatever the precise path of human cooperation, the truth is that as individuals we are each of us keen to find common cause with others.

In economics, positive ideas about cooperation stem from rationalist arguments about the benefits of specialization and market exchange. The Nobel Prize-winning economist Kenneth Arrow expressed this point simply and elegantly:

First, individuals are different and have different talents; and second, individuals' efficiency in the performance of social tasks usually

improves with specialisation. We need cooperation to achieve specialisation of function. This involves all the elements of trade and the
division of labour. The blacksmith in the primitive village is not
expected to eat horseshoes; he specialises in making horseshoes, the
farmer supplies him with grain in exchange, and both (this is the critical point) can be made better off.[9]

This form of cooperation is essentially spontaneous and individualist.
It emerges from specialization and market exchange rather than from
some form of central or strategic plan. But cooperation can also result
from organization. For it is common to find complex forms of cooperation both within businesses and also across business boundaries. In fact,
cooperation is as much a feature of the business world as is competition.
Companies develop management strategies to encourage cooperation
internally. And they also develop organizational strategies to collaborate
with other companies, through formal mergers and alliances or through
more informal partnerships, to improve their combined profitability.
Indeed, the success of market economies rests on the success of very
many large companies. The largest companies produce substantial wealth
and value through staggering degrees of voluntary cooperation between
people working within these companies over extended periods of their
working lives.[10] After all, even Bill Gates didn't work alone.

The choice between acting alone or acting with others is not as difficult as economists would have us believe. Personal ambition sits alongside cooperation for the common good. What's more, it seems to come
naturally. Whether in families or in business, we seem to be able to
judge fairly readily and speedily when to go it alone and when to
cooperate.[11] While past progress is often depicted as arising from the
march of individual achievements throughout history, we can equally
suggest that it has been the cooperation between people that has been
the fuel for progress.

The conflict between personal ambition and common cause seems to
occur when individual actions appear to undermine efforts to build common
effort. And it is to this thorny issue that this chapter is addressed – the
dilemmas and the conundrums involved when individual actions conflict
with the interest of building common cause and building a healthy and
sustainable commons. But why is this important? Well, if the contours of
the state are in flux, if the boundary between the state and the citizen is
more fluid than before, then we need to come to new agreements as to
where responsibility lies – with individuals, with families, with civil
society and/or with the state. We need to know how best to shape common

cause. And furthermore, we need our democratic governments, at national and local level, to foster a new civility, to nurture higher levels of civil literacy, to re-establish civil conventions, to enable civil enterprises to grow and flourish and thereby to encourage a new compact for the commons. However, we may need to face the possibility that engaging in lofty rhetoric about building the common good is fruitless if individual action inevitably cuts away at the roots of practical cooperative endeavour.

Private, social and public choices

If I make a choice for myself it is a private choice. I do so to pursue my personal desires, ambitions, preferences and tastes; and, in part, to capture some of the value in the world to myself. This is something that each of us does every day – whether it is reading a book on self-improvement or buying something in the high street. It is an exercise of building private value. In pursuing my own interests I usually do so with other people whose interests are similar to mine. And my individual behaviour therefore has echoes in the behaviour of other people like me.

One problem is that when many thousands of us act together ('birds of a feather flocking together') the aggregate result may not be what we each individually intended. In the 1970s Thomas Schelling showed, from the prosaic example of how lecture theatres fill up from the back when students start arriving, that people's behaviour depends on what they think others are doing and that the aggregation of purposeful but individual behaviour often leads to perverse and unintended consequences.[12] His insight took another twenty or so years before it prompted the current growth of behavioural economics that is able to explain adverse social outcomes as the aggregate unintended consequence of individually rational behaviour.

The difference between individual and social actions may also stem from intention and motivation. For example, I may decide that for a particular purpose I will eschew individual action and, instead of acting alone, I may decide to get together with others who share some of my interests or preferences; people who live in the street where I live or whose interests and lifestyles are similar to mine, so that we can benefit by mutual association. When we do this together we might make a social choice. When we do so we are acting in a combined way in pursuit of our common interest as a group; we are pursuing our sectional interest, we are trying to capture some of the economic, social or cultural value in our community to ourselves as a group – an exercise of building social value.

However, when across our entire community choices have to be made that balance the interests of individuals and the interests of mutually supporting groups of people with the broader concerns of everyone, we are engaged in making public choices. Public choices for everyone differ from social choices made by and for groups of people. And it is almost impossible for us to make these public choices collectively – there are simply too many people involved, too many voices to be heard. And so these public choices are usually made through the prism of representative politics – by those elected by all of us to govern all of us, and who make choices on our behalf. This is the essence of governing: making collective choices that attempt to build public value for everyone. So private choices are about us acting as individuals; social choices are about some of us acting together; while public choices are about all of us acting as an entire community – usually through the process of governing.

Commonly, it is thought that by encouraging associational activity between people with like interests, government is fostering broader community spirit and strengthening the conditions for a healthy democracy. This is the key idea that springs from Robert Putnam's seminal work studying social capital in Italy in the late 20th century.[13] Putnam's core argument was that voluntary associations produce social capital through which civil transactions can be based upon trust in other people in society – people have the courage to cooperate because they are more likely to trust that others are going to cooperate. In this approach, voluntary associations provide a form of social cement in a locality or across a nation.

This idea is, however, somewhat circular and a little utopian. The supply of social capital in a group of individuals cannot at once be the explanation behind their cooperation while also constituting the cooperation that is being explained. And it is notable that throughout history and across cultures that strong social groups function not only so as to produce generalized trust among those involved in the group itself but also to produce mistrust – even hatred – of other people who are not.[14] Nonetheless, it remains widely assumed that the promotion of social capital through voluntary associations will lead to broader acceptance of civic virtues and the common good.

The most likely first step for individuals in moving away from the egoism of their own private interests is when they decide to act with others for social value out of sectional or group interests. And it is probable that many of the people who have adopted a social or group perspective about their interests may be more likely than others to adopt the broader civic virtues that serve the common good or that serve to build public value.

In this respect perhaps Edmund Burke was right when he said, 'to be attached to the subdivision, to love the little platoon we belong to in society, is the first principle (the germ as it were) of public affections. It is the first link in the series by which we proceed towards a love to our country, and to mankind.'[15] But perhaps also the 'little platoon' is just as likely to suffocate the instinct for the public good as it is to act as its springboard. The Burton Street Foundation is not a 'little platoon', although it hosts the actions of many such platoons; and in so doing it seeks to link the small group interests of each platoon to the wider civic virtues and public values about the common good. In this way, it is crucial to appreciate the distinctions between private choices, social choices and public choices.

Let's say, I choose to follow the sport of rugby and spend some of my money and available time at weekends, watching rugby matches. That's my private choice. If I join a sports association with other folk who want to do likewise and we decide to set up a formal social club and pool some money so that, among other things, we can lobby our local council for exclusive access to the commons on Sunday mornings so that our children can play rugby on the commons: that's our social choice. But if our local council decides that the benefits we gain as a social club are outweighed by the losses to the wider community through our exclusive use of the commons, albeit for a few hours on a Sunday, then they are exercising a public choice.

Governing involves choosing for everyone. To govern is to give a lead on public or common issues; rising above the entrapment of private or social interests. To be involved in government is to be entrusted with society's most complex problems and issues. Serving the public interest requires not just a focus on common problems but also a focus on problems of 'the commons'. Many problems exist in the world; but which of them need fixing now – which problems are urgent and which are important? Which problems if they were solved would, in turn, readily solve other related problems? Which problems should people solve for themselves? And which can be left to them to solve together by mutual adjustment and compromise among themselves? In short, when are problems really 'public problems' that require consideration by government?

The scale of the state and the persistence of the so-called 'wicked problems' have too often led us to believe that the state alone is capable of solving problems. In truth, many problems have been 'nationalized' – they have been captured by the state and described as problems that the state can best solve through government policy intervention. Of course, in some circumstances this approach will be successful. But usually these successes occur only in cases where people's problems are far beyond their capacity for self-help or mutual help. Examples include the street-based homeless or people with high drug dependency. We tend to forget that most people, most of the time solve most of their own problems themselves. And when they are unable to solve their problems, they tend to get together with other people like themselves with similar problems to try to solve them together.

This spirit of mutual aid and support among people with similar problems cannot be imposed or organized from outside – it emerges. This line of reasoning would suggest that it is only when individual self-help and mutual self-help are unable to solve people's problems that people then expect the state to help them. But this would assume the existence of a passive state that acted simply as a safety net. The role of the state – whether national or local – is not just to provide services, it also has an active role to help people help themselves.

While the state's role may be to exercise public choice for everyone, it also has a role in helping people make better private choices (such as not to smoke or drink too much) and also to help sustain better social choices through fostering community action and community enterprise. That is why the confluence of behavioural economics with modern social marketing techniques has been grasped by politicians and public policy professionals in an attempt to encourage some forms of civically virtuous or pro-social behaviour and discourage other forms of uncivil or anti-social behaviour.[16]

The seeds of pessimism about the commons

The notion that individuals and social groups would naturally seek to cooperate with each other for the overall common good has been painted as overly optimistic by a series of connected and pessimistic ideas. And over the past sixty years these pessimistic ideas have served to blight the optimism that seeks to encourage cooperation. If we are successfully to build common cause, we need to understand the deep pessimism of these ideas. They may be conceptually impressive but they are imagined nonetheless. We have to understand them if we are to re-imagine routes to cooperation and common cause.

There are four main seeds of pessimism. First, came Merrill Flood and Melvin Dresher's 1950 ingenuous idea of the 'prisoner's dilemma' which, through competitive gaming, demonstrated vividly why two people may not cooperate even if it is in both their interests to do so.

Second, came Mancur Olson's 1965 idea that, 'collective action was illogical' as people in groups, particularly those in large groups, would inevitably 'free ride' on the efforts of the majority. Third, came Garrett Hardin's 1968 idea of the inexorable 'tragedy of the commons' when people inevitably misuse a common resource that is open to all. And fourth, came John Platt's powerful idea in 1973 of 'the social trap', where he argued that people could not rationally decide to forget the past behaviour of others and that cooperative behaviour will only occur when people judge others to be trustworthy based on their prior behaviour.[17]

The first seed of pessimism – the prisoner's dilemma – essentially pivots on the idea that, without the benefit of discussion or even meeting others, people assess whether other people are likely to cooperate with them or betray them. The prisoner's dilemma is well known in game theory and fascinates scholars in that it produces a paradox where individually rational strategies lead to collectively irrational outcomes. In simple form, the dilemma can be described in the following way:

> Two suspects are arrested by the police. The police have insufficient evidence for a conviction, and, having separated the prisoners, visit each of them to offer the same deal. If one testifies for the prosecution against the other (that is, they betray) and the other remains silent (that is, they cooperate with the other through silence), the traitor goes free and the silent accomplice receives the full ten-year sentence. If both remain silent, both prisoners are sentenced to only six months in jail for a minor charge. If each betrays the other, each receives a five-year sentence. Each prisoner must choose to betray the other or to remain silent. Each one is assured that the other would not know about the betrayal before the end of the investigation.

At its most pessimistic this dilemma suggests that rationally inspired people are simply unable to cooperate with each other. This conclusion has suffocated attempts to foster cooperative endeavour for a number of decades. Its conclusions had widespread impact on public policy and business strategy. The powerful gaming strategies that derive from the dilemma influenced military strategies in the cold war and competition policies in the management of domestic economies, as well as business strategies between companies considering mergers and acquisitions.

The second seed of pessimism stems from Mancur Olson's idea that when people function in social groups, they will tend to 'free ride' on the efforts of others. He presents a very compelling argument that on first blush appears to corrode the case for cooperative endeavour. Let's explain

Olson's idea with a simple example. Imagine that this evening you are going for a meal with three other people to a restaurant. None of the four of you have met each other before, and the only thing you have decided in advance is that you will split the bill four ways. You arrive five minutes early and begin the social process of getting to know your dinner companions' names, where they are from, their family circumstances and the essential details of their working lives. All four of you sit down at the table together. You remind yourself which is the side plate intended for you and which glasses are for you to drink from – after all you don't want to come across as socially gauche! You then look at the menu. There are two starters: a plate of oysters (at £10) or lentil soup (at £4). You begin thinking quickly; 'if I choose lentil soup, I will be subsidizing the cost of their oysters'. Or alternatively you may think, 'I'll have oysters, and if they have lentil soup, they'll be subsidizing the cost of my starter'. In practice, and assuming you like both options and that night you are indifferent in your preference, you will consider both options simultaneously.

All this happens in just a fleeting moment but it involves highly complex considerations about your own preferences. It also involves your coming to a snap view of the likely preferences and motives of your three new dinner companions. Given the uncertainties of the moment, the most likely thing is that one of the four of you will say, 'is anyone having a starter?', followed by, 'what are you having?' What will then unfold will be a generative and emergent discussion between you as individuals about taste and preference with an underlying tone about anticipated costs and benefits.

The calculations that you are making in these moments are not just about money and the cost of your part of the bill but also about the emotional and social aspects of sharing a meal with these three other people. How do you want to come across to them? Are you likely to meet them again? Do you think that you may get to like them and want to meet them again? Your stance towards the starter dilemma will revolve around your assessment of these three other people; how they come across to you and the nature of their responses to the prompting first question. At the table, this will all be worked out through the practice of gossip and chat and general banter before the waiter arrives to take the order. It is a form of informal social deliberation.

Well, if it is that complex for four strangers to share information between one another about prospective costs and benefits over a meal,[18] how difficult is it for four hundred strangers? And what about 400,000? How about if it is for millions of people? This is the intrinsic problem of large groups trying to make common decisions about how they are prepared to share costs and benefits. And it is this issue that lies at the heart of politics: politics as a generative dialogue between people to seek compromise through discussion; and politics as the conduct of elected representatives in the act of governing by public dialogue, making public choice decisions, and finding common cause. Mancur Olson argued that the 'free rider' problem (you buying oysters in the hope that I will order lentil soup and so pay for a share of your costs) is endemic in collective choices and, moreover, that the problem grows with the size of groups.[19] In the past, social groups were based more on static hierarchy, whereas in today's world social groups are characterized by more fluid and dynamic lateral networks. That said, hierarchy remains powerful in social groups and 'free rider' effects are notable everywhere that people function in large groups.

The third seed of pessimism about the commons stems from a short article by Garrett Hardin powerfully entitled 'The tragedy of the commons'. Again, it relies on a simple idea – that when individuals use a scarce resource in common, such as goat herders on an open pasture, the tendency will be for them to overgraze the land. Hardin suggests that each goat herder is motivated to add more goats because he receives the direct benefit of his own animals and bears only the share of costs resulting from overgrazing. Hardin used the metaphor of the grazing commons to capture the problem of overpopulation, although the metaphor has been extended more widely across resource economics generally and in particular where a number of users have access to what are termed 'common-pool resources'.

According to Hardin, the crucial problem of the commons is not that there is confusion between common or overlapping interests, but that the sum of individual or group actions is generally destructive of the commons.[20] Hardin's argument has been made to apply specifically to fisheries and more generally to wider environmental problems such as CO_2 production and climate change as well as to social problems in densely populated urban areas.

This problem, of how to deal with open access demand on finite resources, produced two sets of solutions among economists. The first solution was privatization. If the pasture was divided equally between the respective goat herders and they were afforded property rights in respect of their part of the pasture, they would be more likely to exercise more control and consider the sustainability of their part of the commons. The second solution proposed was public ownership of the land and/or externally imposed enforcement of arrangements for goat grazing. In this latter solution a central authority must assume continuing responsibility to make decisions for a particular common pool resource. These two solutions, and minor variants of them, are proposed and implemented across the world for all manner of common pool resource problems. They apply in highly local communities (such as in access to water wells and access to communal areas on housing estates) as well as in international waters.

The fourth seed of pessimism stems from the idea of the 'social trap' that was developed in the early 1970s and appeared to add a fourth twist of the knife against the prospect of naturally occurring cooperative behaviour. The core of this pessimistic idea was that people's behaviour in relation to other people is based largely on how they believe these people will act in the future. And their judgement of how they anticipate they will behave is based largely on their view as to how these people behaved in the past. In this way, people get stuck in a social trap where they are unable to trust that other people will cooperate with them. Once this state of affairs is crystallized in people's minds, it is very difficult to escape from the trap. People get stuck in a negative feedback of mistrust and non-cooperation.

The practical case for cooperation and the commons

Weighed against these four strong pessimistic arguments are three highly practical accounts of how cooperation develops naturally in the life of a community. The first is found in the work of the evolutionary anthropologists such as Michael Tomasello. From comparative studies of primates and human infants, Tomasello has discovered that quite apart from any socialisation affects, human infants naturally cooperate with each other and with adults. Whether this is "informative pointing", fetching or sharing behaviour, infants appear naturally to develop shared intentionality with others between the ages of 12 months and 36 months. Humans have a remarkable capacity for cooperation which appears to have evolved from interactions from within local groups. As Tomesselo argues, "if people did not have a tendency to trust one another's helpfulness, lying could never get off the ground".[21]

The second account is found in the work of Robert Axelrod and the third is found in the work of Elinor Ostrom. Both Axelrod and Ostrom moved beyond the theoretical description of what happens when people do cooperate to suggest policies and approaches that might trigger cooperation as well as to reinforce tendencies towards cooperation. Robert Axelrod published the results of many thousands of games of the prisoner's dilemma in the mid-1980s. He discovered that (unlike in one-off games) in repeated games, cooperation was actually the most successful strategy for individuals taking part in the game.[22] This led him to conclude that the basis for cooperation lay in the existence of stable and durable relationships where reciprocity could flourish. Of course in real life most games are repeated; we encounter the same people over and over again in the course of our life and we engage with them today in the shadow of our past encounters. Axelrod argued that governments should act to encourage the emergence of cooperation. Here are his five simple and practical suggestions; they may seem overly straightforward but they also seem incredibly sensible:

1. 'Enlarge the shadow of the future' – mutual cooperation is stable if the future is sufficiently important relative to the present.
2. Change the 'payoffs' so that non-cooperation is more heavily penalized.
3. Teach people to care about the welfare of others.
4. Teach people about the benefits of reciprocity.
5. Improve people's abilities to recognize the pattern of other people's responses so as to sustain long-run cooperation.

Again in the 1980s, the political scientist Elinor Ostrom was examining among other things how self-organizing fishing communities operate when they are using a 'common pool resource'. She described how a large inshore fishery at Alanya in Turkey had over 100 fishers operating in two or three person boats using a variety of nets. Half the fishers belonged to a local producers' cooperative. After a decade of trial and error, the fishers adopted a number of rules that they established themselves – these had the effect of spacing the fishers far enough apart and ensuring that boats had equal chances to fish at the best spots. This meant that, among other things, the fishers wasted no time or effort searching for or fighting over fishing sites on the lake.

Tellingly, Ostrom argued that government officials could not have crafted such a set of rules without assigning full-time staff to work (or actually fish) in the area for an extended period. Instead, the fishers had used self-organizing principles to arrive at a workable solution that was both effective and equitable. Ostrom concluded that self-organized solutions for common pool resource problems are more likely to be effective than externally imposed solutions. She then identified a number of key factors for any group of people using common pool resources that enabled them to arrive at an effective self-organized solution.

First, Ostrom showed that participants need a capacity to communicate with one another; second, they need to be able to develop trust within the group; and third, they need to develop a collective sense that they share a common future. One of Ostrom's key insights was that the people who are best placed to monitor and control the behaviour of users of a common pool resource should themselves be users and/or have been given a mandate by all users. These are fundamental principles for creating a sound and sensible basis for communities of people to share resources sustainably. The only surprise is that it took another twenty years for the force and power of Ostrom's conclusions to gain her a Nobel Prize in economics.[23]

The principle of self-organizing solutions to common pool resource problems presents interesting opportunities for the wider development of public policy. Traditionally, solutions are explored in terms of externally imposed enforcement or of sectioning common pool resources between participants. And a good deal of effort is deployed in attempting to find policy instruments and specific fiscal incentives to conjure up these solutions. The key insight from Ostrom's work is that emergent self-organization can solve these problems if the participants understand the nature of the problem they share; if they communicate in a trustworthy manner with each other; and if they establish between themselves that they are most likely to share a common future together.

Elinor Ostrom's work has triggered further research in political science about how trust and social capital develop in societies and how governments could begin to encourage individuals and social groups to trust each other more so as to smooth the path to more cooperative behaviour. These include the American social theorist Robert Putnam[24] and the Swedish political scientist Bo Rothstein. Both of these thinkers have tried to identify the ways in which political institutions could build credibility and trust in society and how it may be feasible for governments to enable different groups to overcome their entrenched 'collective memories' about the past behaviour of each other.[25] Just as it is difficult to get Israelis and Palestinians to say, 'let's forget all the bad things we have caused one another and start all over again in a cooperative spirit', so too is it difficult to get taxpayers who have experienced grave corruption in tax administration (or abuse of authority by those who are elected to govern) to forget about it when their next tax bill arrives. Mistrust is seared into our memories – mistrust of other people and mistrust of government and political institutions.

Together, Axelrod and Ostrom have offered a route around the earlier pessimism about cooperative effort. Their work shows that it is not only feasible to build common effort; in many circumstances it is both natural and optimal. Individual actions do not always undermine the collective effort for the common good. But for cooperation to flourish, what is needed is a prevailing culture that fosters generalized respect and civility as well as trust and trustworthiness between people. What's more, if government action is to be trusted, its actions need to be seen to be trustworthy. To this end, the political institutions of the state and their public agencies will need to provide convincing evidence that change has really occurred in how they conduct their business.

Added to this, people need some assurance that civil society in the area where they live is characterized by respect and civility. For when neighbours are strangers to each other they need to adopt common civil norms. With the waning influence of custom and tradition, it can be ever more difficult for people to relate warmly to each other in communal settings. The 'lonely crowd' that is experienced in large urban settings sees people struggling to conduct their daily life amid a swarm of strangers.[26] And this produces a scarcity of respect, where, according to the sociologist Richard Sennett, 'no insult is offered another person, but neither is recognition extended; he or she is not seen – as a full human being whose presence matters.'[27]

But it is not just the scale of modern society and the pace of modern life that create problems of civility: so too do increasing social diversity and divergent social norms. Across very many nations, incivility is increasingly presented as a growing concern. This may be due to a rise in self-regarding behaviour or a growing disregard for the concerns of others. And while only a minority of people would demand a return to a more genteel and deferential age, there is no real appetite for a rude, coarse and aggressive style of public discourse. The case for a new civility is both strong and urgent if there is to be a revitalized civic life.[28]

Community enterprise and the discovery of common cause

With the retrenchment of public spending, many politicians will inevitably call for civil and community enterprises to enter the space vacated by the shrinking state. At its simplest, community enterprise is social enterprise functioning locally in communities. It is usually mission driven and it is usually grounded in local places. Most local governments are energized by a corresponding civic enterprise – they are not just running public services, they are also trying to foster a sense of civic spirit in their localities.

The Burton Street Foundation that opened this chapter has as its purpose enlivening its local community in Hillsborough, Sheffield. It has no social mission to extend its remit beyond Sheffield, to concern itself with community life in other places. As a community anchor it acts as both a magnet and a form of glue. It draws people into its activities and it cements social relations through the performance of these activities. The sources of community are found not only in people's bonds of belonging and attachment but also in a sense of mutual support and security at times of uncertainty. When the risks people face threaten to overwhelm their resourcefulness, if their community cannot in anyway help, then they live in communities that are characterized by 'bonds without consequence'.[29] By enabling people to offer support to each other during times of need, the Burton Street Foundation encourages bonds with consequence.

However, as elsewhere, the needs, demands and preferences of Hillsborough's local community are liquid. They change as the people in the area change and as the social fabric of the community changes. And so the Burton Street Foundation has to keep abreast of these changes. It needs to make sure that its offer remains relevant and appropriate locally. The Foundation is a host; it enables people locally to discover common cause through social action. But it is not a neutral host – it seeks to promote cooperation and common endeavour. In this way, the Foundation in Sheffield does not seek to build or develop a community; rather it helps community to be discovered by people themselves – people who may share fragments of a common history but who also may share fragments of a common future together.

The practice of getting people to become involved in group or common action is extremely difficult. This is because there are real participatory dilemmas. The larger the group, the more insignificant any individual's efforts appear. If we are to read Mancur Olson's work closely, its pessimism may infect us so that we conclude that it is not possible to motivate and sustain collective action under conditions of 'free riding'. And yet we also know that people are not driven solely by material benefits or expected 'pay-offs' from their engagement with others in any group action. Our life experience tells us that people gain enormously from their involvement in collective action. Being part of a group with others can help people improve their self-esteem, their self-respect and even their sense of self-worth. This is because it is so empowering to be actively involved in contributing to some purpose greater than one's own self-interest.

Of course different countries contain very different cultures around volunteering and community involvement. In the mid-19th century,

Alexis de Tocqueville famously described the rich 'associational' life of American civil society and showed how it differed from the then civil life in France and in Britain. But differences persist to current times. A cross-national poll conducted in 2010, about people's willingness to contribute their time or their money to helping others, showed significant national differences. In Britain, 77 per cent of respondents said that they had personally donated money to charity in the previous 12 months. This compared to 71 per cent of Americans, 62 per cent of Italians, 50 per cent of French, 45 per cent of Spanish and 42 per cent of German respondents. By contrast, British respondents were the least likely to agree that, 'everyone should be encouraged to give up some of their time to help support public services at a time of economic uncertainty and government cuts'. Only 25 per cent of people in Britain agreed with the statement. This was far lower than in the other countries and well below the 42 per cent of Italians and Americans who thought it their duty to participate.[30]

People are driven not just by a positive passion to achieve something for themselves but also to achieve something for a community with which they identify. What's more, we know that people are ruled not just by passions to feel something positive but also by their passions to avoid feeling something negative (like avoiding a sense of shame or guilt that may be felt if they act in a way that they know will bring disdain from others).[31] And we also know that the more an individual's well-being and sense of identity are tied to a group, the stronger they feel a social obligation for mutual assistance. As the social psychologist Albert Bandura suggests:

> many people shy away from collective action not because they can gain benefits without the costs of participation but because they seriously doubt the group's efficacy to secure any benefits at all. They see little purpose in taking ineffectual action that will only inflict troublesome costs with little prospect of benefits. [However] .... social reforms are achievable by a critical mass of activists rather than requiring universal participation. If social change depended on everyone participating, it would rarely be attempted because few would believe that a huge populace can be mobilised. In fact social reforms are typically the product of an efficacious and highly committed minority of people who invest themselves in shaping a better future. They are the driving force for social change. Their belief that they can bring about change and mutual support insulate them against discouragement.[32]

However, not only are the participatory dilemmas in collective action overcome in theory, we know from history that they are overcome in practice. The American cultural anthropologist Margaret Mead famously said, 'Never doubt that a small group of thoughtful committed citizens can change the world; indeed it is the only thing that ever has.' Common cause is not found in the mass efforts of everyone but by the efforts of small groups of highly committed people who share a vision of how their world can be changed for the better and who can best share their energies and efforts to achieving the change they wish to make.

Forms of localized social action are a powerful force in helping cooperation to flourish more generally across society. This is why governments at the national and local level need to enliven mutualism, social action and community enterprise. In doing so they may be able to devise more responsive and lower cost options for sustaining services during a period of public spending retrenchment. They need, however, to beware a philosophy that simply adopts an approach based on Edmund Burke's 'little platoons' for this may encourage fragmenting public interests into sectional interests. Thirty years before Burke wrote about his 'little platoons' another of the American Founding Fathers, Alexander Hamilton, warned of the dangers of this form of sectionalism and wrote instead of the mutual duty of each branch of civil society towards each other:

> In a civil society it is the duty of each particular branch to promote not only the good of the whole community, but the good of every other particular branch. If one part endeavours to violate the rights of another, the rest ought to assist in preventing the injury. When they do not but remain neutral, they are deficient in their duty; and may be regarded, in some measure, as accomplices.[33]

This 18th-century argument has been revised by several current-day thinkers – and in Britain most notably by the Chief Rabbi, Jonathan Sacks. He suggests that because modern nations are now made up of such social difference they need to find new ways to identify shared interests across groups with conflicting values and specific interests. He suggests a model of citizenship based less on individual rights and more on responsibility to wider society. His model is based on the idea that different communities need to do practical work with each other and not simply co-exist.[34]

This is a prime purpose of government – enabling us all to live together with as much harmony and cooperation as we can muster. The secondary purpose of government is to help people share responsibility for the costs and benefits of the commons. Public policies that encourage self-organizing solutions to common problems should therefore be a starting point for governments. For governing involves much more than the managerial tasks of securing effective and efficient public services; it also involves facilitating public discussion, mediating between competing interests, building common ground and assisting people to discover common cause among themselves.

Chapter 5

Deciding in a Democracy

Revealing public preferences and balancing biases

I learnt to swim as a young boy while on holiday in the seaside town of Margate on the Kent coast in England. Rather than brave the waves in the open sea, I chose the beach lido that was refreshed by seawater on the turning tide. Swimming came easy – the salt water kept me buoyant, and the lido walls kept the waves out. Returning to London after my holiday I decided that I wanted to go swimming again – but there were very few swimming pools in London at the time. Finding somewhere to swim was difficult. However, my friends and I got to learn of a swimming pool within reach by bus. It was said to have the warmest water in London. After a journey of some three miles we arrived at the New Cross 'baths'. There were two separate entrances to the baths: one for men and boys, the other for women and girls. The changing cubicles were rudimentary and were set along the edges of the pool – the men and boys on one side, the women and girls on the other. The noise inside was a cacophony of splashing and laughter mixed with the shrill whistles of the attendants, who seemed to be struggling to maintain a sense of order among the joyous chaos. There was no diving board but part of the fun involved lots of jumping in at the deep end. My most vivid memory is of the warmth of the water. The folk tales were true. The water was as warm as a bath. It was so inviting that it made you want to swim for hours and never get out. We all left with skin like prunes and eyes red with the chlorine. But it was tremendous.

The baths in New Cross had been built in 1895 by the vestry board of St Paul's Deptford. In Victorian London, local government was a complex patchwork of church and lay vestries that were responsible not only for the ecclesiastical affairs of parishes but also for the local administration of the Poor Law and various other laws.[1] The Baths and Wash-Houses Act of 1846 gave powers to vestry boards to build baths and wash-houses to promote the cleanliness of London's vastly growing working classes in the context of an increasingly insanitary capital. The population of

London had grown from one million in 1800 to some seven million by 1900 (which at the time was one-quarter of England's entire population). Hence one of the biggest issues for the governance of Victorian London was cleanliness and sanitation. The first wash-house had opened in Glasshouse Yard in the City of London in 1845 and its popularity among London's labouring working class prompted the 1846 Act and spawned many more such wash-houses across the capital. Indeed, the volume of demand for these baths and wash-houses was sufficient to produce quite significant operating profits.

By the end of the 19th century, the various vestry boards in London became incorporated into the newly formed local Boroughs. St Paul's vestry became part of Deptford Borough Council, which therefore took over the running of the New Cross baths. Some 60 years later, at about the time when I started swimming in the baths, London's government underwent a further reorganization and the local Deptford Borough Council became incorporated into Lewisham – one of London's new multi-purpose London Boroughs. By this time the insanitary conditions of London had been transformed and the vast majority of the capital's working classes had baths in their own homes. This meant that the main purpose of the public baths had changed from cleanliness (in the 1860s) to recreation (in the 1960s).

However, the New Cross baths closed in 1991, less than one hundred years after they were first opened. The cost of bringing the old baths up to modern standards was prohibitive and new trends in swimming had emerged. Young families with small children were said to prefer shallower, large leisure 'splash pools' with slides, flumes and more modern changing facilities. The old and small Victorian baths at New Cross with their antiquated changing rooms were no longer fit for purpose; and so when a newly designed leisure pool, Wavelengths, opened in 1991 in Deptford (next to St Paul's church itself which had originated the old vestry board), the staff from New Cross were redeployed to the new pool and the old baths closed down. Their warm inviting water was never to entertain youngsters again. The old building that housed the baths was adjacent to Deptford Town Hall, and to sustain the heritage of the building locally it was transferred to Goldsmiths College, of the University of London, whereupon it was converted for use for lectures and seminars for undergraduate students of politics. A location that was once for wet joy became a place for dry reflection.

Making a decision about a swimming pool

Just four miles away from the site of the New Cross baths, the Victorians had in 1885 built a swimming pool in Forest Hill. This pool had not decayed at the same rate as the one in New Cross but, after 140 years, it was in desperate need of investment to allow it to continue in use for swimming. In 2006, the pool at Forest Hill had to be closed following an inspection of the roof by surveyors. The pool had to be redeveloped for entirely different purposes or it needed to be refurbished or rebuilt. The local campaigns to refurbish the pool galvanized the energies of very many local community activists as well as swimmers. And so two options were considered.

The first option was to demolish the old Victorian pool and rebuild it anew on the same site. However, this was likely to be opposed by those local residents who wanted to preserve the appearance of the old building. The many thousands of users of Forest Hill pool had strong advocates. There were several informal associations and a highly active and successful swimming club. In addition, several local amenity societies argued strongly in favour of the preservation of the pool as a building of local heritage and because of its aesthetically pleasing character. These local amenity societies were active, vocal and well connected. Additionally, while the pool served a wide catchment area, it was itself located in an electoral ward that returned three councillors. These three councillors were elected among some 10,000 electors. By contrast, the mayor was elected 'at large' across the whole of the borough – among some 180,000 electors. Moreover, the three local ward councillors were members of a different political party to the directly elected mayor. To add to the mix, the mayor himself lived in the electoral ward in which the pool was located. The pool was deteriorating, the cost of refurbishment was escalating; it was going to be quicker and cheaper to demolish the old pool and start again, but the campaign to preserve the old building had very many vocal supporters. This example of competing preferences and biases – involving swimmers and non-swimming taxpayers, local amenity preservers and custodians of public resources – is therefore also intertwined with competing views about democratic legitimacy and contested views about who best speaks for local interests and who is best placed to decide.

The decision about whether to rebuild or refurbish the pool at Forest Hill encapsulates how, through public consultation exercises, public officials attempt to reveal public preferences; how any one issue can become a magnet for differing interests; how biases can get mobilized by stakeholders; and how effective decision-making requires all these preferences and biases to be articulated and balanced. Everyone agreed on one thing – that Forest Hill pool was not fit for modern purposes and was in need of considerable repair. But public resources were constrained; public users of swimming pools were unlikely to be willing (or even able) to finance the full operating costs of the pools let alone the cost of their construction. In addition there were many other competing investment priorities including social care, social housing, school building, road resurfacing and so on. This meant that the problem was about more than balancing the supply and demand for swimming pools. It was also about the quantum of scarce public resources that ought reasonably to be allocated to swimming pools at the expense of other public priorities.

Before any formal decisions were made, three different phases of public consultation took place about the future of the pool at Forest Hill. In October 2005, the Council undertook public consultation on two options: the first option involved retaining and refurbishing the existing pool at a cost of £4.0m; the second involved rebuilding a new pool on the existing site at a cost of £4.7m. To consult on these two options, over 20,000 leaflets were distributed to local residents and other methods were used including an online resident questionnaire, focus groups, exit surveys (of pool users) and two well-attended public meetings. The responses to the consultation were fairly evenly split: broadly, local residents and amenity societies preferred the refurbishment option that retained the existing building, whereas swimmers preferred the rebuild option.

It was after this consultation exercise had been completed that the roof in the pool deteriorated further and the pool had to be closed. Ironically, this created a space to conduct further consultation on the future of the pool. At this juncture it was considered that to make the scheme viable it might be sensible to consider redeveloping the adjoining building (another Victorian public building) to make the scheme larger and include some housing or retail use as part of the overall development. Independent architects were appointed and they produced three options. These options involved different mixes of housing and retail development, although each option included two pools. These options were rendered redundant when one of the amenity groups locally successfully lobbied English Heritage to get the adjoining building 'listed' because of the value of its heritage and its architectural merit – this effectively prevented the larger development from happening.

The Council then returned to the drawing board and came up with two final development options that it put to wide public consultation in the spring of 2009. The first option was to build on the original site while retaining the Victorian facade; the second option was to build the pool on a nearby site. The benefit of the second option over the first was simply that it could be delivered sooner. The consultation undertaken in early 2009 included postal surveys to local residents, online surveys, in-depth public interviews, focus groups and a telephone survey of residents, local businesses and schools. The results were equally balanced: again, swimmers mainly wanted the pool delivered earlier and so tended to choose the second option; whereas local residents tended to be more concerned about preserving the amenity of the building and therefore supported the first option.

At the final meeting when the mayor considered these options, there were over 100 members of the public present. The atmosphere was tense, as this issue seemed to have dominated local politics for about five years. At the meeting three sets of voices were heard. First, the mayor asked the professional officers to present their considered view of the issues, the technical and financial factors and their views as to what public opinion was on the basis of the online, written and interview responses. Then, representatives of swimming groups, local residents and amenity societies spoke for nearly an hour on their preferences and gave their account of what should be decided. And finally, the locally elected councillors spoke for ten minutes or so on what they thought should happen.

The mayor then made his decision. He spoke for ten minutes. He outlined the different voices that he had heard and the different factors that he had to weigh in the balance. He said that he couldn't please everyone and was bound to disappoint some of those present. But he also said that avoiding a decision was worse than making a less than best decision. He chose the option that preserved the Victorian facade. The pool at Forest Hill is now being rebuilt at a cost of some £12m. It will be completed just before the London Olympics starts. While the facade will be kept intact, the pool will be unrecognizable. Making this decision had been very difficult – almost painful. And the factor that was most complex and that took most time was the consultation with the public and local stakeholders. The mayor could have made the same decision earlier but he judged it important that the decision made was one that was based on the widest consultation. This is because he felt that to do so would make it easier to implement any decision that he made. Electors may want decisive politicians who lead but they also want accountable politicians who actively listen to as many voices as possible.

As individuals we can decide to go swimming, but we can't decide to build a swimming pool – that's a matter for us all to decide collectively. But we find that we can't do that. Our interests are too diverse, our perspectives too varied and our voices too disparate. That is why we elect people to represent us. They can decide for us. But their democratic legitimacy is inherently fragile. In most democracies, elected politicians are seldom voted into office by a majority of their electors (although some may have the majority support of those who voted). This factor weighs heavily with many elected politicians and therefore they rightly attempt to connect the requirement on them to make decisions on our behalf, with participatory approaches to governance. In short, they recognize that their democratic legitimacy can be strengthened through complementary deliberative approaches. Well, at least the best of them do.

When public decisions are made, the public want to know that those making the decisions are accountable and that those engaged to provide advice about these decisions are themselves open for scrutiny. Of course, in making their decisions these politicians are bound to have regard, somewhere in their personal calculus, to the bearing of the decision outcome on their subsequent electoral prospects. But we hope that this factor is marginal and does not routinely bias their considerations. For in making these public decisions, we expect politicians to act reasonably and to consider analyses and proposals on the basis of best available evidence. Moreover, we expect public decisions to be made in the light of considerations as to what consequences might flow from these decisions. That is why making any public decision requires care and considered judgement.

In the case of the pool at Forest Hill, this could be done over a fairly leisurely period. Many other public decisions need to be made much more quickly under the urgent pressure of the moment and the demands of unfolding events. However, it is not the pressure of the moment that leads to flawed decision-making – rather it is the inherent biases of the human mind. Decision makers can have too much regard to irrelevant issues and too little regard to relevant factors and they can be confounded by attempts to work out 'what is best?' This is because decision-making is not a straightforward process of rational logic: what counts for 'the best decision' is extremely difficult to judge; and furthermore it requires emotional intelligence as much as an appreciation of costs, benefits and potential consequences. The science of decision-making is a new and growing multidisciplinary domain of knowledge. It involves psychology and ethics, as well as economics and politics. In the case of public decision-making there are two main sets of boundaries and biases: first of ethics; and second, of cognition or understanding.

Making decisions: ethical boundaries and cognitive biases

Making any personal decision is a matter of will as much as it is a matter of reasoned choice – whether it is to choose to swim today, to swim tomorrow, or never to swim at all. Making a personal decision, such as whether or not to swim, involves a fairly complex calculus. Making a public decision, such as whether or not swimmers should be supported by public subsidy, is even more complex as it involves moral reasoning. Personal decisions require individuals to give reason to their inclination and will – so that they can answer the question 'why did you chose to do that?' Public decisions by contrast require decision makers to pronounce on the ethics of why they chose one course over another. Ethical considerations swamp all others when making public decisions. Ethical issues, about choosing between right and wrong options, dominate public decisions. And in the real world, right and wrong are matters of ethics not logic.

Having a solid ethical framework helps public decision makers think through the moral basis for their decisions – why they feel able to describe some outcomes as fairer and more morally just than others. But when public decision makers wrestle with practical problems, they find that they often have to delineate new ethical boundaries. This is because ethics centres on practical reasoning applied to real-life problems. Public ethics assists us to address current practical problems, dilemmas and quandaries.

The source of ethical approaches to public decision-making can be found in the mainstream religions of the world as well as in some central tenets of philosophy stemming from Ancient Greece and the Enlightenment. In the West, the ethical bases for public decision-making stemmed initially from the practical application of the ancient virtues of justice, temperance, prudence and courage (virtues that were developed over centuries by philosophers and theologians alike).[2] However, much of what passes for ethics and public decision-making rests on the 'utilitarianism' that was developed in the late 18th century by Jeremy Bentham. In his approach, the moral worth of any decision or any action is best judged by its utility in providing happiness or pleasure to people. If public decision makers adopt a 'utility principle', they should as a matter of course, 'chose whichever will bring about the best consequences'. Following in Bentham's footsteps,[3] John Stuart Mill argued that because people tended to know what was best for them they should be free to follow their natural inclination as long as it did not cause harm to others. Thus the 'best consequences' rule that promoted 'the greatest good to the greatest number' became modified in the 19th century to the rule to 'minimize harm to others'.

This utility-based approach is known as 'consequentialism'. It is a cogent and widely accepted approach to public policy. However, it has its limitations and the practical application of utilitarian principles is not as straightforward as the language that describes them.[4] The aim of achieving 'the greatest good for the greatest number over the long run' seems both right and admirable. But then if you consider the outcomes for those in the smallest number it doesn't seem quite so just. Moreover, the suggestion that your happiness ought not to rise at the expense of mine, seems OK at first mention but if you are penniless and miserable and I am wealthy and extremely happy, the suggestion seems rather odd. On something as fairly simple as whether or not to use public money to rebuild a swimming pool, public decision makers can quickly become enmeshed in a tangled web of conflicting interests where people want different outcomes and adopt contrary positions on what should be done. In these difficult situations, the correct course for public decision makers is one that holds fast to five core ethical principles:[5]

1. Treat people according to their own wants and intentions and not by what you think others want of them (the principle whereby other people are treated as ends not means).
2. Let people chose for themselves (the principle of autonomy), unless you can be absolutely sure that you know their interests better than they can.
3. Empathize with the needs of others and be true to your obligations to them (the principle of selflessness and service).
4. Provide direct help to people if the help you give is worth more to them than it is to the public at large (this help principle means that help is afforded to where it is needed but not if it is too difficult to give or if the help would be wasted).
5. Encourage people to help each other through fostering mutually reciprocal behaviour (the principle of community).

The ethical boundaries on public decision makers describe one set of constraints on decision-making in respect of public choices. The other is found in the cognitive biases that public decision makers share with all human beings. For example, neurological research has shown, from case studies involving people with damage in the relevant parts of their brain, how those people who are incapable of experiencing emotion are unable to come to decisions.[6] Decision-making requires emotional maturity not emotionless detachment. People who lack emotions suffer the disease of indecision. But procrastination is not simply limited to people with serious brain damage – the tendency to procrastinate vies, in all of us, with the tendency to jump to judgement. That is why making decisions can be as exhausting as it is empowering. However, in coming to decisions we seldom do so based on an emotionally detached examination of the issues: habit, preference and prior belief come into play to motivate our reasoning.

This factor is something that cognitive researchers and decision scientists refer to today as 'confirmation bias'. This is a potent bias that acts so as to contaminate even our most reasonable of beliefs. In short, we tend to pay more attention to stuff that fits our prior beliefs than stuff that might challenge them. Every memory we have, every choice we make, and every belief we hold is subject to this confirmation bias – in short, we prefer to believe what we want to be true. What is more, experimental research has demonstrated clearly that our capacity to make decisions is subject to powerful contextual biases; such as 'halo effects', focusing illusion; framing and priming effects; anchoring and adjustment impacts; and the familiarity effect.[7] That is why even the most experienced public decision makers can make flawed, even catastrophic, decisions. Most commonly, they either place over-reliance on the lessons of their previous personal experience or they become emotionally attached to pursuing particular solutions.[8]

Those at the fringe of decision-making often know that the decision being made is the wrong one, but they are subject to powerful social norms to say nothing. Sometimes people are keenly aware of the risks and perils of a chosen course of action but they stifle their doubts, speak too quietly or fail to register their disquiet because of organizational or group cultural pressures to pursue a particular goal. This 'bystander' effect has been shown to have disastrous consequences in a range of cases – from the *Challenger* space shuttle disaster in 1986 to the corporate finance fiascos of 2008. Bystanders within organizations can institutionalize incaution in the face of known and foreseeable risks. The Gulf of Mexico has been subject to two highly visible examples in the recent past. First, the denial of peril and risk by public authorities and the incomplete development of a flood control levee system, led to 1800 deaths and the spending of $200bn of public resources in the case of hurricane Katrina in New Orleans in 2005.[9] Second, the known risks of deep sea oil drilling, and the gradual incaution that led to the disaster at the BP oil rig at Deepwater Horizon, killed 11 workers and caused the biggest ever oil spill in the world (4.9 million barrels) during three months of 2010.[10]

Conventional approaches to decision-making assume that the underlying cognitive process is hyper-rational and that the key problem is to account for the pursuit of self-interest among the parties to any decision. In truth, decisions are made as much from fear of the consequences as from a drive for self-interest. Motivation to decide, to choose, is like all motivation – a blend of desire and fear: searching for attachments and affirmation as well as searching for comfort and safety in habit and routine. And decisions are based as much on prior conviction as freshly minted evidence, for as Bertrand Russell remarked, 'every man, wherever he goes, is encompassed by a cloud of comforting convictions, which move with him like flies on a summer day.'

Over fifty years ago Herbert Simon suggested that decision-making is in practice characterized by 'bounded' rationality.[11] In the main, people are happy with results that are 'good enough' as opposed to always pursuing the ideal. And they do not want to be confronted with a blizzard of information. The human brain can only cope with so much information at any one time. When it is grappling with too many facts, major mistakes can be made through confusing important issues with trivial issues.[12] Cognitive scientists have discovered that, just as too much information can produce bewilderment, so too much choice can create indecision.[13] People can become overwhelmed and unable to cope with the combinatorial possibilities involved in a myriad of trade-offs. This can apply to the purchase of jam in a supermarket as much as to the decision about where to spend one's holiday this year. All these factors together mean that public decision-making (like all types of decision-making) is a complex business involving a blend of emotion and reason. Some of us may be subject to a strong personal sense of prudence, temperance and self-control, while others may be more wanton and be blown by the winds of the moment. But whatever our personality and our motivation, all of us choose in the context of the circumstances before us and with the same set of cognitive biases.

This means that most public choices tend to involve intricate layers of questions. It is not simply a question of 'how best do we make public choices?' but of what constitutes a public choice and how are the claims, interests and inevitable biases taken into account in the framing of these public choices: decisions such as spending public money refurbishing a swimming pool; or demolishing it and building a new one; or not building a new one and advising those who want to swim to go to other pools instead.

We should perhaps start by acknowledging that every discussant is subject to some degree of bias, cognitive or otherwise. Those who want to swim in a public pool that is built and operated at taxpayers' expense are biased. Those who live nearby and wish to preserve the amenity afforded by an iconic Victorian building in their vicinity are biased. The politicians who seek office and/or who wish to sustain themselves in office are biased. And the professionals who advise and who manage the services are biased for a whole range of career-enhancing reasons.

Second, we need to acknowledge that everyone involved will want to mobilize bias in the decision-making for their own benefit or towards the solution they favour the most. One of Jeremy Bentham's early fears in the development of his utilitarian approach was what he termed, the 'sinister interests' of politicians who may be motivated to pursue their own collective group interest rather than the common good.[14] The mobilization of bias in political decision-making (and in 'non-decision-making') has long been reported but the truth is that all stakeholders will attempt overtly or covertly to mobilize bias to their favoured solution or away from their least favoured solution.[15] Therefore it is crucial in framing public decisions that the principles of disclosure, openness and transparency are adopted explicitly at the outset and are maintained throughout the process of choice making. What's more, public decisions usually involve some form of moral calculus: is it fair to decide this in this way; or is it morally just that this particular outcome occurs? Moral questions that pose issues of fair process and just outcomes are demanding for those involved in decision-making. For at their core these questions require sympathy, generosity, consideration for others and a public spirited sense of practical justice.

There is no algorithm for making public decisions

It would be so much easier if an algorithm existed for making public decisions. Algorithms are step-based instructions or rules that enable a problem to be solved (such as, 'why doesn't the light work?') so that decisions can be made (such as, 'change the light bulb' or 'fix the wiring in the switch'). It would also be easier if some formula could be devised: one into which all the possible advantages and disadvantages could be loaded; all the factors could be weighted according to some collectively agreed set of principles; and a decision emerge that was of optimum public utility and was fair to all. Many people involved in government across the world are searching for some algorithm or some formula. Some are searching, more prosaically, for some form of measuring rod: one that enables national or community 'well-being' to be measured. This search is rooted in a Benthamite stance – a search for a community calculus: of measured losses and of measured gains. But despite

Bentham's elaborate calculations, it remains impossible to devise an algorithm to combine incommensurable factors or to devise some mechanism that enables us to choose between, say, competing claims for public resources.

In his book *The Idea of Justice*, Amaryta Sen describes the problem of deciding between competing claims by use of a simple illustration.[16] Imagine, three children squabbling over a flute. Anne claims the flute because she is the only one who can play it. Bob claims the flute because he is poor and the only one of the three without toys or musical instruments at home. Carla claims the flute on the grounds that she spent a long time making the flute herself. The point is not just that the vested interests of the three children differ but that the three arguments they advance to support their claims each rely on a different type of impartial and non-arbitrary reasoning. Incompatible claims may rely on incommensurable values that cannot be sorted by reference to a simple formula.

The achievement of satisfactory solutions to competing claims relies on a healthy functioning democracy that is plural and inclusive: one that enables participants to invoke their claims and that ensures that these claims are heard and discussed widely. This is easier said than done. Sensible elected politicians are cautious at over-interpreting public views. Those who are recently elected may place a little too much reliance on the strength of their 'mandate' in deciding public questions; although most will acknowledge the authentic and genuine claims on public resources of different local interest groups. But many elected politicians will want to have a reliable canvass of general views to weigh against the specific demands of particular views that are more routinely brought to their attention. To this end, extensive public consultation is a conventional precursor to any final public decision. In this way, representative democracy bleeds into participatory democracy through the engagement of the public in discussing and debating public interest issues and questions.

Deliberation: the prospects and perils of participation

The word 'deliberation' conveys two meanings at once: to balance, and to decide. The latter of these meanings is perhaps the oldest. The 17th-century British political philosopher Thomas Hobbes argued that before performing any action we may be said to possess 'the liberty to do or not to do' the action concerned. The process whereby we arrive at a decision is thus the 'taking away of our own liberty'. Hobbes described this process as de-liberating ourselves. When we decide to act we choose between our appetites that incline us to act and our fears that withhold us from acting. In this old interpretation of the word, deliberate, it means arriving at a decision. However, for Hobbes, true liberty also consisted in not being a slave to the passions.

At the same time that Hobbes was writing, there was a fashion for 'emblem books'. These books contained picture–text combinations intended to inspire their readers to reflect on a general moral lesson derived from the reading of both picture and text together. One such lesson was contained in the emblem book by Jean Jacques Boissard, which depicted liberty as 'balance', through the image of scales for comparing weights, rather than as decision. The idea ran as follows: many people are slaves to the body. The man who is able to avoid such licence and may therefore be said to flourish in true liberty is he who prudently weighs his passions in balance with reason and care. The moral is that we must learn to keep our balance (*librare*) if we wish to free ourselves (*liberare)* from the passions that will otherwise reduce us to servitude. In this sense, deliberation is about balance as much as it is about deciding.[17]

When many people deliberate they inevitably want different things. They start from different points of origin and they may want to go to different destinations. Moreover, their personal experiences differ. Experiential diversity provides the backcloth against which all other forms of diversity are cast. The point of participatory governance is to ensure that as many people as possible have their say so as to try to encompass difference in the public decisions that are made. When people have relatively fixed views it is easier to take account of them; however, when they have fairly unclear or unstable preferences, it is much harder to take account of their views. This deficit in the democratic process is the problem to which 'deliberative techniques' are the answer. These techniques include:

- **Citizens' panels** – these tend to be based on the deliberative polling technique designed by James Fishkin. This approach relies on informing a randomly selected large group of citizens who then discuss the merits of various positions without reaching a consensus or a collective choice.[18]
- **Citizens' juries** – these tend to be a randomly selected small group of citizens who are convened to consider and debate an issue on which they then issue their collective findings and recommendations.

- **Community conferences** – these tend to be large 'Town Hall' style events where citizen participants debate contested issues in small groups and may then use collaborative technologies to create common views that are then shared and discussed further in a recursive fashion.
- **Direct democracy** – this includes techniques such as binding or non-binding referenda as well as delegating decision-making to those closest to the problem. The populism of this approach is attractive to many but it contains a number of obvious problems. First, all citizens participating should, as far as is feasible, do so on the basis of a common information base (referenda on capital punishment differ in nature from, say, referenda on the adoption of an alternate currency of exchange – the euro or the dollar). Second, the consequences of the decision should bind only on those invited to participate, regardless of their participation.

The prospect of participatory and deliberative forums is that they offer chances for citizens to engage with each other and with public officials (both elected and appointed) in ways that strengthen popular accountability, through reasonable public dialogue, and so begin to address the dilemmas involved in making public choices. However, these techniques, while powerful as a means of informing and educating citizens who participate, suffer two fundamental and insuperable problems. First, that deliberation can be debilitating for those involved. In a well-honed joke, Clement Attlee famously quipped that, 'democracy means government by discussion, but it is only effective if you can stop people talking'. To overcome this problem a very old solution exists – in ancient Athens, the cradle of democracy, people were randomly selected by lot to make public decisions. However, even when citizens are selected randomly to decide for everyone, for those taking part:

> the equal right to address one's fellow citizens as they take their sovereign decisions, has always been offset by the less agreeable (but accompanying) duty to hear out the persuasions of every fellow citizen who chooses to exercise it, and by the still more painful duty to accept whatever these fellow citizens together then proceed to decide.[19]

In short, if you attend a meeting of 60 citizens and proceed to talk for five minutes about your views on a particular vexed issue that affects you and your family, then you have a corresponding duty to listen to the other 59 citizens for almost five hours. These compound arithmetical problems increase as the number of people involved increases. It is why practical attempts at deliberative democracy often descend into 'talking shops', and why deliberation can be debilitating for those taking part. After all, there is only so much discussion that the average person can put up with.

The second fundamental problem with deliberative techniques is the truism that no amount of deliberation can overcome the impossibility of achieving majority decision if there are more than two options available. This problem was identified in the late 18th century through the work of two French encyclopaedists, Compte de Borda and Marquis de Condorcet, who tried to apply mathematical rigour to voting systems. The two examples below show the irresolvable problems that occur when more than two people attempt to combine their preferences on more than two topics.

For the first example, imagine you are cooking a meal for three friends. You ask them their preference in respect of three different starters. Figure 5.1 shows your imaginary friends' preferences. There is no way of aggregating or collating these preferences into a collective choice. If choosing a starter by majority decision is not feasible then the only options left are randomly assigned or imposed choice. This result often offends democrats who advocate the importance of collective choices – but despite their dispositions, they cannot buck the arithmetic.

Figure 5.1 *Aggregating the ranked preferences of individuals does not necessarily produce agreed majority preferences*

Ranking	Jim	Janet	John
Best	lentil soup	Caesar salad	lobster tails
Middle	lobster tails	lentil soup	Caesar salad
Worst	Caesar salad	lobster tails	lentil soup

Now let us consider the problem of first preference majority voting. Imagine an election when just 21 people are voting for a representative; and imagine that they have just three candidates to choose from. As can be readily inferred this is a very small election between a small number of candidates and a tiny electorate. In this case let us assume that the outcome of the vote, in preference order, is as shown in Figure 5.2.

Figure 5.2 *The dilemma of aggregating votes for the most and least favoured candidates*

21 voters in total	8 voters	7 voters	6 voters
1st preference	Amy	Bert	Charlie
2nd preference	any order of	Charlie	Bert
3rd preference	Bert or Charlie	Amy	Amy

Plainly the majority of voters prefer Amy least; and yet Amy obtains the majority of first preference votes. So-called 'approval voting' and 'proportional voting' systems try to get around this problem but they also contain their own weaknesses and problems in return. The 18th-century calculations of Borda and Condorcet were revived in the 1950s by the economist Kenneth Arrow who devised a new approach to studying what he called 'social choice' – or the difficulties of arriving at group decisions. Arrow demonstrated the impossibility of arriving at group decisions when there were multiple preferences – he called this the 'impossibility theorem'.[20]

This 1950s finding generated deep pessimism among democrats at the time but it has since prompted a rich body of constructive work which has sought to inform social decision procedures. The lesson learnt from these exercises is that arriving at majority views is fraught with profound problems of method and that the process of revealing public preferences is highly complex. The lazy convention of revealing public preferences through simple forms of 'opinion polling' denies the participants the prospect of developing an informed view and deludes decision makers into believing that they are tapping into deeply felt public attitudes.

As we saw from the case of the pool in Forest Hill, community participation in public decision-making was crucial not only for the popular accountability of that decision, but also to smooth the path for the implementation of the decision. Of course citizen participation in public decision-making occurs across a spectrum from 'manipulated tokenism' through to fully delegated community decision-making. But the sensible course to adopt is one that informs and educates the public in the issues involved and which privileges no set of stakeholders in respect of their leverage on the ultimate decision. Deliberative democracy requires a reflective style and a commitment to dialogue. But there are different forms of dialogue and it is crucial to appreciate which form works best to generate options and consensus around those options. Some dialogue works to build a consensus, while other forms of dialogue serve to accentuate points of disagreement. The purpose of public discussion is not to manufacture acquiescence but instead to develop a critical citizenry – one that is engaged with the issues and that seeks common solutions to common problems or problems about the commons.

From this we can see that much of what passes as dialogue is, in fact, defensive and controlled debating. In these instances, discussion is characterized by advocacy and produces, at worst, adversarial styles of debating where people speak past each other. However, it is possible to build useful styles of dialogue that encourage skilful conversations between people who can then agree to disagree in tolerant and respectful ways. But if people are genuinely to listen to others with a minimum of resistance, they need to engage in a reflective dialogue with each other. It is perhaps this form of generative dialogue that offers the best possibilities for new insights.[21] The rhetoric of public consultation often leads participants to expect opportunities to generate fresh community insights, whereas in practice it too often stifles imagination through the rehearsal of practised and defensive routines.

Some political commentators argue that the claims of deliberative democracy are overplayed and possibly dangerous. They suggest that the public's reticence towards involvement in deliberating on public issues is reasonable given the pressures on people's lives and time, and that the public's unwillingness to become involved may be a good thing as the public are generally ill-equipped to engage in deliberation. This line of reasoning has merit and it presents a fairly strong case against deliberation.[22] However, it is also clear from in-depth research in people's willingness to deliberate, that it is not the issues themselves that put off the public but the process of partisan politics and interest group politics that frame how these issues are debated in public. Most people actively avoid close involvement in partisan politics – which often appears to be a central condition for full participation in public decision-making. However, ordinary citizens will engage with public issues if they are framed reasonably and are not overly linked to partisan or interest group politics.

The challenge to enthusiasts for deliberative democracy is therefore twofold. First, there is a need to move from a sterile debate on public issues to a more generative dialogue that enables creative public choices to emerge. Second, there is a need to blend deliberative approaches for ordinary citizens with the particularities of partisan and interest group politics. This requires considerable political maturity – and yet it can be achieved. It requires the adoption of Karl Popper's famous dictum: 'I may be wrong and you may be right, and by an effort we may get nearer to the truth.'[23]

Four differing perspectives on public choice problems

In deciding what should happen in respect of any vexed public choice problem there are always four different perspectives. Each has a legitimate angle on the problem and each could claim, for different reasons, that it is 'best placed' to make decisions about how any one problem should be solved or how any one service ought to develop and change. Consider the case of the development of any particular service – let's choose public museums. The four different perspectives are:

- **Users** – the users of the service (and/or their advocates) know most about it from a customer perspective and perhaps they are best placed to decide how it should develop and change. They attend museums and they will know what sorts of subjects and forms of engagement will attract them to attend more regularly.
- **Experts** – those experts who work in the service, who have most service-specific knowledge and whose personal careers are bound to the development of the service. They think about the service throughout their working life and regularly pick up ideas from other museums about how to attract new visitors and repeat visitors.
- **Citizens/Taxpayers** – if all taxpayers finance the service (or heavily subsidize it), then perhaps as citizens they are best placed to decide the scope and scale of the service. The exhibitions are provided in the name of civic virtue and the common good and some visitors and even museum curators may wish to present material that offends public sensibilities (say, exhibitions of Nazi war memorabilia).
- **Politicians** – if politicians are elected by all of us to direct and oversee the institutions of the state and if this particular function or activity falls within the aegis of a particular group of politicians, perhaps they ought to decide the broad scope and scale of the service and arrange for the museums to be overseen by a regulator.

And so users, experts, taxpayers and politicians vie for leverage and control of any one public choice problem or any one public service. The case of museums is fairly simple and straightforward (although some museums are the responsibility of national government, some are the responsibility of city-regional government and others are responsible to the local tier of government). Other services present much more complex and knotty problems to solve – services such as prisons, child protection and development control. Figure 5.3 depicts how any one public interest question involves a process of tension between the four forces of users, experts, citizens and politicians. It also shows that each force has both a legitimate claim as well as a distorting bias. Service users are closer to the issue or problem. And therefore they have a strong claim to be involved in determining the future for the problem or service. Indeed, some argue that by far best source for creative innovation in public service design and delivery stems from service users. And in large part they are correct; however, users may also tend to want to particularize service outcomes to meet their specific needs as users. This tendency to 'capture' the value for themselves may be even stronger if the service is free at the point of use or is heavily subsidized.

Figure 5.3 *The public interest and the four forces*

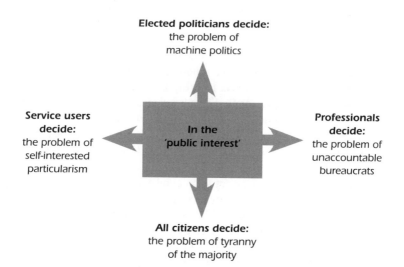

Elected politicians decide:
the problem of
machine politics

Service users
decide:
the problem of
self-interested
particularism

In the
'public interest'

Professionals
decide:
the problem of
unaccountable
bureaucrats

All citizens decide:
the problem of tyranny
of the majority

Of course, professional experts could decide the future of a service. They are usually qualified in a body of expert knowledge and can claim to know most about the intricacies of the service or the related policy problem. Moreover, as professionals their training includes an expectation of emotional detachment. They are expected to balance interests in arriving at recommendations and to consider matters in impartial and objective ways. And in large part this is true. The best professionals are well placed to consider issues in a well-rounded way. However, they too have a distorting bias. They may be more accountable to their professional bodies and institutes than they are to the public they serve. And they may also be prone to career-enhancing behaviour by promoting innovations that serve the purposes of their personal careers as much as they serve the public interest.

A third approach to deciding on a public interest question is to let everyone decide through some form of citizen engagement process. This can involve direct democracy techniques or deliberative techniques. This may be considered the 'ideal' solution in a democratic society – everyone deciding together. The problem of this is not just the methodological impossibility of arriving at a collective decision but the bias that is known as the 'tyranny of the majority'. As described above, agreeing to pursue 'the greatest good for the greatest number over the long run' sounds perfectly sensible until you realize that you may never appear in this greatest number and that your minority interests may well be trampled over by a large majority. That is why a key feature of a democratic society is how it determines public interest issues in the context of safeguarding minority interests.

Finally, elected politicians can rightly claim that they uniquely have a legitimacy to make decisions in the public interest. Elected politicians plainly have a privileged position in this diagram – and so they should. They do sit above all other interests in determining issues in the public interest. Their privilege stems not from their proximity to the problem (the service user is best for that); nor from any multifaceted conception of the public (citizens at large are best for that); nor from any depth of knowledge about the subject (professional experts are best at that); but instead because of their democratic legitimacy and the fact that they are elected representatives of all of us. They and they alone are elected to choose. The quality of their choosing is crucial but it is the quality of their democratic legitimacy that is vital. And it is the fragility of their democratic legitimacy that serves to undermine their case.

The operation of 'machine politics', among other things, bedevils the practice of representative democracy. In the most part, politicians are able to make decisions free from considerations of party advantage but from time to time the issue of gaining or sustaining office inevitably clouds political perspectives. Of course, political parties are crucially important for electors and activists alike, but they can also present problems for the conduct of decision-making. Individual politicians' fidelity to party and their perceptions of party advantage sometimes act to distort good judgement. Of course the precise character and dynamic of machine politics varies across institutions. Parliamentary systems have their own political arithmetic, as do local government systems that involve executive political control by a single political party.

The point about the diagram is that service users, citizens, professionals and politicians all have legitimate claims to be best placed to decide on any given policy problem or public service. Each claim has its merits and each claim carries its own biases. None are privileged above the claims of elected politicians. But even they need to acknowledge their own biases and the fragility of their democratic legitimacy. Perhaps the best approach is to consider a public interest question or a public choice problem and ask, whose voices are most dominant? Whose voices are least heard? Is the issue sewn up between service users and professionals? Are politicians overly dominant in determining the issue? Have wider citizens' (or taxpayers') views been adequately factored into the consideration of this issue? In short, public choices are best made by politicians but only after all four sets of voices are heard and when the competing claims of each and their attendant biases are open and transparent to all.

Summary

Someone once said that the world is divided between two sets of people. There are those who procrastinate and cannot make decisions, people who look for more analysis to perfect their judgements after weighing all the evidence painstakingly. These people are cautious calculators, destined to advise. And then there are those people who jump to judgement. They hold their opinions weakly (sometimes weekly) as the circumstances that give favour to certain choices are always changing. These people are entrepreneurs, destined to decide. This caricature conveys an element of truth – but only an element. For we know that decisions are hard for all of us to take. And decisions about public choices are even harder to make. Public choices are fraught with general ethical quandaries as well as specific cognitive biases. We would like to think that collective choices can be made democratically and with ease but we have discovered that this is not the case. Very small groups of people are unable to make clear collective choices when faced with more than two options. This has enormous implications for those responsible for framing public choices. Moreover, we know that each stakeholder to a public choice will sensibly want to exercise leverage on these choices and, in addition, each will carry a distorting bias in the very act of considering these choices. But the vexed issues of choosing in the public interest are not confronted because they are easy but because they are hard.

Deliberation involves weighing and balancing, but it also involves deciding. Deciding in the public interest is usually the prerogative of elected politicians. But politicians cannot decide alone. They need to be informed about what the public think, what special interests demand, as well as what best professional expert advice suggests.[24] If public decisions are to be made and to stick, those impacted need to feel that the process involved was a reasonably fair one. Of course, not everyone can agree with the final public decision (the world we live in is too complex for that). But at least they can agree that it was handled fairly by the public authorities concerned. For fair process is as important as just outcomes.

Public decisions are, at their centre, moral decisions – about how we live together and what we owe each other. Those deciding need to demonstrate not simply their judicious approach but their sympathetic and compassionate nature. This is why the demands on public leadership are so heavy. Citizens want authentic and sincere political leaders and they want them to be empathic and careful. These are demanding requirements. Moreover, citizens want to be assured that those public officials appointed to advise public decision makers are focused principally and impartially on how best to solve public problems, rather than how best to enhance the reputation of those for whom they work. That is why a productive relationship between elected politicians and public officials is central to good government. Politicians lead and set the tone, officials advise, politicians choose and then officials implement the chosen way forward. Balancing issues requires poise, moving a community forward requires willpower. And at the deepest of levels, leadership requires sympathy for others combined with the courage to choose in the midst of uncertainty.

Chapter 6

The Geography of Governing

The uniqueness, distinctiveness and power of place

Consider a world in which everywhere was exactly like everywhere else. A world of indistinct landscapes of bland uniformity. A world where the experience of arriving at a destination evoked the same emotion as when leaving the point of origin. And while travelling, everything seemed so eerily familiar – nothing about the terrain through which you travelled was novel or distinctive. The journey from A to B involved the passage of time, but nothing else. The visible landscape undulated with the same overall gradient towards the horizon. Buildings had the same form and feel, streets had the same grey curves and cambers, and the topography of open spaces was wholly unremarkable. In this world, places have no character; neither charm nor edge. No locality, no place is imprinted on anyone's memory and so no place has a special meaning to any of us. The place you first called home, first rode a bike, first attended school, first felt real sadness, first kissed another, would be just like any other place. Locality would only mean where you were now: a place just like any other. It would not offer you any prospect of emotional bonds or ties of attachment – wherever you are now reading this would be just like wherever I am now writing it.

Well, how weird would that be? This thought experiment reminds us of the importance of place and locality to our lives. Place helps to define our lives: where we began, the journeys we have taken, and the locality where we live now. Place is central not only to how we live, but also to how we are governed. In this chapter, I shall examine the impact of place on the character of government and the implications of local geographical variety for the successful delivery of public services. Traditional books on government or public policy stress the balance between differing tiers of government: at national and at sub-national levels. They tend to focus on whether the national level of government is overbearing in relation to local or regional government or whether new forms of localism, devolution or secession offer the better routes to community self-governance.

But while the relationship between national level or federal government and regional or local government is important, it is not my main focus here. My aim in this chapter is to set out some key aspects of how geography impacts on good governance. We know that an appreciation of history is important to crafting good governance. But so too is an appreciation of geography.

This is why it is important to explore the impact of geography on life-chances; why geography is critical to our well-being and sense of identity; and why geography is vitally important to the very fabric of government. Geographical scale, geographical variety and the spatial impact of clustering and proximity are highly relevant to any discussion about how places are best governed.

Different democracies approach the issue of geographical variation dependent upon their scale and internal variety as well as their population density and clustering. Among democratic nations of the world, India stands apart with its 1.2 billion people and a population density of 355 people per square kilometre. Japan's population of 127 million people live at the next highest density (345 people per sq. km) and among Western democracies, Britain has the highest population density (255 people per sq. km). Perhaps this is why the British appear overly anxious about geographic variations that other nations would consider as extraordinarily minor. Only Germany and Italy among other large Western democracies have population densities comparable to that in Britain. By contrast, the urban population clusters in the US, Canada and Australia belie the exceedingly low population densities of these countries (31, 3.5 and 3 people per sq. km respectively).

Spatial scale, population density and clustering have a bearing on political identity and governance but they also have a strong bearing on the extent to which public services can be designed and delivered in ways that ensure reasonably fair and consistent service outcomes. It is important that democratic governments learn from each other's experiences but they need to situate this learning in the geographical contexts of each nation. Lessons about government and public service from, say, Sweden can be very insightful but it has to be remembered that there are nine million people in Sweden, one in four live in the three largest cities, seven in every ten people are of the Lutheran faith and the largest ethnic minority are 50,000 Sweden Finns who live near the Finnish border. By contrast, just 5 per cent of Americans live in the largest three US cities and almost one-half of the populations of both Australia and New Zealand live in these two countries' three most populous cities.[1]

At the most personal level, our experience of place mingles with our streams of memory to help us create not just a sense of where we are but also a coherent sense of who we are. Memories of landscape tell us who we are as well as where we are.[2] For most of us, our life's journey sees us move along complex pathways from a place of origin to a very different destination. Our origins have their consequences on our potential destinations. Some of us may live as adults in places where we were born and grew up but very many of us will have journeyed many miles to live and settle. As a result, our sense of personal identity depends in part on where we started our lives, and partly it depends upon the journeys we have taken. In this way, our landscape becomes part of our lives rather than a stage on which we act. It is how geography becomes woven into the very fabric of our lives. This impact on us personally finds a broader and deeper echo in the impact of geography on politics and community self-governance. The impact of geography on the character of a locality and its governance is key to any appreciation of how communities develop, how public interest decisions are chosen by governments, and also how public services are best designed and delivered for communities. It also helps us to understand the politics of identity and the geopolitics of emotion.

Geography may not be destiny, but it stamps its imprint on our life and our life-chances. And while both opportunity and constraint have strong cultural preconditions, they are themselves subject to an underlying geography. Fortune favours those born into wealthy families, but it also favours those born into wealthy places. And while in the developed world, absolute measures appear to matter less than relative measures, the poorest families in the wealthiest places on earth will have children with far better life-chances than those born to the wealthiest families in the poorest places on earth. Place matters. And in this chapter I shall start by examining geography through a tale of a tiny village called No Place.

A place called No Place

There is a place in England called 'No Place'. It is a tiny village in County Durham in north-east England. It is near the town of Stanley, some eight miles south of Gateshead and fifteen miles from the city of Sunderland. No Place is just to the south of the A693 between Stanley and Beamish on the road towards Chester-le-Street, a historic market town just five miles to the east. Originally the village consisted of just four terraced houses in what was an outlier to a coal mining pit village community. The Beamish Mary coal pit is nearby. In 1937, the residents of a large series of terraced houses named Co-operative Villas adopted the land on which the four houses stood and they took the name of No Place for their area. These 19th-century linear terraces of Roseberry Street, John Street and Gladstone Street comprise some 160 workers' homes built to high density; whereas the adjacent and much more recent development in Beamish Hills comprises 50 lower density, higher value detached commuter homes.

In the 1980s, the local council tried to change the name of the entire village to Co-operative Villas. But this met with strong protests from local residents who wanted the signs to No Place to be left intact. The authorities plainly thought that the name was unacceptable. Local sentiment among people who lived there rather enjoyed the tease involved in living in a place called No Place. The origin of the name is uncertain. Perhaps it derives from an abbreviation of 'North Place', 'Near Place' or 'Nigh Place'. One theory is that the original four houses stood on the boundary between two parishes neither of which would accept them and hence, by default, it became known as No Place. Currently as a locality, No Place has just one substantive claim to fame – it has an award-winning real ale pub, the Beamish Mary Inn. This inn dates back to 1897 and is a classic mining pub that now serves as a source for 'heritage drinking'. Although the origin of No Place, like a great deal of settlements in County Durham, is found in coal mining, its future depends more upon the urban renaissance of the easily commutable Newcastle–Gateshead conurbation and of the city of Sunderland. An economy that was centred on coal and steel is now rebalancing towards car manufacturing, service industries and the creative sector.

The central city regeneration of the Newcastle–Gateshead conurbation has been based on very significant public sector investment over the past two decades. Newcastle itself has been a focus of inward investment. And across the Tyne, the Gateshead Quays development includes an enormous art gallery (in the former Baltic Flour Mill); the £70m Sage conference centre with its 1650 seat concert hall; as well as the eye-catching Millennium Bridge and the associated renewal of the riverside.[3] Despite this investment in regeneration, the north-east of England was hit hard by the 2009 recession: the two biggest impacts being the scaling back of car production by Nissan in Sunderland (with 1200 jobs being lost in January 2009) and the partial closure of the Corus steel plant in Redcar (with 1700 jobs lost in January 2010 in what was then the biggest remaining industrial plant in the north-east).

However, in March 2010, Nissan announced plans to build its 'Leaf' electric car in Sunderland after receiving a £20.7m government incentive grant.[4] This was a turnaround for the fortunes of the car plant from the previous year. And producing such a ground-breaking car locally may not only safeguard over 550 highly skilled jobs at their Sunderland plant, but may also act as a magnet for inward investment into green technologies in the area. What's more, over the past decade, the Newcastle–Gateshead conurbation has become the focus of major cultural investment in the creative industries.[5] It seems that the residents of No Place can no longer rely on the natural resources of their physical landscape for work. Instead, they rely on their proximity to the manufacturing cluster emerging around Nissan in Sunderland and the cultural cluster being forged in the Newcastle–Gateshead twin city. What's more, the people there have a strong sense of connection and identity to the north-east. This sense of identity is based on an emotional attachment to place and to region.

This brief account of a place called No Place shows clearly that while places may be distinctive and unique, they are never entirely separate from other places. No Place exists as a settlement because of the discovery of coal in the 19th century; it persists as a thriving settlement at the early point of the 21st century because of its proximity to the developing economic success of Sunderland and the Newcastle–Gateshead conurbation. Every place connects to other places. Sometimes there is a discontinuous break between one place and another but mostly places blend into places adjacent to them. Many places are defined by the principal features of their physical landscapes, such as highland outcrops, the confluence of large streams or the existence of tidal rivers. And rivers, in particular, play a crucial role in the history of human settlement – as both the source of geographical advantage and the site of symbolic power. Their importance may stem from their specific history in trade (such as the 19th-century coal exporting and ship building on the River Tyne in the north-east) or as the nexus for general trade or a site of power, as is the case of the River Thames in London.[6] Thus despite their uniqueness, localities are often defined less by their intrinsic characteristics of their physical landscape and more by their connection to, or their proximity to, other places. In short, location still matters and geography retains its power.

And yet geographical considerations barely feature in discussions about politics, government or public policy. This is surprising given the astonishing differences in the socioeconomic geography of democracies. The degree of internal socioeconomic variation, clustering and sociocultural diversity in a nation is central to any understanding of its politics and its governance as well as vital to the appropriateness of the design of its public services. We happily discuss the apparently vast differences between nations while describing nations themselves as though they are internally homogeneous – places with little variety. But when it comes to governing and designing public services, geographical variation matters as much within nations as between nations.

Unique places, uniform processes

Our personal geographical experiences tend to be of places and localities that are distinctive to us, and that in some way we consider to be unique. However, the pressures of modern life seem to generate within us a corresponding desire for reliable, predictable uniformity. This paradox was eloquently described by Thomas Friedman in his book *The Lexus and the Olive Tree*, when he characterized modern life as a struggle between a drive for prosperity, development and standardized quality (the Lexus) and a drive based on identity, tradition and unique attachments (the olive tree).[7] This duality is witnessed in No Place. The success of No Place rests upon its unique character as a place to live, while its local economy is dependent in part on the success of Nissan's mass-electric car just fifteen miles away. The production of a reliable, high quality, cost-effective car relies upon global economic integration and standardized processes.

Approaches to 'modernizing' government or improving public services easily slip into discussions about how best to standardize processes, outputs or outcomes. And standardization has as its aim the imposition of uniformity. This can often develop into a system-wide approach to public service reform that attempts to ensure that public services are designed and delivered to uniform standards and with uniform characteristics. After all, a feature of the modern world, in services as much as in cars, is the expectation of consistently high quality products and services. The houses built in No Place were constructed to nationally set standards, the cars that the residents of No Place drive were built to international standards, and the televisions that they watch were designed to globally accepted standards of quality. Uniformity pervades modern life in No Place as elsewhere in England. And people want uniformity in their lives – they want quality, reliable goods and services. Many of the residents of No Place shop weekly at Asda in nearby Stanley, or at Sainsbury's in Chester-le-Street, and some travel further to Morrisons in Sunderland or to Tesco in Durham. But people also desire and thrive on uniqueness. Where everywhere is the same, we experience tedium and monotony. Where every offer is the same, we experience stasis and routine.

And yet every place is unique, locationally and historically; and every place offers the prospect of unique experiences to residents and visitors alike – what's more, people enjoy this uniqueness. Thus when governing localities, a key question becomes how best to balance the modern drive for uniformity with the human enjoyment of uniqueness. To govern a place well requires a deep understanding of the physical and cultural landscape of a place, the history of its people and their social diversity. To govern a place well also requires a strong appreciation of the sources of locational comparative advantage of that place to its neighbouring and adjoining places. Governing is not an aspatial activity. It is rooted in geography as much as in history. Those who govern well don't just make good public interest decisions. They make decisions that are relevant to the scale and variety of the area for which they have responsibility. If, as Tip O'Neil, the former Speaker of the US House of Representatives famously quipped, 'all politics is local', then perhaps the best government is also the most local – the most in touch with the variety of the places it is elected to govern.

Mental maps, identity and the geography of emotion

Our mental map of the world derives from our memory of maps together with our experience of travelling through the world. Usually the mental map of the world we inhabit (as opposed to the world we know about) is burnt into our memory by our daily experience of travelling through the world. And in most cities it is the transport network that acts as the dominant force in creating the mental urban map for most people.

Our mental maps can create a sense of comfort as well as a sense of alarm. Familiar places and familiar routes offer reassurance through routine. We have clear mental maps of places near where we live – of places we know. We travel daily to work using the same route through the same places and we often arrive without any intense memories of how we got there. This familiarity can be comforting. But when we travel to new places, on new journeys, we tend to be more alert – for the unexpected, for the novel. The boundaries of our mental map stretch to include new places that we have visited through new journeys that we have taken. But our mental maps remain highly distorted representations of geographical reality. Indeed, the ubiquitous nature of Google maps serves to create a 'neogeography' where we have access to space and place regardless of our current location.[8] It enables me to check out the house my son is moving into in Brisbane, Australia via 'Street View' despite the 10,000 miles of distance between that house and my own.

Our perspective of the world is not just through our memory of maps or our invasive use of Google maps and the geographical tags but, more importantly, through strong cultural filters. We see the world we expect to see – and what we expect to see depends upon the extent to which our thinking is governed by open-minded enquiry or more by the claims of tradition and custom. For example, when we think of other places in terms of their prospects as a holiday destination we tend to think principally about landscape and the prevailing climate. But in most other respects our view of other places depends less upon the landscape and more critically on our attitude towards the people who live in these places – their customs and their traditions. Fifty years ago, differences between peoples and places used to be described in nationalistic terms. People's nationhood described their 'difference from us'. And for much of the 20th century, differences between nations were described with reference to the cold war between the West and the Soviet Bloc. But in the post-cold war period these differences have crumbled along with the Berlin wall.

In a cogent but ultimately reckless line of argument, Francis Fuku-yama claimed that liberal democratic ideas had, at that time, become triumphant and that history had effectively 'ended'.[9] In a response to this argument the American political scientist Samuel Huntington countered that what had replaced the cold war was a 'clash of civilizations'. In this clash, Huntington suggested that religious and cultural identities would serve as the principal sources for conflict in the world.[10] At a surface level, Huntington's thesis seems to have been proved correct. But his rather shallow distinctions between cultural and religious differences are far too superficial to explain both the roots and routes of conflict in the early 21st century. What characterizes political difference in the world today is the politics of identity and emotion as much as the claims of custom, culture and religion.

In a refreshingly insightful account of emotion and its global political expression, Dominique Möisi contrasts the despairing fatalism of some affluent young students he discovered while teaching in Morocco, with the positive optimism of the much poorer students he taught in Mumbai. Why, he asks, do material circumstances seem to bear so lightly on people's sense of their future and why are some people infused with hope and opti-mism while others seem suffocated by despair and fear? Möisi suggests that three primary emotions fuel major political forces in the world – the emotions of fear, humiliation and hope. He suggests that all three of these emotions are closely linked to a collective sense of confidence.[11]

At the broadest level, Möisi suggests that the fear of others currently dominates the developed world; that many in the Arab-Islamic world harbour historic senses of grievance against other nations who, over generations, even centuries, have acted so as to humiliate them; and that other peoples, in rapidly emerging economies, are fuelled by a more open-minded sense of hope about the future. Importantly, Möisi does not paste these emotions straight onto national, religious or cultural groups; rather he makes a more nuanced point about the geopolitics of emotion. He suggests that the best way to understand the outlook of the peoples in, say, Japan or Russia or the Arab-Islamic world is not simply through cultural or religious lenses (important though these are) but also through the historical path that each nation has taken.

Where Dominique Möisi seeks to explain differences between nations, similar issues of political identity and emotion can help us to understand differences at the more local level. In particular the pace of social change through migration can lead to strong and sometimes polarized emotions in communities. For example, concentrations of minority populations in small urban areas often produce a cocktail of social issues for communities themselves. This is because residential segregation crystallizes 'difference' into daily life – a sense that 'we live here, they live over there'. When difference is coupled with a sense of injustice about the distribution of public goods and benefits ('they receive more than they deserve, while we lose out'), a strong negative emotional response develops. In this way, Möisi's observation about grievance and humiliation at the level of national governments applies at least as forcefully at the level of local communities.

A sense of distinctive separation can be found in all communities that are economically or culturally 'trapped' in localities. In the West it can be found in poor white communities as much as in poor ethnic minority communities. It is as much a function of impoverished ambition and aspiration as it is a function of fear of others. Bounded communities, of all types, live frozen in localities, looking inwards and backwards. These communities often struggle to preserve traditions and customs (of kinship, work and sense of place). These communities often feel threatened by the uncertain character of modern life and the pace of change in the locality in which they live.

When examining internal differences within any nation, issues of demography and social diversity are vitally important. But perhaps the most powerful contrast to grasp is the difference between a close community and a closed community. Closed communities exclude others by a mix of economic, social, linguistic and cultural barriers. They mark their boundaries stridently and their welcome to outsiders lacks genuine warmth and engagement. When engaging with communities with these characteristics the key task for civic actors is to attempt to foster openness and connections with others. Closed communities are unable to integrate with the wider society in which they live and they certainly are unable to thrive in the fast pace of the modern world. Closed communities have a tendency to look backward and they can become overwhelmed by a collective sense of fear or humiliation. As a result, very many of the individuals within them have closed horizons and low aspirations.

By contrast, open communities thrive in the context of difference. Open communities expand dialogue between people and thereby expand peoples' horizons. They enable communities to discuss with each other, on a fair and reasonable basis, how best to pursue a good society.[12] They promote opportunities and expand horizons for the individuals within them. They look outward to the wider world, to connect to others in other places. They tend also to look forward and they are more likely to be fuelled by a collective sense of hope.

Uniformity and centralization: two sides of the same coin

It is a shared sense of citizenship that generates a sense of common obligations and entitlements within national boundaries. Paying taxes to the same government and having legal obligations that are enforceable by that same government can drive a sense that everyone is entitled to similar levels and standards of public service. Countries, like the UK, that centralize their tax raising powers also centralize their legal authority and tend therefore to be anxious about variable outcomes across their geography. For if everyone has common obligations to contribute through a common tax system, perhaps everyone should have commensurate entitlements to public facilities and services. This can apply at any spatial scale – across nations, across states and across local government jurisdictions. And citizens will be alert for those governments at all levels who appear to favour one locality over others – in terms of investment, resources and political attention. A sense of 'geographical fairness' underlies mental models of consistency and spatial standardization. Variations in all manner of public services, their activities, outputs and outcomes are claimed to violate the principles of geographical fairness.

The drive for evenness or uniformity in the distribution of public goods is entirely understandable. Public sentiment may well support the case for similar standards of service outcomes in all parts of the city, the county, the state or the country. But these sentiments will depend crucially upon the degree of variation, diversity and clustering in a city, county, state or country. Electors and taxpayers are bound to be concerned if they discover that variations in public service outcomes arise from unaccountable discretion exercised by local politicians or appointed public managers. However, arguments in favour of geographically consistent outcomes very often stem from a strong underlying presumption that decentralization feeds unfair outcomes and that to remedy this more centralized control is necessary.

There are two main reasons why decentralization can lead to unacceptable variations in public service performance: either local public servants have too much discretion and are differentially competent; or there is inequity in the distribution of resources available to start with. Only the first of these receives much attention. In the UK, variations in service outcomes received an immense amount of attention under the Blair governments (from 1997 to 2007). These governments sought to drive more equitable outcomes through, among other things, a blend of 'top-down targets', and the convergence of capabilities and competencies across public service providers.

Much of the emphasis of public service reform in the UK during the period 1997–2010 was to minimize variation that arose from differences in the competence of teachers, doctors, police officers and public managers. The promotion of improved 'public leadership' in these sectors and the adoption of 'best practice' principles in each of these areas was a further attempt to improve outcomes and reduce variation. And finally the development of a very strong framework of public service regulation and inspection was devised to minimize the range and distribution of service outcomes. However, variations in service outcomes may not stem from the exercise of discretion at the sub-national level nor may they stem from variations in competencies and capabilities of public leaders. Instead they may arise from the underlying and unequal distribution of resources (natural resources or tax resources).

In an insightful paper on the political economy of local public goods, the economists Timothy Besley and Stephen Coate posit that the competing arguments for centralization or decentralization depend upon the interplay of two factors: first, whether there are marked differences or similarities between localities; and second, whether there are strong 'spillover' effects in respect of the local public good in question.[13] A spillover effect exists if, for example, a locality decides to invest in a facility that is then used by people from neighbouring localities. Where this happens, the cost of the facility is borne by one locality but its benefits spill over into other areas.

Basically if local public goods are to be organized from the centre, it requires a style of governance that balances interests across regions or localities. Centralized systems tend to produce 'one size fits all' approaches that are unable to reflect the variety of all local needs.

Decentralized systems by contrast are more susceptible to 'free rider' problems – which occur if one locality provides a public good or service that can be used or consumed, at no or lower cost, by people in a neighbouring locality. According to Besley and Coate, when it comes to public goods and services, the case for decentralized decision-making is strong when localities are markedly different and when spillover effects are small. By contrast, they argue that the case for centralized decision-making is strong when localities are markedly similar and when spillover effects are large.

And yet discussions about geographical variations rarely start with an appreciation of these two key factors. This is mainly because the forces of centralization fuel the argument more than any concern with geographical fairness or equity. In public discussion on policy matters we may accept that there is variation and patterns in all things (in resources, in needs, in deserts, in managerial competence, in democratic legitimacy and so on) but we seem unable to conclude what range of variety is acceptable and what is not.

Irregularity and spatial variety occurs in everything. But what we often forget is the truism that, even in an interconnected world, local factors are more likely to give cause to observed variation. And while the 14th-century logician and friar William of Occam had a point when he argued that simple explanations should be preferred over complex explanations, most complex social conditions have complex, multiply intertwined causes rather than simple linear causes.[14] Moreover, proximal causes need to be distinguished from ultimate causes. And as the English cosmologist and physicist John Barrow argues, it is a simple law of non-quantum physics that:

> things occurring here and now are directly caused by events that occurred immediately nearby in space and time: this property we term 'locality' to reflect the fact that it is the most local events that exert the predominant influence upon us.[15]

That is why even in a globalized world, where according to a simple version of complexity theory the flap of a butterfly's wing today in South America may eventually result in stormy weather in the north-east of England, observed differences between places are far more likely to be caused by local factors. Of course not every observed difference arises from local factors – but most of them do.

The fact that there are extensive variations of public service delivery and of public service outcomes has to be confronted by policymakers. For it is undoubtedly the case that some of these variations will produce unfairness between people that is not acceptable to society as a whole. But knowing how best to address this problem, and remedying this unfairness, requires a proper understanding of what causes the variation in the first place – is it best understood as arising from different patterns of needs and demands; from different patterns of resource availability; from different patterns of institutional capability and performance; or instead from different patterns of community self-help?

Concerns about geographical variation may be reasonably expressed but sometimes they betray a centralizing motive. We need to remember that while there are many similarities between places, every locality has its unique geography. And we need to remember that almost nothing occurs in uniform or spatially even distributions and that there is irregularity and variety in everything. And while our tidy minds may want to classify and measure all manner of geographical variations, the act of measurement will not of itself advise us how best to act to reduce this variation. Of course there may be glaring geographical inequities at local, sub-regional or regional levels – the point is we need to understand the underlying economic, demographic and social causes of these spatial inequities. So-called 'postcode lotteries' may offend our presumed geography of fairness but even in the most equitable of systems, spatial variation in social results and service outcomes will persist.

The difficult challenge for any government is to assess in each locality the public appetite for managing difference in service standards or outcomes based upon local views about resource allocation and local views about how best to meet similar types of needs in very different types of places. People living in densely populated urban areas are bound to have different views about the right access to some public services than people living in remote and sparsely populated areas. In short, their experience of good government is therefore related to their experience of place.

The experience and power of place

When we think of a 'place', it can sometimes be a natural landscape devoid of other people – a dramatic coastline, an awesome mountain range or a simple meandering stream in a lowland meadow. So much about place is learnt by living in it – through the soles of one's feet and the experience of just being there. What's more, the sight of the natural landscape greatly informs our appreciation of place: the rugged outcrop of rock, the smooth line of an escarpment. But sight is just one sense. We can also hear the sound of a place, we can smell its essence and its atmosphere, we can touch the texture of the topography, the soil, and we can experience the landscape's gentility or its grandeur.

Different places evoke different emotions – of wonder or of fear. Most of us avoid places that induce a sense of foreboding or fear – such as scary heights or deep and dark caves. Instead we seek places that inspire a sense of calmness and instil a sense of safety. But place is not experienced statically – we move and flow through it. In this way our sense of place is dynamic, because we relate it to our journeys – today's brief journey or our longer journey through life. Is the place where we are now, a place of origin, a place of destination or a transit point from one location to another? Paths between and through places are therefore as crucial as places themselves. Open and convenient paths help us gain access to new places, while constricted paths limit the scope of our access.

Moreover, in witnessing today's landscape we can sense its past. For in urban landscapes, what we witness today is a palimpsest of place – layer upon layer of settlement and development. Post-modernist buildings sit easily or awkwardly alongside historic buildings of substantial heritage. The design of the modern architectural form rests comfortably or clumsily upon the ancient street pattern of yesteryear. In this way, the legacy of the past is imprinted on the geography of today. However, most people's experience of place is not structured through visual encounters with the built environment but through the interplay with other people who happen to live or work in that place. For we seldom experience wilderness landscapes devoid of people; mostly our experience of place is of locations enlivened by other people – their histories, their cultures, their current ambitions and their hopes for the future. Our experience of place is mostly set through our encounters with other people in those places. And most people in the world people rub shoulders with lots of other people like themselves in densely populated urban areas.

The geographer Harm de Blij writes of the enduring 'power of place' in shaping the uneven distribution of opportunity in the modern world. As de Blij argues, the staggering situational differences between the world's places continue to shape the lives of the vast majority of people on earth.

In their lifetimes, this vast majority will have worn the garb, spoken the language, professed the faith, shared the health conditions, absorbed the education, acquired the attitudes, and inherited the legacy that constitutes the power of place: the accumulated geography whose formative imprint still dominates the planet.[16]

In his account, de Blij differentiates between 'locals, globals and mobals'. Most people in the world are 'locals' – they live their entire lives near where they started. A very small number of people are 'globals' – relatively wealthy cosmopolites who travel the world for work and for leisure in a post-modern bubble of experience. The very different life experiences of these localized locals and the globetrotting globals stem from the highly variable geography of opportunity and constraint into which they are each born. 'Mobals' by contrast are the risk-taking migrants who are willing to leave their places of origin to take a chance on new and different surroundings. Most of these mobals move within nation states, from rural areas to urban areas, from the periphery to the core of the nation state. But some move internationally across borders in search of refuge or opportunity, such that by the turn of the year 2000 there were some 150 million international migrants in the world – 2.5 per cent of the world's population. Very few places in the world are composed of locals, globals and mobals – cities like Paris, London and New York are among the few.

Cities of production or consumption?

In traditional economic geography, towns and cities were viewed as arising from advantages of production or exchange. In this way, the sources of urban dynamics and growth lay in the geographical conflu-ence of resources, skills, and institutions of coordination. In short, there were economic advantages from the clustering of resources and talent. However, clustering inevitably produces higher density, which in turn produces congestion effects as well as other negative social effects (such as higher crime rates). So the conventional approach was that towns and cities were good for production but bad for consumption. Firms and workers may earn more in cities but they pay higher rents, commute longer, suffer worse public services and are subject to more crime.

This view was challenged in the latter part of the 20th century by urban scholars who argued that cities were attractive centres for consump-tion. The influential American urbanist Jane Jacobs had long pointed out how cities fuelled economic growth by using social and cultural diversity to replace imports.[17] But the American experience of declining 'rustbelt' cities and growing 'sunbelt' cities (with warmer winters) pointed to the prospect that jobs might be following people rather than people following jobs. As a result, it was increasingly being argued that cities had positive consumption advantages that attracted migrants.

The case for the 'consumer city' was based on a number of advantages that cities were alleged to have: (1) greater variety of services and consumer goods; (2) better aesthetics and physical settings (such as the architectural form of San Francisco, and the year round warmth of San Diego); and (3) the sheer speed of access to services and goods.[18] Central city locations, for example, were seen as possessing significantly higher amenity value, arising from their dense but diverse offerings, than the more mundane offering of suburban or edge city locations. And the renaissance of urban centres and the decline of outer city suburbs would appear to support this argument.

This view of the city as a bundle of consumption advantages that grows in size by attracting a diverse array of in-migrants and that grows economically through the dynamism of their creative talents finds its strongest expression in the work of the American geographer Richard Florida.[19] For him, it is the lifestyle preferences of talented workers that are changing the shape of cities, reviving them and ordering their relative economic functions and importance. And there is some strength to this argument. Talent does choose where to spend its time – but economic advantages of cities continue to arise from the underlying dynamics of production; and the path-dependent character of many businesses means that there is often 'localized lock-in'. In short, many firms and sectors are centred where they are because that is where they started some while ago and that is where they now have deep roots.[20] As a result, some cities are trapped in declining sectors simply because that was their economic specialty a few generations ago, while others are searching for new economic specialties that might attract talented and mobile in-migrants. Whatever the trajectory of historical development of any individual city, it is clear that cities offer their residents substantial economic and social advantages. Close proximity assists collaboration and competition – which fuels innovation and success.[21] Very large cities may require substantial infrastructure investment to realize these advantages but they are places where human skills and talent can be nurtured and developed.

Liking where you live

Each and every one of us has to live somewhere. And where we live is crucial to our well-being, our connection with community, our sense of self as well as to our ability to fashion opportunities for ourselves. A number of separate studies in the US and in the UK have recently highlighted the importance of place to our satisfaction with life generally. These studies have each attempted to untangle the contribution of place and locality to our collective sense of happiness and to a sense of contentment with public services and government generally.

Together these studies point to a number of interlinked findings. The first is that geographical mobility and social mobility are connected. People who move home from one place to another tend also to be upwardly socially mobile. Indeed it is usually their ambition and drive that generated within them a desire to move – to discover new opportunities for work and for their life. Those who decide to move home are by definition more outgoing and experimental than those who choose to stay. And the act of moving home encourages people to become more adaptive and flexible – all attributes that are positively associated with upward social mobility. The second finding is that living in a pleasant place creates a deeper sense of life satisfaction and well-being. There are very many factors that contribute to a positive sense of well-being but it seems that place is a very critical one. The third finding is that people's attitudes to the place in which they live have a significant bearing on their attitude towards public services and governance in their locality.

According to Richard Florida, choosing where to live is one of the three most important decisions you will ever make in your life (the other two are choosing who to share your life with, and choosing what you want to spend your working life doing).[22] For those who are able to move home the choice of where to live is not just a product of happenstance. People want to live where opportunities abound. Location attracts people; great location attracts a great number of people. In a highly competitive and global world, life's opportunities are clustered in successful urban areas. Richard Florida stresses the continued importance of economic 'clustering' forces and the obvious truth that mobile people with ambition and talent will choose to move to locations that offer them a good quality of life as well as good quality of life-chances.

To investigate the impact of place on well-being, Richard Florida undertook a 'place and happiness' survey. The survey had over 27,000 respondents across 8000 communities in the US. He found that when asked to rate happiness in relation to things like work, finances, personal life and place on a 1–5 scale, place scored 3.63 – ahead of everything but personal life and work. The place in which people live is more important to their happiness than their education or indeed how much they earn. By contrast only 3 per cent of his respondents identified their locality as a source of stress in their lives. Out of all the possible factors that act as a source of stress, place came last. Attitudes towards place are not universal – urbanites do appear to value different factors to those who live in rural locations. Three factors emerged from his analysis – first, that place is a major source of excitement and creative stimulation, an essential component of our psychological well-being. Second, place offers people an environment that they can adopt and call their own, an essential component of identity. And third, place gives us something to which we can belong, providing a sense of attachment and pride.

In a parallel but more localized study in the UK very similar findings emerged. The quality of the place in which people live came third in a poll undertaken by the BBC in 2005. And a project that examined the prospects for enhancing well-being in three localities in England (Manchester, Hertfordshire and South Tyneside) identified a number of contextual factors, such as social deprivation and a sense of local community, that were associated with the geography of happiness.[23]

More specifically, the British government introduced a requirement on English local authorities and their partners to conduct a nationally determined 'place survey' to gauge, among other things, people's views and opinions of the success of public agencies in improving service outcomes in local areas. This place survey was conducted in 2009 but abandoned in 2010. It was meant to examine the relationship between people's view of local public institutions and local public services with their views about the local area in which they lived. The place survey in England found that 80 per cent of respondents throughout England were satisfied with their local area as a place to live, while a much lower 45 per cent were satisfied with the way in which their local council ran its services. However, the factor that was most important in explaining people's satisfaction with their local council was their degree of satisfaction with their local area.

In-depth research into this nationwide data set produced a five factor explanatory model that described 82 per cent of all variation in people's satisfaction with their local area.[24] These five factors showed that it is the nature of other people in our locality that shapes our views of the locality itself. People's levels of overall satisfaction with their local area depended positively on the presence locally of educated middle-class people or negatively on the presence of poor, overcrowded, and young people. One of the key factors for explaining people's negative assessment of localities is simply the ratio of young people to older people in a local area. For when examined at the locality level, this factor alone accounted for almost half of the variation in satisfaction with locality. It is plain that locality is socially significant as much as it is geographically distinctive.

The existence therefore of a 'rubbing shoulders' effect at neighbourhood level is also unsurprising. People like where they live if they like the other people who live there. This is one of the underlying reasons why it is easier to govern in socially homogeneous and upwardly mobile areas and why it is much more difficult to govern in socially diverse areas that are subjected to severe comparative disadvantages.

An international online survey of 24,000 people conducted during 2009 among 23 separate countries discovered that citizens in the Netherlands, Canada and Australia were happier with their local area as a place to live than those living in the other twenty countries. The researchers attempted to examine the relationship between citizen satisfaction with locality and citizen perception of: (1) ability to influence decisions locally; (2) the level of corruption of local governments; and (3) community cohesion in these countries. Critically, this survey concluded that there was no clear link between feelings of influence over local decisions and satisfaction with local area. Respondents in Latin American countries felt that they could influence decisions locally but they had relatively low levels of satisfaction with their local areas; however, this may be because of the relatively high level of perceived corruption in the local governments in those countries.[25] In this way, perceptions of place mingle with perceptions of democratic authority, its openness and transparency.

Governing amidst uniqueness and variety

A decade ago, at the earliest stage of the internet 'hype cycle', geography was supposed to be history. We were supposed to be witnessing the death of distance and the levelling of the landscape for opportunity. According to these accounts, two profound changes were killing geography. First, came the rapid growth of technological and communication networks. The argument was that these new networks served to flatten geographical advantages by negating the benefit of clustering. You could now work remotely from wherever you wanted, delivering your services down a length of wire. And as it would take just one-eighth of one second for any of your work to travel around the entire world – you were now footloose. Or if you chose not to be footloose and resisted the call for flexibility, others could take your place. Perhaps your work could now be done remotely and more cheaply in Mumbai or Bangalore. In this new flattened world of cheap ubiquitous communications, everyone was supposed to be on a level playing field where there was no centre and no periphery and opportunities were ever less subject to the 'friction of difference'.

The second profound change was the accelerating pace of economic globalization. Of course the world's nations have always traded globally but the advent of instantaneous communication together with more liquid capital markets and the re-entry of China and India into the global bazaar accelerated further the integration of economies across the globe. Basically, you borrowed money in the United States or in Britain to buy goods made in China, while overnight, as you slept, the credit on your account was being administered in India.

But geography is not history. It is alive and kicking. It is true that the 2009 recession underscored the interdependent nature of global market economies – as financial crises reverberated across the globe in minutes, weeks and months. But at the global level, the geographical distribution of natural resources (of water, food and energy sources) is as vital to 21st-century geopolitics as it has ever been in the past. The power of the Gulf States speaks to their strength in the oil economy; the dampened effect of the 2009 global recession on Australia speaks to that country's comparatively rich mineral deposits. But the injustices that people experience everywhere are not driven by geography. Instead they stem from the imposition of bad ideas by powerful people or from the unintended consequences of bad systems in human affairs.[26]

Geography refracts injustice and it also refracts opportunity. Human activity and talent continue to cluster in cities. Some 600 of the largest cities in the world house one-fifth of the world's population but they generate 60 per cent of the globe's GDP and all indications point to a further clustering of people and productive talent in these cities. Of course, the centre of gravity in global cities is shifting with the urban world moving south and east (with new large cities emerging into the top 600 such as Haerbin, Shantou and Guiyang in China; Hyderabad and Surat in India; and Cancun and Barranquilla in Latin America).[27] Indeed, cities develop their own distinctive personality from the cultures and psychologies of the people who move to them and who flourish in them. In this way, the collective personality of New York varies from that of, say, Kansas or Seattle because these different places are made up of different people who not only share different collective histories but who may also share differing personalities, drives, ambitions and outlooks.[28]

Think back to No Place in the north-east of England – a small village within commuting range of Sunderland and the Newcastle–Gateshead conurbation. The district in which it is based has been deeply affected by the global recession with a collapse in demand for the region's steel-making. As the region with the lowest gross household income and the highest economic inactivity rate, it is perhaps unsurprising that during a 10-year period to 2007 the north-east saw its population stay the same (at just 2.6 million people) while the rest of England grew by an average of 4.6 per cent. The contrast with London is stark. Labour productivity (measured by gross value added per worker) is substantially higher in London than in the north-east.[29] These two places show the continuing power of geography. Different places may have similar challenges but even these are refracted through unique character of localities.

For geography refracts how our economies work and function. Labour is local; people have to live and work somewhere. But capital is global; it seeks out opportunities to make returns – in assets, in the urban form, in the supply of labour; and across the world. The radical geographer David Harvey writes of how capital flows across the globe are intertwined and interrelated so as to produce uneven geographical development that is:

> infinitely varied and volatile: a de-industrialised city in northern China; a shrinking city in what was once East Germany; the booming industrial cities in the Pearl River delta; an IT concentration in Bangalore; indigenous populations under pressure in Amazonia; the conflict ridden oil fields in the Ogoni region of Nigeria; the staid middle-class suburbs of London, Los Angeles or Munich; the garment factories of Sri Lanka; the shanty towns of South Africa; the new mega-cities in the Gulf States ...[30]

However, while the interconnected nature of capital flows across the world may ultimately provide the fuel for this variety, they may not be its proximal cause. But Harvey makes a powerful case when he argues that disruptions and discontinuities in capital flows are the clear source of volatility in the economies of these different geographical locations. The foreclosures on low-income housing in Cleveland and Detroit in 2006 that preceded the foreclosures across suburban USA in 2007 arose (as shall be seen in the next chapter) from global capital disruptions involving trade imbalances, asset bubbles and debt-fuelled economic booms.

Summary

Each geographical location needs its own government. And all government is self-government. Government that rests upon a dry and abstracted understanding of the communities it serves without proper regard to their unique histories and geographies will fail. To succeed in the 21st century, governments will need to know the rhythm and pulse of the communities they serve, their dynamism and their uniqueness. And to govern well in the places they serve, they will need to honour the past, capture the present, and shape a better future.

Until quite recently the gulf between the governed and the government was great: the governed were deferential and their government was authoritative. The 21st century brings not only a steepening in the decline of deference but also an incline in the profile of social difference. To govern is to lead a community as well as to choose between competing claims.

If all politics is local, then perhaps the best governance is also that which is local. But in human affairs we need to be mindful of the limits to localism: for there are perils in parochialism. Advocates of localism need to acknowledge that, like all things, it has its dark side. After all, the claims of local tradition and local custom can suffocate initiative, foreshorten horizons and limit ambition. At its worst these effects can be seen in some local communities as well as in some local governments. Each of us has to live somewhere. And if we live in a locality that encourages us to cooperate with our neighbours and find common cause with other citizens locally, then we can be part of a strongly bonded social capital. But we don't just want to live well with others, we want to make the best of ourselves and that may involve us in reaching beyond our locality to the challenges and opportunities of our region, our nation, our globe. Helping citizens to be self-reliant and resourceful by building their capabilities and confidence is therefore an important aspect of good government.

If there is a danger to avoid it lies in a localism that serves to strengthen the ties within communities while weakening the ties with other localities. This form of localism strengthens the bonds of community too tight, potentially turning close communities into closed communities.

Chapter 7

Results Driven Leadership

Managing and leading for public purpose

Malcolm is focused on delivering results. He has a high-pressure job in charge of a high-profile public project with a tight budget and an even tighter timescale. Malcolm is the client project manager for the 6000-seat Velodrome that is to be the venue for the indoor cycling events in the 2012 Olympics in London. This is an £80m scheme being delivered by a specialist contractor – Malcolm leads the overall design consortium to make sure the contractor and suppliers keep to target. His project is highly complicated, it involves a complex web of suppliers, and it has a deadline that simply cannot be missed. In 2008, a large contaminated site in Stratford, East London had to be treated before any building work could start. Over 48,000 cubic metres of material had to be excavated to create the bowl for the venue; and more than 900 steel piles were driven to depths of up to 26 metres to form the venue's foundation. With just 36 months to go before the start of the Games, over 100 workers were on the site building the concrete base structure. By the spring of 2010, work was complete on the steel structure of the stadium; and by July 2010, with 24 months to go before the Games begin, the awesome sweeping design of the building's iconic roof was in place and the track installation was underway.

For Malcolm, getting things right involves exceptional skills in project management and relationship management. The pressure of the work excites Malcolm; he is someone who learns by doing but he is also highly conscientious. Previously he had worked as a project director, rebuilding hospitals in London that were funded through the government's private finance initiative. Getting involved in the Olympics was a mouth-watering prospect for Malcolm – a keen cyclist, this was his dream job. A lot of emphasis had been placed on the innovative design of the Velodrome; but designing the building was arguably easier than executing such a complex design and sustaining the supply chain of companies to deliver the project to time and budget.

Getting a public project of this high profile built to design, time and cost is extraordinarily challenging for Malcolm and his team. If they were to get something significantly wrong amid this complexity, it would be costly – not simply in terms of money but crucially to everyone's reputation. It would be very damaging for the reputation of the Olympic Delivery Authority itself and damaging to the London Olympics team more generally. What's more, the Mayor of London would find it reputationally damaging, with the mayoral election scheduled just three months before the Games begin; as would the UK government and the people of London generally. So Malcolm is under considerable pressure to get this right. That suits him as he thrives on the adrenaline of complex project delivery to tight deadlines. Moreover, it places a premium on his naturally innovative spirit, to attempt new ways of delivering to meet the architectural design goals and to meet the Olympic Delivery Authority's specific targets for the scheme.

Ann is focused on delivering results: she is the manager of one of England's most hard-pressed child protection services in a city in the East Midlands. She manages and leads about 65 people in seven discrete teams that have interlinked work objectives. Each team is focused on a different part of the process of safeguarding children and young people. The teams work to a highly pressured daily and weekly rhythm that is intensely stressful and presents real emotional demands on the staff themselves. Each month about 460 formal referrals of children are made to Ann's service. Each of these referrals involves children and young people who are thought to be vulnerable and at risk in their family settings. The referrals are made by teachers, doctors, police officers and concerned members of the public. Assessing whether children are safe in their family settings is a complex business. It involves a three-stage process: an initial assessment is undertaken, usually within a week. Where there is cause for serious concern, a multi-agency 'core assessment' will be completed for each child – this takes usually over a month. In those most serious cases were social workers have significant concerns about the safety of children, they institute care proceedings.

In the average month, Ann's staff undertake 275 initial assessments and about 80 core assessments. Her teams are performing at the average level for services across the country. They complete 67 per cent of all the initial assessments within 7 days and 85 per cent of the core assessments within 35 days.[1] Over a one-year period 430 children in this East Midlands city are made the subject of child protection plans – that's eight each week. Every working day her staff are in court representing the interests of children, usually in cases which present the parents and carers in a poor light. 'Preparing for court appearances is one of the most nerve-wracking aspects of these jobs', says Ann. Child protection plans are prepared after the social workers have met the families and evaluated the extent of independence and vulnerability of each child in the family, and usually after a multidisciplinary case conference has discussed the many aspects of the family and the individual children concerned. Across England as a whole, some 37,900 children were made subject to a child protection plan in 2008–9. Of these, 44 per cent were because of concerns about general neglect; 26 per cent were because of concerns about emotional abuse; 15 per cent were because of concerns about physical abuse; and 6 per cent were because of concerns about sexual abuse. In 9 per cent of cases, children were thought to be subject to multiple forms of abuse and/or neglect. In the overwhelming majority of cases referred to Ann's staff they were able to help the families cope better with family life and improve their parenting. However, in about one case in every eleven her social work team leaders had to institute care proceedings so as to place the children in safer settings: either in foster care or in other forms of care.

For Ann, getting things right requires exceptionally sound judgement, great people management skills and high levels of personal resilience. At work, Ann exudes grace and calm despite the ever present pressures. She is someone who learns by reflection. Her management style is thoughtful, considered and calming. Child protection social workers have to balance compassion with detachment. They are making life-changing judgements for families. Each case involves different people with different risks and vulnerabilities. This places a premium on innovative thinking on the part of the social workers. For 'knotty problems' in families require highly personalized solutions if they are to work. Getting things wrong, by taking children unnecessarily from their families or by leaving them with their families when they should not be, poses very significant risks for the children concerned. Additionally, serious failings in assuring the safety of children at risk can be professionally damaging to the social workers involved and reputationally damaging to the local multi-agency partnership board that has oversight of child protection, as well as to the local authority for whom Ann works. The fear of making a wrong decision or missing an opportunity to intervene to prevent a child suffering serious harm looms as an ever present danger over Ann's service.

Tyrone is focused on delivering results: he manages a waste collection, street cleaning and recycling service in a large London borough with a population of 270,000 people. Overall he manages and leads about 185 people. The waste collection service is a very important service locally – among a range of public services it regularly scores highest in terms of overall resident satisfaction. The service collects waste from 110,000 local residential properties and about 3000 local businesses. It is a 'general good' service to everyone – and everyone has a view about the quality of the service: the timeliness of the arrival of the refuse truck, the tidiness of the refuse staff and the overall convenience of the service to them. Less than half the costs of the service that Tyrone manages are labour costs. This is because his service incurs high costs in terms of the financing and maintenance of vehicles and plant. What's more, his 30 vehicles, 18 of which are very large refuse trucks, take up a lot of depot space when they are not active and thereby incur high capital charges (the accounting equivalent of rental costs). The collection rounds involve four operatives in hard manual work each day of the year (barring Christmas day). Each day the loading staff walk an average of five miles and each truck collects some 20 tonnes of waste. The task of supervising, managing and motivating these staff is itself a challenge.

Ten years ago when he was first appointed to his job, Tyrone's management task was simpler – the focus was mainly on delivering a quality, reliable and cost-effective service. There is a reasonably competitive market for waste collection services – he knew his competitors, their likely costs and their innovative practices. However, the economics of the waste business encourages a 'vertical integration' between waste collection and waste disposal. Critically, Tyrone's service collects waste; it does not dispose of it. Instead it has a very large service contract with a local incinerator that, through burning, converts refuse to energy. He therefore sends a comparatively low proportion of the waste collected to landfill. However, this also means that his service achieves comparatively low recycling rates – although it may prove that burning recyclables is more energy efficient than transporting them elsewhere. Tyrone is acutely aware that it costs about £80 for each tonne of recycled materials collected compared with £20 for each tonne of refuse collected from the very same homes.

In his own time, Tyrone has pursued a passion for computer software design and, out of curiosity, he devised some web-based solutions to some of his work problems. He designed a mobile phone application that enables anyone to take photos of environmental problems and report them via GPS-linked multimedia messaging. The work is assigned on receipt of the image and a team is despatched to deal with the problem (such as graffiti or vandalism). When they have sorted the problem, Tyrone's staff take a photo and send the image of the cleared up site back to the person who reported it originally. A simple idea has spread by word of mouth over the past two years. It has dramatically altered the effectiveness of the environmental maintenance service as well as reduced its costs – mainly through engaging citizens in smart reporting. The system has now been adopted by ten other localities. This approach means that Tyrone is now involved in the management of demand as well as the management of supply – he is now tasked with helping residents reduce their volumes of waste production as well as improve their overall recycling rates.

For Tyrone, getting things right involves managing a slick fault-free refuse collection service but it also involves discovering ways in which residents' behaviour towards waste production can be modified. Tyrone learns by experimenting and prototyping. As a manager he delegates to his staff and empowers them. Many public services are invisible to the public at large – but not refuse collection. It is one of the very few services where all citizens have a view of the effectiveness and efficiency of the service overall. Every political leader and public manager knows how important it is for the refuse collection service to be high quality. Getting things wrong in this service can be reputationally very costly as well as environmentally very damaging.

Malcolm, Ann and Tyrone are all managers of public projects or public services. They are not administrative functionaries dispassionately delivering services they do not care about. Each of them is actively seeking to improve the performance of their services and the outcomes of these services for the population locally. And each of them cares deeply about what they are doing. They all have to achieve set performance standards but they also need to be highly innovative. They have targets, deadlines and standards imposed upon them as well as a battery of reporting requirements. But the measures they use most are the ones that they have devised themselves. They are not dancing to someone else's targets; each of them is personally driven to achieve results and together with the managers to whom they directly report, they have set themselves stretching goals. In different ways they each operate within a framework of accountability to elected politicians, although in each case politicians expect these managers to deliver. Politicians rightly conclude that daily oversight or inappropriately close political influence in the management of these public projects and services will divert managerial attention from the essentials of delivery. Having the right framework of accountability between public managers and those who govern is an essential building block for effective delivery.

Building a high-profile public project, like the 2012 Velodrome, involves programme and project management skills of the highest order. Delivering a responsive but robust safeguarding service for highly vulnerable children requires extraordinary sound judgement and high order skills in complex risk assessment. Managing a general public service that is known and visible to everyone requires attention to the grinding detail of routine service delivery and the possession of exceptionally good management and innovation skills. Each of these three managers is doing more than just managing services; they are also delivering public goods, regulating public bads, and managing public risks. And each is doing more than simply delivering results; they are also building a licence to manage with their stakeholders and with citizens generally. The most effective public managers go beyond just delivering what is initially required of them; the most effective public managers seek to engage the public in the nature of the service they are delivering so as to inspire, excite and educate their stakeholders. In the case of our three managers, they want their stakeholders to know how the Velodrome fits into the overall spirit of the London Games, how we can help families and communities to care better for children at risk, and how we can all take better responsibility for reducing our volume of household waste and contribute to a greener environment.

Each of these three managers has a mastery of the detail of their service area; they are experts in their respective fields. They have each introduced strong programme management and performance management approaches. They sense opportunities to deliver better and they manage risks well. They manage by measuring what they are doing and how successful they are in doing it. But they each know that measurement is not management. Over the years they have each improved by learning. And they know that you learn by doing – in particular, you need to learn quickly when you make mistakes.

Managers of public projects or public services like Malcolm, Ann and Tyrone may be directly employed within the public sector or instead they may be engaged through contract by private companies, through special purpose agencies or via not-for-profit voluntary organizations. It doesn't really matter which. For it is not their status as public sector employees that is their defining characteristic – rather it is what they do, the results they are seeking to deliver, and how they go about managing and leading their service. A good deal of public sector programme and project management is outsourced to private companies; by contrast, hardly any children's safeguarding services are managed within private social work practices; while most waste collection services are outsourced to private sector providers.

Blueprints, recipes and the essence of learning

Malcolm, Ann and Tyrone are successful because they are each disciplined in their approach to management. And put at its simplest, effective management occurs as a consequence of disciplined thinking and disciplined execution. Disciplined in doing 'business as usual' and disciplined when approaching innovation.[2] But why is there such apparent variation in performance across public managers and public agencies? Why do some projects overrun; why do some child protection services insufficiently safeguard children at risk; why do some refuse services perform so poorly at recycling; and why are some public agencies much more successful at achieving their goals than others? These questions tend to elicit two types of response that suggest two similar sorts of remedies. The first is what I shall call the 'blueprint' remedy. The second response could be described as belonging to a 'best practice' school of management.

Blueprint thinking is useful in some management tasks, usually the manufacture of products. But it is a style of thinking that tends to infect all management. Consider this. The first purchasers of a new car made by Honda are its competitors. They want to know everything about the new Honda car as it is a straight competitor with cars that they make. When they buy the Honda they can deconstruct it bit by bit and then rebuild it, restoring it to its original state. Or if they do not have the car, they can build it by obtaining a blueprint and developing it from scratch. Cars are like that. They are developed to a blueprint – they are engineered. They can be deconstructed and rebuilt. Most management that is focused on delivering products tends to think in these blueprint ways. Sometimes there are different standards of blueprint or different levels of quality.

Think of men's suits. The vast majority of men who buy suits, buy them 'off the peg'. An off the peg suit is cut off a block standard pattern and is sold to consumers categorized by chest measurement. It fits at the chest – and hopefully elsewhere too. By contrast a 'bespoke' suit is one that is based on individual body measurements and that is then made by hand uniquely to fit an individual client. These bespoke suits involve three to four fittings, hours of hand stitching and generally cost several thousands. Suits that are 'made to measure' are midway between off the peg and bespoke as they are cut from a block which is then adjusted to fit the client. In 2008, there was a fierce legal case in the UK involving the exclusive tailors of Savile Row in London about the definitions of 'made to measure' and 'bespoke'. The Savile Row tailors wanted to protect the term 'bespoke' because mass market retailers of suits were using laser cutting technologies and new manufacturing capabilities to produce personalized suits from a block. They lost the case. Blueprint technologies for making more personalized suits at lower cost had effectively reduced standards of fitting from three levels of quality down to two.

By contrast, the management of services that involve people delivering value to other people involve recipe thinking more than blueprint

thinking. Recipes involve ingredients and sequencing. They
similarities to blueprints – for one thing they still involve
scripting. But crucially they do not rest upon an engineering mindset.
Think of a cake. Cakes are made according to a recipe, with ingredients
and sequencing instructions. But once baked, it is not feasible to deconstruct a cake and then reconstruct it again. Cakes are not like cars. And
everyone accepts that different people will make slightly different
versions of the same cake based on the same recipe. Of course, many
public services gain from blueprint thinking (in terms of standardizing
levels of service and assuring consistency) but for very many public
services it is recipe thinking that better reflects the nature of the
relationship between the service user and the front-line service provider.

Governments will understandably want to orchestrate public services
that are of good quality but that are also of lowest feasible cost. This means
that they will want public managers to get the best approach to standardizing – using economies of scale through copy-based approaches that
replicate consistently. This drives a search for best practice solutions –
ideal approaches that can be adopted and applied everywhere. The case for
standard operating procedures for building velodromes, taking children
into care and collecting household rubbish is fairly strong. And standardized approaches will help lower the cost of service provision. However, the
school of management thinking that focuses on best practice tends to over-
look the natural way that people and organizations learn. Learning is
central to how people and organizations perform – and they don't learn
best by copying.

Effective learning helps people to turn errors into successes; and
effective organizational learning helps organizations keep pace with their
ever shortening life cycle. Through more systemic learning, organizations cope better with the inevitable errors and mistakes that accompany
innovation and that tend to spread caution throughout organizational life.
Organizations perform well if they have embedded work-based learning
that helps their staff (and often their service users) reflect on past performance and helps them envision how better to deliver services in the future.
Successful organizations will have focused on the general way in which
they learn and in particular they will have focused on the way that their
people learn from error and mistake. And they will understand that there
are different styles of learning and different types of error.

Conventional learning involves 'reactive learning'. This occurs when
people and organizations react to changes in their environment. And
when they react they tend to rely on routine and habit. They learn by
repeating old ways of reacting to events – 'this seemed to work then,

perhaps it'll work now.' The power of learning from direct experience was identified by Tyrone Kolb in the early 1980s. Kolb identified the main ways in which people differed in how they perceived things and also in how they processed information.[3] His work suggested that people had a small number of different learning styles (such as theorist, reflective, activist and pragmatist) and that their learning would improve if they gave more thought to how they as individual best learnt new behaviours.[4] This approach was developed further by the management theorist Peter Senge who argued that when people and organizations are confronted by profound change in their environment, they respond best through deeper levels of learning based on more in-depth reflection on what needs to be learnt.[5]

Learning from error is the cornerstone of learning. But in management as in life generally there are two types of error. A 'type 1' management error involves choosing to do something that events subsequently prove to have been a wrong choice. A 'type 2' management error involves deciding not to do something when subsequent events lead to the conclusion that it would have been right to have done it. Most managers in most organizations focus entirely on type 1 errors. They tend to focus on their obvious mistakes – when they have chosen to do things (pursue a particular strategy or implement a strategy in a particular way) that go wrong. And they draw their learning from these sorts of errors. This does not happen in Ann's case. For, almost uniquely, child protection services involve 'serious case reviews' which focus on type 2 errors. Serious case reviews are instituted in the event of a child's death or a child is the subject of a seriously harmful incident(s). These reviews attempt to identify 'missed opportunities to intervene to safeguard a child'. The focus in these serious case reviews is on things that weren't done that should have been done.

Learning from error is crucial and avoiding bad practice is fundamental. And yet the best practice school of management tends to forget this vital aspect of human nature. It overlooks the human truth that we are just as likely to want to avoid worst practice (including our past errors as well as the known errors of others) as to want to chase best practice. What's more, the best practice school tends to draw its evidence only from successes and in so doing it makes a number of methodological errors. The first of these is the truism that success is assigned retrospectively and moreover, success is usually assigned ad hominem to those at the top of organizations. In a famous illustration of this point, the physicist Enrico Fermi was introduced to a general in the US army during his time working on the Manhattan Project in the 1940s. 'Mr Fermi, let me introduce you to our best general', said the senior intelligence aide. Fermi responded, 'but how do you know he is your best general?' He went on, 'if armies are equally matched the chance of a general winning one battle is 1 in 2; the chance of winning two battles is 1 in 4; the chance of winning three battles is 1 in 8; four battles is 1 in 16; and five battles it is 1 in 32. – how many generals do you have?' The aide said that there were about 2900 generals in the US army. Fermi replied, quick as a flash, 'then 90 should have won five battles simply by chance'.[6] This story illustrates the retrospective and ad hominem bias involved when evaluating success.

What's more if you only examine successful managers (or organizations) and you find that they did A, B and C, you really cannot conclude that they succeeded because they did A, B and C. This is because you have not identified others who may also have done A, B and C but who, by contrast, have failed. In an attempt to remedy this problem, researchers at the Kennedy School of Government in Harvard created two groups of public service organizations: one group that had succeeded in achieving its goals and another group that had failed. They compared the practices used by the apparently successful group with those of the failed control group. The researchers found that compared to agencies which failed, successful public agencies focused more on organizational performance, had a collaborative and participatory style with employees and also had lower levels of political involvement in their day-to-day operations.[7] This is one of the very few pieces of research that have systematically sought to identify 'what works' by examining both successes and failures.

Three building blocks for effective management

As the case studies of Malcolm, Ann and Tyrone show, public sector managers must, first, be good to do good. Excellence in project management, professional judgements, and people management underlie each of our three managers' approaches. Competence and capability are the starting point for effective delivery. In addition they need well-directed strategies, appropriate resource controls and effective performance management. Highly competent and capable people can under-perform significantly if they are misdirected in their efforts, under-resourced or ill informed about the impact of their performance.[8]

Second, public managers need to be imaginative, innovative, adaptive and agile.[9] They may not be operating in a fiercely competitive market for service but nonetheless they need to be sensing opportunities and adapting their approaches to ever changing circumstances. The best

' innovation are found more at the edge of practical service
 are discovered among the policy community. Innovation
 ᴏᴏ adaptive behaviour are particularly important for public managers as
they receive weaker signals about changes in the external environment
than do managers in the private sector.

Finally, public managers, like all managers, have to be able to blend
their need to be intellectually energetic (such as when they are involved
in designing accountabilities, choosing strategies, and managing
performance) with the requirement on them to offer 'emotional labour' to
the people they manage. This aspect of management is usually described
rather coldly as 'people management'. That underplays how demanding
and draining it is for most managers.

The requirements of emotional labour vary between management
roles. For example, head teachers in schools are subject to different
demands to, say, police commanders or highways engineers. Most of a
head teacher's emotional labour is focused on the school's pupils and not
the school's teachers. But teachers are also demanding of a head teacher's
attention. Each of our three public managers (Malcolm, Ann and Tyrone)
is subject to different demands with regard to their suppliers, staff and
service users respectively. Managers need to offer emotional labour if
they are to build an esprit de corps, nurture a positive attitude among staff
generally; and tap into peoples' personal motivations so that they may be
better aligned with organizational goals. In short, to be any 'good at doing
the job', a manager must be good at managing people and relationships.

These dimensions of managerial effectiveness are tied together by
cultures and systems of accountability within organizations. Front-line
staff may be subject to supervision (to ensure consistent quality of
response or judgement) but they will more usually be subject to management. Managers direct and control while supervisors oversee and check.
Front-line managers are themselves subject to line management accountabilities and line managers, in turn, are subject to strategic and corporate
management accountabilities. Organizations that have good systems of
accountabilities are those that have the right layers of management
(which seem to have a natural tendency to increase) and the correct spans
of control for each layer of management (which correspondingly appear
to have a natural tendency to reduce).[10] Regular periods of organizational
pruning therefore become a key activity among the most senior executives in the most successful organizations. More generally, the most
successful managers are those that exercise both 'grip' as well as 'delega-
tion' and, critically, they know the precise circumstances when it's best
to grip and when it's best to delegate.

Figure 7.1 shows the dual character of organizational leadership. The main emphasis in the conventional accounts of good management practice is on what I term the 'organizational hardware' – the strategies, the structure, the programmes and projects and so on. It is the hardware that academics, auditors, inspectors and regulators want to see, to read and to judge. However, effective hardware is merely a necessary condition for organizational success; it is not a sufficient condition. That is because organizations (in the private and public sector) are made up of people – organizations are socially constructed. And so it should come as little surprise that successful organizations tend to be those that are highly effective at inspiring people. They connect and help people to discover for themselves a tangible and palpable sense of personal contribution to wider organizational goals.

Figure 7.1 *The dual character of organizational leadership*

Organizational leadership involves intellectual
drive and emotional labour

Hardware	**Software**
Strategies and plans	Ambitions
Structures	Relationships
Reporting lines	Responsibility
Programmes	Hopes and fears
Projects	Dynamism
Products and services	The act of becoming
Activities	The craft of work
Deliverables	Confidence
Output	Pride

When people arrive at their place of work they do not leave their humanity, their hopes and fears at the door. Their sense of personal ambition, their need for productive relationships with others, and their desire to experience craft and pride at work comes with them. Organizations that understand their people's software needs as much as their organization's hardware needs will stand a much better chance at success in achieving their goals.

Leadership, management and a sense of collective efficacy

Good leadership and good management are essential for the successful governance of a community and the successful delivery of public serv-

Good leadership can be found in everyone – in politicians, in senior managers, front-line managers, in professional and service experts, and in communities themselves. Good management can also be found in everyone. Leadership and management may be complementary but they are not always two sides of the same coin. Leadership and management may have distinctive practices but they are not separate domains. Some people have both strong leadership qualities and deep managerial skills; but in truth most people possess these qualities and skills only in small measure.

The theory of leadership, with its focus on setting direction and inspiring people, may differ from the theory of management, with its focus on maintaining stability and harnessing resources,[11] but frankly the distinction is irrelevant in the everyday life of organizations. As the organizational theorist, Henry Mintzberg argues, the past two decades have seen a growing focus on leadership development and a declining emphasis on management development.[12] Perhaps Mintzberg is correct and organizations are now, in consequence, over-led and under-managed. And perhaps he is correct that the art, science and craft of management need nurturing in this era of leadership. But what counts for success in any organization is that it has sufficient leadership and sufficient management involved in a coalition for change and improvement.

Leadership is not conducted in an armchair. It is a field activity. What's more, it often involves personal perils – leaders have to go out on a limb, take risks, and stray into uncomfortable places. Accounts of political leadership tend to focus on the practice of politics at the federal or national level, although one of the most insightful accounts of recent years is that produced by Rudolph Giuliani the former mayor of New York. He not only drew on the immensely difficult challenges of dealing with the atrocious attack on the World Trade Centre in Manhattan on 9/11 2001, he also offers sound and practical advice on political leadership. His advice includes simple policy suggestions such as 'under promise and over deliver' as well as more emotionally important political prompts such as why politicians should always attend funerals.[13]

It is clear from Giuliani's experience as well as the lessons from many other political leaders that maintaining perspective and focus during times of great uncertainty and tumult is crucial.[14] And when introducing new initiatives it is also important to hold one's nerve. For as the management guru Rosabeth Moss Kanter is fond of saying, 'every success feels like a failure in the middle'. And it is 'in the middle' when people lose their nerve: when innovation in practice does not seem to be producing the desired results; when people want to return to old ways of working.

This is why change is so difficult to embed. People need to see m
the benefits of the new. They need first to draw their own conclus......
the current way of working is simply not good enough – either for their
service users or for themselves. Too often people in leadership positions
believe that their role is simply to establish some compelling vision of
the future and then devise some practical first steps to achieving change.
Of course compelling visions are needed, as are agreements on next
steps. But organizational inertia will never be overcome if most people in
an organization consider that the way things are done now is really not
that bad. That is why 'spreading dissatisfaction with current reality' is an
essential starting point for any form of leadership. Every manager seems
to devise their own personal formula for change. The one I prefer is a
formula expressed as follows.[15]

$$(AG + ANS) \times DCR > OI = change$$

When AG is agreement on goals; ANS is agreement on next steps;
DCR is dissatisfaction with current reality;
and OI is organizational inertia.

People are critical for any organization's success; and the craft of
developing success in organizations is the conversion of a mass of critical
people into a critical mass of people. To this end, we need reminding that
every human being has the same basic drivers – they want to acquire
objects and experiences; they want to connect with others; they want to
learn and make sense of the world; and they want to defend themselves
from harm.[16] At work, they want to experience a sense of personal
accomplishment – of tasks performed well; they want to be involved in a
team effort with others to accomplish something together; and finally
they want a sense that they are involved in progress through their
combined efforts with others.[17] It takes exceptional people management
skills to connect people with these deep drivers and wants.

At work, particularly in public service, people want their managers
and leaders to give them a sincere and open appraisal of the issues. They
want an objective assessment of the facts of why this problem matters.
Why does the work on the Velodrome, on child protection or on recycling
really matter? But more than this, they want their managers and leaders
to offer them a sincere and transparent revelation about themselves –
about their hopes and fears as managers and leaders. And they want to
know why the problem, that they are engaged to work on, matters to their
managers and leaders.[18]

All organizations, whether in the public or private sectors, need a blend of both leadership and management. For managers to be successful they need to be able lead others, for leaders to be successful they need to be capable of managing. To be managed by someone who doesn't lead can be dispiriting but to be led by someone who doesn't manage can be equally as disengaging. Good management builds an organization's capabilities. Good leadership inspires an organization's confidence. Management makes sure that people have the right skill set. Leadership makes sure that people have the right mindset. In this way, managerial focus is on building a sense of 'how to'; while leadership focus is on a sense of 'can do'.

Whether it is for individuals, teams or organizations, a sense of 'confidence' is the bridge connecting expectations and performance. Confident people make things happen, they don't wait for them to happen. Confidence helps people to take control of circumstances rather than be dragged along by them.[19] The right level of confidence (neither too overconfident nor too under-confident) delivers optimum performance. People know the precise nature of their day-to-day challenges at work; and they know their capabilities in meeting these challenges. With the right level of confidence they will not only deliver on these challenges, they will also use more initiative and be more innovative. Within organizations, leaders and managers create the emotional climate that builds or corrodes confidence. At their best, they build an atmosphere of personal accountability; at their worst they build a climate of fear and blame. At work, a sense of confidence operates at three levels. First, there is confidence in oneself – in one's own capability to perform a given task or service. Second, there is confidence in one another – in the team in which you work and in the team's means of internal support and help in performing tasks and services. And third, there is confidence in the overall system of the organization to support and sustain individual and team efforts and to successfully manage progressive change

Confidence arises from a sense of self-efficacy. This differs from the more commonly used term of self-esteem. Self-esteem centres on judgements of self-worth, whereas self-efficacy is concerned with judgements of personal capability. People need much more than high self-esteem to do well in life. Personal efficacy creates the goals that people set for themselves as well as their performance attainments. People with high levels of self-efficacy set themselves stretching goals. As the social psychologist Albert Bandura has argued, outcomes arise from actions. How one behaves largely determines the outcomes one experiences.

Performance is thus causally prior to outcomes. 'People do not jud
they will drown if they jump into deep water and then infer they n
poor swimmers. Rather, people who judge themselves to be poor swimmers will visualize themselves drowning if they jump into deep water.'[20]
Hence it is crucial that people's judgement of themselves is optimal. A
high standard of self-efficacy will generate higher performance and
better outcomes – for themselves and for their teams and the wider
organization in which they work.

For hard results acquire soft skills

Elected politicians set the tone for public institutions. The style and
substance of their leadership is central to how public institutions are
viewed by their staff, their service users and their stakeholders. Their
conduct and their behaviour set the atmosphere, the microclimate in
which the institution functions. Their role in governing the institution is
vital – they lead, they speak for the public, and they choose direction and
strategy. They set the intent of policy and they also choose the instrument
of policy. They decide what is to be done and often how it is to be done.
But they are not usually involved in execution. They are not closely
involved in the implementation of policy. And failure of execution,
failure of implementation, is often the key to understanding why public
agencies fail.

To deliver results in both the public and the private sector requires
extraordinary attention to implementing things correctly. The three case
study managers that opened this chapter describe the range of skills and
expertise required to deliver public results. And the case studies show
that while government worries a great deal about how to incentivize good
management, the best managers are intrinsically motivated; they need
neither carrot nor stick.

Every organization needs managers to plan, budget, organize and
review. And every organization needs managers of people, resources,
projects, tasks and processes. In all people-intensive organizations,
managers need to focus the attention of others on those critical factors
that are central to ensuring organizational success. And they also need to
shape people's behaviour so as to achieve common cause. This common
cause is achieved not simply by managers encouraging collective
endeavour ('It's better if you work with others rather than work alone')
but, rather, because individuals themselves realize that they are unable to
achieve big outcomes through just their little actions.

Part of the role of all managers in all organizations is to promote the intrinsic benefits of strong cooperation. It is essential for managers and leaders to achieve this sense of common cause across their organization – whether it is in the private sector or the public sector. But responsibility for motivating people requires managers to recognize individuals' personal contribution; they should neither focus solely on a common agenda nor focus solely on how people's efforts compare one to another.[21]

From time to time people may look for comparison ('am I doing well compared to others?') but ultimately they want their personal contribution to be of value and not just compared. No one has etched on their tombstone, 'he was better than his brother!' This deep psychological need to be recognized for one's personal contribution underlies people's anxiety of ranking systems, league tables and comparisons generally; even though comparisons are inevitable and can be quite useful in assessing how well a team or an organization is performing. As a manager of other people, the 'rule of thumb' should be: first acknowledge the value of someone's contribution before appraising how their efforts compare to others.

Valuing contribution may be crucial, but contribution to what? Most managers would say, 'contribution to organizational purpose'. But they would be wrong. People want to contribute to far wider goals than the narrow objectives of any organization. And this is where public service organizations have a massive motivational edge on their private sector counterparts. In local government this is easier still. The common cause that conjoins those who work in local public service is the welfare of the local community. The purpose of local government is crystal clear – 'to improve the quality of life and quality of life-chances of people who live in this locality'. The focus on place is in reality a focus on the lives of the people in that place.

Why is this so important? It is because connecting with the deep purpose of an organization is known to be very important to people – it harnesses people's intrinsic motivation and it enables heightened organizational effectiveness.[22] Helping people to connect with deeper purposes requires high order emotional intelligence on the part of an organization's managers and leaders.[23] This can be seen in the leadership of the best private companies and the best not-for-profit organizations – it needs to be spread more broadly throughout government and across public institutions. Public service was for some a vocation. The combination of professional capture ('I'm an accountant') and the simple commodification of work ('I'm employed by public agency X for £30,000 per year') may have corroded this vocational sense – but it can be re-energized. Organizations succeed when their people understand deeply the 'spirit' of the organization: not just its rules and procedures but, rather, what the organization is for.

In public service this ought to be easy – for the goals of public organizations are directed at overall welfare or the common good. Their mission is therefore more likely to resonate with their employees' own sense of personal purpose. It ought to be easier for leaders and managers to foster both a sense of self-efficacy and a sense of collective organizational efficacy in public service organizations. However, three different factors often serve to undermine this.

First, public managers need to have world-class interpersonal skills to generate sufficiently high levels of self-efficacy in their organizations. Second, political partisanship can sometimes get in the way. Public service purposes can get hijacked by party political positioning to the point where pursuit of a particular policy goal or use of a particular policy instrument is branded as part of the core propositions of a given political party. To some extent this process is inevitable, as parties will need to differentiate themselves to the electorate and in so doing position themselves in respect of particular policies. Third, as public agencies are accountable through the political process, there may be a too formal relationship between elected politicians and executive managers – such that the latter are considered by their organizations as little more than neutral implementers of politically determined policies.

The public entrepreneur

Politicians and public managers are usually cooperative in their drive to achieve progress through public action but they most definitely walk to the beat of different drums. As public executives they need to work together – with complementarity. Political rationality and managerial rationality are different lenses through which government and public services can be viewed. Mostly, politicians and public managers work well together in pursuit of public aims and to build effective public action – but not always. As Geoff Mulgan, the former Cabinet Office strategy advisor remarked, 'everywhere there are well-intentioned officials trying to make sense of the wishes of flailing politicians, and principled politicians driven to distraction by incompetent and complacent civil servants'.[24]

The conventional caricature of a public manager is of an objective, impartial, emotionally detached man or woman who is an implementer of policies agreed by their political masters. This caricature misses completely the role of public managers in providing disinterested, impartial advice to

.iticians and it also misses their vital role in building capacity within their organizations. Not least of which is their leadership role in motivating their staff to align their energies to organizational strategies so as to deliver politically agreed goals and desired social results. To do this well, they need continually to walk the fine line between giving disinterested advice and being passionately committed to implementing agreed policy.

The extent to which managerial tasks in public organizations are distinctively different from managerial tasks in private sector companies is a quietly controversial topic. Undoubtedly there are differences in the sectors between how inputs and outputs are measured. However, while it is true that private companies are more able to reduce their performance to simple money-based measures, public managers need to be equally rigorous in how they assemble evidence to track progress in the achievement of their objectives.

Some of the most prominent organizational theorists of the past century (Max Weber, Herbert Simon and Peter Blau) have argued that there is not much difference between large private companies and large public sector organizations.[25] They argue that the managerial problems of scale, complexity, the development of specializations and the need for appropriate coordination between specialisms beset all large organizations regardless of their context or environment. And they are right – there are considerable similarities between public organizations and private companies.

But there remain a number of ways in which managing public services differs from managing private companies. These include the sheer closeness of political oversight, the assumption of fairness in outcomes and, in the absence of market mechanisms, the difficulties in eliciting the public's preferences in respect of public services.[26] One area where there is a strong commonality between public managers and private managers is the need to ensure organizational effectiveness. Public managers need to develop their organization's capabilities so as to deliver social results just as private sector managers need to mobilize their company's energies to improve their overall competitiveness. Mobilizing an organization is difficult to achieve from a position of detached neutrality – hence public managers need to embrace impartiality but avoid detachment. That is why public managers need to have a repertoire of skills. Yes they need the soft skills of people management but they also need the hard edge disciplines of resource and project management.

In a review of the extent to which organizations in the public (or social) sector need to adopt private sector practice, Jim Collins adopts his usual directness:

We must reject the idea – well-intentioned but dead wrong – th primary path to greatness in the social sectors is to become, 'more like a business'. Most businesses – like most of anything else in life – falls somewhere between mediocre and good. Few are great. When you compare great companies with good ones, many widely practiced business norms turn out to correlate with mediocrity, not greatness. So then, why would we want to import the practices of mediocrity into the social sectors?[27]

Perhaps at the highest level, leaders of public agencies need to develop what business psychologist Howard Gardner has described as a fivefold approach. They need to be disciplined, have a synthesizing style, be creative, be respectful of others, and approach issues and people from a strong ethical stance.[28]

Managers lead, leaders manage

A disciplined approach to delivering public value and improving social outcomes is what differentiates Malcolm, Ann and Tyrone from their less successful contemporaries. It explains their relative success: for not only are they disciplined in their approach to managing their projects and their services but they are also disciplined in how they manage the people who work with them and for them. Their focus is fixed on outcomes and results. But they know that to achieve better results they need to galvanize their people's energies to deliver their organization's goals. In this way managers need to lead. They approach things with strategic intuition. They synthesize – in that they draw on a range of concepts and evidence. And at their best, they are driven by a strong ethical frame about their work and its purposes.

What's more, this is true of elected politicians as well as appointed public managers. In his seminal work on American mayors, Douglas Yates created a typology of mayoral leadership based on the dimensions of political activism and the scale of resources they could bring to bear on any problem. If anything, he revealed that the image of 'boss' political mayors is a caricature of American city government. The plural demands of diverse cities were instead creating the conditions for 'broker' mayors who became ever more successful in the kaleidoscope of competing interests of US cities.[29] Since then the comparative effectiveness of facilitative approaches to political leadership has been evidenced in several further empirical studies in American cities.[30] A more generalized study of high performing public agencies in the US found that they had leaders who defined their key role as enhancing employee productivity. These leaders typically hold the following values – learning; a focused mission; a nurturing community at work; and an enabling leadership style.[31] A canvas of leadership by women executives across organizations in every sector found that to frame organizational meaning and direction, to mobilize people's energies, and to connect staff productively with each other required a 'centred leadership' approach that was personal, authentic and appreciative of others.[32]

All organizations are built around people. Public organizations may be built for the public, but they remain built around their people. These people are not in it for themselves but rather they are driven to deliver better public value and higher social results. Of course, organizations can be stultifying, boring places to spend one's time – and there is evidence that people are least happiest when spending time with their manager at work.[33] As the late Sumantra Ghoshal argued, at their best, organizations are 'versatile and creative, they are prodigious amplifiers of human effort.' He argued that organizations need the invigorating, life-giving force that foresighted, determined and energetic leadership and management can bring. This is as true of public organizations as it is of any organization.

> From being the builders of systems, leaders transform into the developers of people, adding values to all employees and helping each individual become the best that he or she can be. The leadership doctrine of strategy, structure and systems that is derived from current theories is replaced by a new doctrine focused around purpose, processes and people.[34]

Chapter 8

Risky Business

Governing and delivering in uncertainty

It was a hot, humid April in Mexico City – one of the largest and most vibrant cities in the world. At its centre live nine million people, surrounded by a sprawl of 59 municipalities containing another ten million people. Mexico City's notoriety for appalling air pollution had waned a little over the past five years thanks to the efforts of the 'ecoguardia' – a task force of some 50 environmental police who stalk polluting cars and trucks throughout the city. Their practice of confiscating the licence plates of the worst polluters had proved fairly successful. Only a few years earlier cyclists routinely wore surgical masks, birds reportedly fell dead in mid-flight and school children were said to use brown crayon to draw the sky. Ranked the world's most polluted city by the UN in 1992, it had successfully cut air pollution by three-quarters. And now in early 2009 the new president of the US, Barack Obama, was visiting. It was an opportunity for Mexico City to show the world how it had improved the quality of its public health. The trouble was, no one had thought about the health of their pigs.

Pigs routinely have influenza. But unusually, pigs can be infected with particular influenza strains that infect three different species: birds and pigs as well as humans. This makes pigs a potential host for particular forms of influenza viruses that might exchange genes producing new and more dangerous strains. Shortly after Obama's visit, Mexico City was effectively shut down by an apparently virulent influenza outbreak among humans. By the end of April, Mexico City had a suspected death toll of over 100 people and over 1000 people were diagnosed with serious breathing problems. All schools were closed, and large public gatherings (such as football matches) were banned. The outbreak appeared to have started in a pig-breeding area in Perote, a municipal area in the Veracruz region to the south-east of Mexico City.

One of the first people reporting the outbreak was Guillermo Vazquez, the mayor of Perote. Mayor Vazquez announced that 800 people in the Perote area had been taken ill and that his office was engaged in house to house monitoring.[1] The first case of swine flu was alleged to have been identified in a five-year-old boy, Edgar Hernandez, who lived in La Gloria, a small rural town in Perote. La Gloria was near an enormous pig breeding farm run by Carroll, a subsidiary of the US food giant Smithfield.[2] With farm work in steep decline in the region, many locals make a long bus commute to work nearer to Mexico City. Hence it was not only pig-breeders who were anxious about the impact of the news on their business – so too were many locals. Mayor Vazquez chose to speak the truth quickly and to make sure that his local municipality was involved in solving the problem rather than ignoring it. In this respect, Mayor Vazquez's approach differed markedly from the response of Mayor Stockmann in Ibsen's play *Enemy of the People*. In Ibsen's play the mayor tried to cover up the contamination of the local baths and spa so as to sustain tourism, while his brother, a local doctor, was pilloried as an 'enemy of the people' for identifying the problem and bringing it to public attention.[3]

Mayor Vazquez's public spirited activism excited the regional and then the national news media. And when the outbreak reached Mexico City itself the news spread around the globe in hours. This was no longer a local problem for Mayor Vazquez; it was internationally significant. All of a sudden a trip to Mexico, or simply a meeting with a Mexican, seemed somehow risky. But real information about the actual risks to people were much more difficult to assess because Mexican record keeping, on the incidence and intensity of influenza among humans, did not appear to match the requirements of international public health experts. The director of the global migration and quarantine for the Centres for Disease Control said that the central question that flu experts wanted to know about Mexico was how many mild cases they had – knowing the numbers of deaths from influenza was simply to know one variable among many.[4] However, within just a few weeks, 150 countries around the world had drawn up flu pandemic contingency plans and were producing public health surveillance reports to the World Health Organization.

Global flu epidemics occur in humans every 30 to 50 years. These are linked, among other things, to generational changes in immunity levels. The horror of the Spanish flu pandemic was a major feature of the early 20th century. It swept the globe at the close of the First World War and is believed to have killed at least 50 million people worldwide. An estimated eight million people died in Spain with some 250,000 dying in the UK. The lessons learnt from this pandemic and subsequent pandemics, such as the Asian flu of 1957 and the Hong Kong flu of 1968, caused public health officials globally to coordinate their work on contingency plans across national boundaries. These contingency plans swung into action with immediate effect in April 2009 – when among many other measures, anti-viral vaccinations and travel restrictions to Mexico began. The globalized nature of the modern world means that a new virus will spread rapidly. Within just two weeks, swine flu cases were reported in Alberta in Canada, in California, New York, Scotland and in London. By the second week in May, three schools in London had closed. The first two schools to close in London were both independent schools, Alleyn's in Dulwich and South Hampstead High School in Camden, where parents or pupils had just returned from trips to the US and Mexico. Public health officials were understandably anxious but they were also rather professionally excited by the prospect of a flu pandemic. Thousands of anti-virals were distributed to affected schools and the multi-agency preparedness and readiness plans, involving hospitals, doctors, pharmacists, local councils and other public agencies, began to be implemented. Globally, the World Health Organization found its purpose and its voice.

Over the next three months, stories of swine flu dominated the world's media and concerned groups of parents, teachers, healthcare workers and others did their own research and made their own decisions for themselves and their families. By the beginning of August 2009 there were 180,000 confirmed cases of swine flu in humans across the globe (one-quarter in the US) with 1100 confirmed deaths (again one-quarter in the US). The UK had over 11,000 confirmed cases of swine flu and had declared 30 deaths.[5] The growth in numbers abated during the school summer break but, as expected, numbers begun to creep up again when children went back to school in September. Speaking in October 2009, Sir Liam Donaldson, the Chief Medical Officer, said that the UK may have had a lucky break with the way that swine flu was spreading. He said that the 'second peak was proving to be a slow burn' which was buying time to get the new vaccine programme underway. Numbers of new infections were declining in Scotland, and in England the rate of spread was not rising as rapidly as feared.[6] In England, the number of cases continued to fall during late October, again something that health experts linked to school holidays. The flu pandemic was declared over in August 2010 some 16 months after it began. A disease that emerged in Mexico City in April 2009 took just 12 months to lead to at least 17,700 deaths worldwide.

In a detailed one-country review, Dame Deidre Hine concluded that nearly 30,000 people in the UK were hospitalized by the flu and, of these, some 457 died, although admittedly the majority of those who died had underlying health conditions that were present before the virus took hold. The independent review concluded that the British government's £1.2bn outlay preparing for the flu was money well spent. However, of this total some £1.01bn was on the cost of anti-virals, doses of vaccine and relevant antibiotics. And the critical juncture in the planning for the flu was when, in July 2009, the World Health Organization 'upgraded' the outbreak from a phase 5 to a phase 6 (a pandemic). This effectively triggered the relevant authorities to begin advanced purchasing of the flu vaccine globally and, in consequence, it raised the costs of these drugs. Across Europe there were allegations that pharmaceutical companies, who had the most to gain from this reclassification, were overly influential. This is yet another example where governments need to balance self-serving private interests with acutely pressing public interests.

In the UK, between 2000 and 4000 people die annually as a result of seasonal flu. The swine flu outbreak was different in that it affected younger people, while seasonal flu targets the elderly. But the response of the UK authorities to swine flu had the effect of reducing the incidence of seasonal flu. And so bizarrely the 'pandemic' may well have saved many lives.[7] In the UK, as elsewhere, the government and public authorities acted swiftly. Partly this was because the government expected up to 65,000 deaths to be caused by the pandemic. It ordered 90 million doses of the vaccine but after several months had used fewer than 5 million of them. At its peak some 40,000 people a week were receiving anti-virals through the UK's national pandemic flu service. By February 2010, ten months from the start of the outbreak in Mexico, the figure had fallen to below 5000 a week.[8] By the middle of 2010, governments across Europe were trying to resell their huge stockpiles of swine flu vaccine.[9]

However, despite these concerns, the overall story is one of qualified success. The dangers posed by Mexican swine flu may have been overestimated and public authorities may have, as a result, overreacted to these fears. And while it is difficult to prove, the flu pandemic may have been contained by battery of public health measures that were organized in a coherent and coordinated fashion. And many more people might have died without the measures that were put in place by public health experts and public authorities generally. Importantly, there is much to be cautiously optimistic about in respect of future battles against flu pandemics. This is not because the measures adopted in 2009 will prevent future pandemics but because the global healthcare planning system has been seriously tested.

Risk-based contingency planning is important – and public health preparedness and readiness plans have been thoroughly tested. So too has the quality and timeliness of public health information. Service coordination has been broadly effective. It involved schools, hospitals, health trusts, local councils and many other public agencies. And in the UK, the expert preparation of new vaccines in the volumes required, in the National Institute for Biological Standards and Control in Hertfordshire, has been hugely impressive. But beating the H1N1 virus in 2009 does not mean that the virus will not reoccur nor does it guarantee against any future flu variant producing a pandemic. Vigilant monitoring, great science, strategic planning and international coordination will all be important in developing an adaptive and resilient approach to responding to new flu strains in the future.

The nature of natural hazards

Swine flu pandemics are part natural hazard, part synthetic hazard: arising as they do from how animals are cultivated. By contrast, the world is subject to the real and present danger of very many different types of environmental hazards (not including the extraneous threats of asteroid impact – of which there is an inverse relationship between the size of the object and the frequency that such objects hit the earth). Most of these environmental hazards disproportionately impact upon the developing world. This is because (aside from Northern California, New Zealand and Japan) the world's most dangerous tectonic plate boundaries are in the developing world – and what's more, in these locations those who live there have not had the resources to construct buildings that are sufficiently resilient to withstand earthquakes. But wherever environmental disasters occur their consequences leave deep scars across the humanity of the globe. In the 20th century, the most deadly environmental hazards took the form of famines – mainly arising from rapid desertification. However, in the early 21st century, the three most potent forms of hazards are earthquakes (and where they occur at sea, their accompanying tsunami); hurricanes and cyclones; and floods.

In the first decade of the 21st century, some 770,000 people have died as a direct result of environmental hazards. These include the 230,000 people who died in the Haitian earthquake in January 2010; the 230,000 people who died as a result of the Indian Ocean earthquake and tsunami in December 2004; the 130,000 people who died as a result of cyclone Nargis in the delta region of Burma in May 2008; the 79,000 people who died as a result of the earthquake in Kashmir in October 2005; the 68,000 people who died as a result of the earthquake in the Sichuan province of China; and the 26,000 people who died as a result of the earthquake in Bam in Iran in December 2003. This shocking toll of deaths has led to calls for more advanced geophysical analysis of earthquakes, and better and more resilient building design in these countries, as well as for more effective tsunami, cyclone and flood warnings.

At the start of 2011, a 7.1 magnitude earthquake (on the Richter scale) near Christchurch, New Zealand, caused the deaths of 180 people and devastated the central city area such that the insurance costs that fell to Lloyds of London were estimated at £3bn. This human misery paled against the tragedy that resulted from the 9.0 magnitude earthquake that struck one month later off the north-east coast of Japan. This earthquake produced a complex weave of interconnected disasters. The advanced nature of construction in Japan enabled the vast majority of buildings to survive the earthquake, but the enormous tsunami produced by the earthquake led to the deaths of some 20,000 people and the destruction of many coastal towns and villages, and rendered hundreds of thousands of people homeless.

One building in Japan that failed to survive the earthquake without damage was the Fukushima nuclear power plant. Four of its six reactors were damaged by the earthquake, many thousands of local residents were evacuated in case of a nuclear explosion and safety crews battled for months to control and contain the disaster. The cost of the Japanese earthquake and tsunami was estimated at some £144bn by the World Bank and it was expected that it would have a 4 per cent impact on Japan's GDP and take at least three years for this advanced nation to recover. The horrific impact of this disaster on the people of Japan demonstrates vividly the role of government to anticipate large-scale risks; to minimize their depth and range of impact; and then help manage the consequences once they occur.

In addition to an incredible number of large earthquakes, the first decade of the 21st century witnessed significant, although substantially lower, numbers of deaths arising from cyclones or floods. The impact of hurricane Katrina in August 2005 in the Gulf of Mexico was the deadliest in the US for over 70 years. In total, some 1840 people lost their lives in the hurricane and then in the subsequent floods. The economic cost of the hurricane amounted to over $90bn and over one million people left the central Gulf coast area in the largest internal dispersion of people in the US in modern times. Some five years later, the city of New Orleans had regained most of its population (back up to 360,000 although still some 100,000 less than it had been before the hurricane struck).[10]

The flood of the River Indus in Pakistan also led to the death of some 1800 people and, moreover, it was also the worst flooding for 80 years.

However, the widespread nature of the flooding led to a diaspora of over four million people within Pakistan. The River Indus regularly floods and many flood control measures have been put into place over the years: but the floods of 2010 were at a scale not previously witnessed. Whether cyclone and flooding occurrences will increase in extent and intensity over the future as climate change exaggerates and amplifies climatic changes is a possibility. But the facts of these occurrences are real and governments – whether the developed democracies of the US or the more fragile democracies such as Pakistan – need to plan for them and be ready to respond.

In those developed economies that do not sit astride dangerous tectonic plate boundaries, the most common natural hazard involves climatic extremes (Canada, the US and Australia), floods and, even more erratically, forest fires or bushfires in areas with significant human settlement. Each year the US is subject, usually somewhere in California, to the threat of forest fires although the fire with the worst death toll was that which occurred in the 'Black Saturday' bushfires to the north-east of Melbourne, Australia in March 2009. These bushfires destroyed 2100 homes, led to 173 deaths and caused over $1bn of losses across 4500 square kilometres in the State of Victoria.[11] The cause of the Black Saturday bushfires is disputed but the two most likely points of ignition were thought to have arisen from clashing power lines as well as from arsonists.

Other environmental hazards can impact on governments in unpredictable and unforeseeable ways. For example, in April 2010 an ash cloud rose from the volcano beneath the Eyjafjallajökull glacier in southern Iceland. It caused air travel to be halted in northern Europe and created travel chaos with all planes grounded in some countries, including the UK, for safety reasons. The main fear was that commercial jet engines would not be able to cope with flying through ash clouds. During this period, the ash clouds rose to 26,000 feet. The British Isles was particularly hit because the ash cloud plume extended from Iceland in a south-easterly direction across Britain.

The decision to ground planes in Britain effectively stranded some 150,000 Britons overseas, causing transport chaos as people tried to return home after their Easter break. The six-day cessation of flights over Europe was estimated to have cost the airline industry some £780m overall. At one point British Airways, which claimed to be losing up to £20m each day, was conducting test flights that it said demonstrated it was safe to fly. Some argued that the safety measures were an echo of the overreaction evidenced in the swine flu pandemic of the previous year. And yet – no one was sure.

The decision to enable planes to fly again was taken by European transport ministers on the advice of safety regulators. These regulators had themselves to blend together two separate streams of advice. First, they needed to consider the advice of volcanologists and meteorologists. And second, they needed to take account of the advice of the aircraft and engine manufacturers on the safety tolerances of engines flying through clouds containing specific types of volcanic ash particulate. After a few months it became clear that this was not a one-off problem and that there was an outside prospect that volcanic activity might interrupt flying in northern Europe at any point in the near future. Governing in such an uncertain, novel and fast moving context, with the full glare of the international media, places an immense strain on everyone concerned – those who are governing as much as those who are governed.

These natural hazards present an uncertain environment in which governments have to operate. They are a challenge to the predictive powers of environmental science (to geology, meteorology and oceanography) and they are a challenge to the construction and environmental maintenance industries that have to develop human settlements that are sufficiently resilient in the face of foreseeable environmental change. But governments need to be focused on more than external environmental hazards – they need to be attentive to risks and hazards of all types that threaten the communities they govern. These include man-made external threats and internal risks to life and well-being.

Man-made risks

Real risks are all around. Risks exists in an objective sense but there is also a strong subjective quality to the nature of risk. In a sense the reflexive character of the post-modern world redoubles and convolutes our judgement of risk.[12] And in the governance of nations and communities in the developed world, the risks posed by man-made threats often seem more real and more palpable than those that derive from natural hazards. These man-made risks may be internal threats or potential harms that arise from within a nation or a community; or instead they may be external threats and potential harms that stem from outside a nation or a community. The internal threats include increasing incivility, community tension, crime and disorder, as well as individual or concerted acts of violence. The external threats include the prospect of terrorism, economic calamity or dramatic climate change.

The demands of governing and managing these public risks or preventing other public 'bads' differ markedly from the demands of delivering public services or allocating public goods.[13] Added to this is the uncertainty of popular response to government policy towards any future threats. For example, in the case of swine flu it is possible that people may be less inclined to believe the next threat given that the last threat appeared to be less deadly than public authorities at first feared. The story of the 2009 swine flu pandemic (that maybe wasn't) speaks loudly of the interconnected nature of the world; the decline of deference to governmental and expert authority; the porous character of nations and communities; and the need for ever more flexible and fluid responses from government and public agencies to new risks and fresh challenges. It also demonstrates how managing risk and uncertainty is a core purpose of government.

The quality of public risk management has increased notably over the past twenty years. One event served to increase global awareness of systemic risks and raise the standard on system preparedness – the event was Y2K. Widespread corporate anxieties of the time stemmed from the theoretical threat of computer failure given the abbreviation of a four-digit year date into a two-digit number within computer systems. At the end of the 1990s, governments and public authorities were deeply entangled in dealing with this entirely manufactured or synthetic risk – the prospect that computers would stall when their internal clock tripped over into the year 2000. On reflection it seems incredible that governments collectively spent hundreds of billions preparing for this event. Special government committees and task forces were convened across the globe to deal with the threat of widespread computer malfunction. But good outcomes can come from even the most pointless of exercises and the main consequence of the Y2K experience was a major improvement in systemic contingency planning and project and programme management as well as preparedness testing. For these plans, programmes and techniques would subsequently prove extremely useful in all manner of risk management exercises and for delineating all manner of risks.

Governments focus a good deal of their attention on the potential risks from hostile and foreign threats. State sponsored aggression is one of the easiest threats to detect; more difficult are the hostile intentions of individual terrorists who may be motivated by fundamentalist or merely eccentrically unpredictable ideologies. For example, the Al Qaeda-inspired attack on the World Trade Centre on 9/11, killed over 2970 people and triggered step improvements to major incident planning and disaster preparedness. The tools adopted to deal with these terrorist risks owe much to the contingency and preparedness plans developed for Y2K. The basic approach is twofold: reduce the vulnerability to the known risk; and reduce the threat of the risk occurring. In Britain this lesson was grafted onto over three decades of government experience in dealing with Irish terrorism (where over 3500 people died between 1969 and 1998). The British government's strategy in tackling terrorism became codified as 'pursue' (stopping the attackers from attacking); 'prevent' (stopping people from becoming terrorists); 'protect' (strengthening those points of potential vulnerability); and 'prepare' (mitigating the potential impact of any attack).[14]

But governments are also focused on minimizing internal risks – by preventing citizens from the potential violence of each other. At its simplest, citizens trade their fealty to their government for their personal security and protection. However, in reality citizens are more likely to be murdered in their beds by the people they live with than by an evil stranger possessed of malicious intent. In a 30-year longitudinal study of homicides in the US, it was found that the victim and offender were strangers in just 14 per cent of all murders. And in the very year of the 9/11 atrocity, nearly 7000 Americans were murdered by an intimate, a family member or by a friend. That accounts for some 77 per cent of all cases where the relationship between victim and offender was determined.[15] We choose who we live with (although we don't chose our parents) and if in so doing we make risky choices, then that is our doing and we must deal with the consequences ourselves. But if we find that dangerous strangers live around us, we tend to look to government (and the agencies involved in the criminal justice system) to help us directly.

As the Mexican swine flu story reminds us, the goals of government involve more than simply delivering services. They involve minimizing public risks and mitigating public harms. As a result, it is perhaps unsurprising that so much effort is spent by democratic governments protecting citizens from each other rather than protecting them from the hostile intentions of foreign governments. To this end, the police and criminal justice system is at the forefront of minimizing public risk.

The art of risk management has existed for centuries but its practice as a 'science' probably took off in the 1960s with the development of the space industry. From then it has become enveloped within the managerial world. By 2009 an internationally accepted standard operating model for risk management was agreed. This standard (ISO 31000) seeks to minimize the effect of uncertainty on the achievement of objectives. It involves the identification, assessment and prioritization of risks followed by the coordinated and economical application of resources to minimize, monitor and control the probability of unfortunate events or to maximize the realization of opportunities. In this way, risk management has become a method by which managers try to control the future in the context of the uncertainty in which their organizations operate.

One approach to risk minimization is to reduce the incidence of human error in systems. The problem of human error can be viewed in two ways: through a person-centred approach or through a system-based approach. In a person-centred approach, the focus is on the unsafe acts of individuals – their errors or procedural violations. These tend to generate approaches to risk minimization based upon compliance and reducing performance variability. By contrast, system-based approaches start from a presumption that people inevitably make errors and they tend to view human errors as consequences not causes. System-based approaches focus on how systems can be improved and made more reliable. The groundbreaking work on risk management in real world situations is James Reason's 'Swiss Cheese Model' of system accidents.[16] Basically, he uses the metaphor of holes in various slices of Swiss Emmental cheese. When these holes become aligned, it enables an 'accident trajectory' to occur, permitting accidents or mistakes to happen. In a mistake-free world the cheese would have no holes but in the real world, holes act as conduits for mistakes. Mistakes or accidents remain unnoticed if they penetrate only one or two holes in the slices of cheese. Reason argues that the defences, barriers and safeguards against mistakes break down for two different reasons: active failures and latent conditions. He suggests that nearly all adverse events involve a combination of these two sets of factors and that 'high reliability' organizations anticipate the worst and equip themselves to deal with it at all levels.

But in the governance and management of public services, risk is not simply the coincidence of accidents or mistakes with opportunities; it also includes an appraisal of the chance of service delivery going wrong. This is why risk assessments are undertaken in respect of any given policy – appraising the risks to successful delivery. This approach has generated considerable programme management effort in public agencies, with political leaders and managers having to consider their 'risk appetite' across a risk spectrum from the highly cautious to the highly adventurous. Being highly adventurous with your own money may be a sign of boldness, while being highly adventurous with the public's money may be a sign of wanton recklessness. The challenge is to be entrepreneurial while carefully calculating the risks that are being taken with both the public resources and the public interest.

The main professional advocates of risk management are, of course, auditors. They rightly attempt to strength test managerial assumptions about what counts for effective control in the achievement of organizational objectives. The application of risk management and the development of rigorous risk registers has been a positive feature in the management of organizations over the past few decades. However, two problems arise from the dominance of audit in the world of risk management: first, there tends to be an overconcentration on the financial dimension of risk; and second, a culture of overly cautious calculation or risk aversion can dominate considerations.

Chancing it – a goal of government

Despite the fact that this is possibly the safest time to be alive as a human being, anxiety about risks in the world often causes systemic overreaction to perceived man-made risks.[17] However, it is also likely that our confusion about risk stems first, from our cognitive inability to reckon actual probabilities from percentages;[18] and second, from the fact that the character of very many risks is far more complex than simple probability models assume. At its simplest, most of the public and very many of the professional experts simply can't figure out the probabilities for themselves. For example, when a 4 per cent chance of dying becomes a 6 per cent chance, has the prospect of dying increased by 50 per cent, two percentage points or has the chance of dying gone from 1 in 25 to 1 in 17? And if all three answers are correct, which is the easiest way for the public to understand the change in the chance and which is the most reliable as a benchmark for future behaviour? One way is to explain the chances by way of natural frequencies (such as 23 in every 1000 people are likely to have such and such a condition) than in percentages or ratios.

Simple models of chance that are based on coin spinning, dice throwing and the normal distribution of phenomena (on a 'bell curve') only weakly explain the risks in the world. Instead many risks, whether in financial markets, the environment or in the social sphere, may be better understood by reference to discontinuous, irregular but repeating measures – what the mathematician Benoit Mandelbrot terms, fractal. He suggests that very many risks may be better explained by reference to irregular repeating patterns and power laws than by simple distributions around the mean. After all as Mandelbrot argues, 'clouds are not spheres, mountains are not cones, coastlines are not circles, and bark is not smooth, nor does lightning travel in a straight-line.'[19] Given that Mandelbrot's fractal analysis has more powerfully explained global financial risks, perhaps it could also be used to cast light on developing societal and economic risks.

It may be the case that the chances of a negative incident occurring are subject not to arithmetical chance but to the viral behaviour of people who copy and mimic each other and who behave in ways that interpret and reinterpret the behaviours of others. This makes the task of calculating the probability of harm very complex indeed. If criminal behaviour is described in terms of dispersion around the mean then an expected quantum of the public (more specifically young men) may be viewed as potentially harmful. But if criminal behaviour has the capacity to spread like a virus then a much more significant quantum of the public might be viewed as potentially harmful. This is the sort of thinking that altered judgements about the latency of terrorist behaviour in young men but it could equally apply to sexualized behaviour and attacks on women or on face to face robbery in the public domain.

Figure 8.1 provides a diagrammatic outline of the varied purposes of government. Of course a good deal of the cost of government rests on the design and delivery of public services. But it is not the whole purpose of government. Governing also involves critical questions about the allocation of public goods, the regulation of public bads, the minimization of public risks, and the need to foster a civic spirit and promote the public or common good. Deciding between competing claims in the allocation of public goods is an essential attribute of good government. Protecting people from external threats (whether man made or natural hazards) and internally generated harms are other key attributes of an effective government. Seen in this way, the simple view of the state as the deliverer of core public services misses so much of the role of government.

Figure 8.1 *The purposes of government*

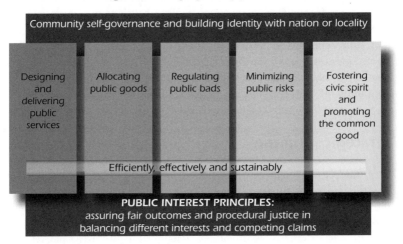

Governing involves leading, guiding and choosing

The story of Mayor Vazquez is of a politician alerting his citizens about a real and present danger in his locality. To alert people to threats without unduly alarming them about unknowable risks is the finest of distinctions that can only really be evaluated post hoc.

In a complex and reflexive world, governing involves so much more than delivering public services. Governing involves dealing with potential failure in the market, in society and in government itself. Governing is not an elite activity undertaken by wise and knowledgeable people in darkened rooms. It is a participatory activity. Where feasible, it involves self-governing, popular involvement, participatory engagement and citizen involvement. At its most basic, governing is about leading, guiding and choosing for all of us. But where some fifty years ago the 'knowledge gap' between those governing and those being governed was quite large, it is now extremely small. Government can seldom rely on its expert authority on any given subject. Instead it needs to offer itself as a means of informing, advising and guiding the public. As the swine flu and ash cloud cases show, governments are required to decide (to choose, to guide, to lead) even when uncertainties are great and imponderables abound.

In relation to public risks, the role of government may simply be to offer a trusted channel of information about the nature of the risks being faced so that citizens can address the issues for themselves. In respect of some public risks, it may be possible to defer, to await more evidence, to seek advice from differing perspectives. But the urgency and pressure of events may mean that choices simply have to be made – necessity has its own time demands. In these circumstances, to govern is to choose in the public interest despite the fog of uncertainty. Least-worst choices may need to be made urgently as making no choice may be utterly ruinous to the public interest.

Strategic intuition

With the rise of business management in the public sector, many corporate approaches to organizational management have transferred from the private to the public sector. One of the most pervasive of these has been the adoption of strategic planning techniques. Strategic planning has dominated public organizations, which, arguably, have placed too much reliance on it as a single tool and by contrast have placed too little reliance on developing strategic intuition within their organizations.[20] The word 'strategy' entered the English language 200 years ago, following the study of the military successes of Napoleon Bonaparte in the first decade up to 1810. At the time, a young Prussian army officer, Carl von Clausewitz, was beginning his studies of military strategy. He subsequently published a highly influential book, *On War*, in 1832.[21] One of von Clausewitz's key concepts was 'the flash of insight' and the accompanying resolution or determination to execute. He claimed there were four elements to successful strategy. These were: studying the lessons of history; having a presence of mind; developing a flash of insight; and possessing a strong resolution – that is, the determination or will to execute the desired actions.

At the same time, Baron Antoine Jomini published his summary of *The Art of War*.[22] Where von Clausewitz gives us strategic intuition, Jomini gives us strategic planning. For Jomini, in a battle, you win because you have greater force than your enemy at the objective point. For von Clausewitz, you win because you have the greater force at the decisive point. In strategic planning, you choose your objective point in a battle and then plan to reach it. In strategic intuition, the decisive point arises as part of an overall picture of the battle scene that comes together in your mind.[23] For the next 200 years, we seem only to have followed Jomini. We have worshipped at the altar of strategic planning, even though we know that many plans fail and that half of all successes arise emergently rather than deliberately.

Of course, we need to improve the discipline of our plans if we are to stand a chance of successfully dealing with crises and catastrophes, but we also need to improve our capacity to exercise our strategic intuition. There is no point having a strategic plan if you lack the insight to know under what circumstances you should act and you lack the confidence to carry through the actions that these circumstances demand. This is the lesson we learn from dealing with crises. We prepare our resilience plans and devise our strategic response and recovery arrangements. But we also know they will inevitably fall short of what is needed when the real events happen.

Summary

All risks are a mixture of the real and the imagined. Imagined risks can pose as much of a threat to the public mind or to the public purse as real risks. Nassim Nicholas Taleb used the metaphor of the Black Swan to explain how hard to predict, unexpected and high impact events that only have a tiny probability of happening, nonetheless do occur in the real world.[24] His account is often misdescribed as the big risks of unpredictable events. However, Taleb's focus is on the inability of statistics to predict rare events and on the often misplaced subjective interpretation of these risks. His key point is more about the delusion of retrospective prediction and the need for a form of 'Black Swan robustness' that would enable societies to withstand high impact rare events. And it is this robustness towards rare but dangerous events that is one of the core purposes of government.

Government is not simply about the provision of services but the socialization and regulation of risk. Government regulates risk on topics as varied as house building materials; the availability of over-the-counter medicines in pharmacists; the use of pesticides in agriculture; the size of the capital cushions required of retail banks to ensure their continuing liquidity; the residence of predatory sex-offenders on their release from custody; and the ownership of dangerous dogs. The regulation regimes that governments use vary across different policy domains but they tend to relate to the precise nature of risks that are anticipated or specific harms or threats that have actually occurred.[25]

Government enables society to be more collectively resilient to natural hazards, economic shocks and man-made threats. But government's first role is to help people reckon and reduce their own risks for themselves. Only when these risks jeopardize the public interest, the common good, the welfare of everyone, should government actively manage risk for the whole nation or the whole community. One perennial question is how much time and money should be spent preventing any given risk? The calculus of public risk incorporates the likelihood that a negative event could crystallize, multiplied by the likely impact of the event across the community, and compares it to the cost of precautionary measures. In this way a focus on risk should be commensurate with its potential harm to the nation or the community as well as to the likelihood of its occurrence.

Natural environmental hazards and man-made threats generate different forms of risk but the resources required to prepare for them and to respond to them may be very similar. For example, there is no objective comparison that can be made between a localized flood and a local violent gang problem. But the harm caused by violent gangs is a risk in a community every bit as real as the risk of a flood. Plans to prevent both sets of harms as well as being prepared to act when either shows signs of occurring raise strikingly similar challenges. Kenneth Sparrow is a professor at Harvard and former police officer. He lectures at Harvard about how public agencies need to focus on minimizing harm rather than simply delivering public goods. In his account of *The Character of Harm* he suggests that a focus on reducing harm or fixing problems is difficult because in public authorities work tends to be more conventionally organized around functional responsibilities and process specialties.

In the organization of public sector work, Kenneth Sparrow argues, 'functions and processes take over; and it pays to understand why. Functions are comfortable. They group employees together with others who share common training, celebrate a common set of skills and knowledge, share a specific professional culture, and climb a well-established disciplinary ladder.' By contrast, the business of organizing around specific harms, and devising solutions for one problem or another, seems vague, amorphous, and entirely optional. Kenneth Sparrow is right when he argues that, 'when staff gather in functional units, they gather around their shared past, their shared training, their shared skills. When staff gather around processes, they gather around a visible and tangible flow of calls, files, transactions or reports. Little imagination is required, in either case, to understand the nature of the work.'[26]

Organizing work around a social problem or specific harm is so much more difficult than organizing work to perform a set of activities. For when organizing work around a threat or harm, exactly what is it that work is being organized around? This is why interdisciplinary approaches to solving public problems so as to reduce public risk are very difficult. However, government needs to organize much of its work around specific harms and threats.

Whatever the circumstances, when pursuing the public interest, governments need to reduce the threat and reduce the vulnerability to the threat. And this applies whether the threat is an environmental hazard, an economic calamity, an atrocious act of violent terrorism or a more generalized community disorder. Governments are not simply delivering public value, they are involved day by day in the practice of reckoning with their citizens about the risks they are taking and, when collective action demands it, acting so as to reduce public risks.

But government and its public agencies need also to get things done – and there are a myriad of risks to successful delivery of change and innovation. Risk management techniques have been developed to enable risk to be assessed and appraised but too often these tend to dampen innovation and risk-taking.[27] They focus predominantly on financial risks (such as poor budgeting, impropriety, waste, poor value for money, poor investment decisions, fraud and malpractice). They focus to a lesser extent on environmental or health and safety risks; and they pay too little attention to the threat to the achievement of service goals and objectives. Those governments and public agencies that are scaling back their activities in response to tighter financial constraints need to reconsider their overall risk appetite. To innovate successfully to lower costs and sustain service activities, they need their managers to be suitably empowered to take measured risks to change services. In times of economic growth and rising public spending the risk is that resources are inappropriately targeted and wasted. In times of retrenchment and cutbacks, the biggest risk is that poor judgement is exercised in how public spending or welfare payments are to be cut or how taxes are to be raised. For just as there is a risk to government so, from a citizen's perspective, there is also a risk from government.

Chapter 9

The Crunch and the Big Squeeze

From private recession to public retrenchment

There was just one more week to go before Christmas. It was near the end of 2008 and there was no sign of snow. Jenny had worked in the same high street store for over twenty years. Business had not been so good that year. The high street was looking tired, and all the talk had been about shoppers buying presents online. Her store had been an anchor in this parade of shops for 45 years. It was one of 807 stores of its type in Britain; a well-known brand with roots in every part of the nation. The store was Woolworths.

The deadline for cash offers to buy Woolworths as a going concern was Wednesday, 17 December – no offers arrived. And so the closures that were being planned by the administrator had to be announced the next day. Jenny's store was among the first 200 to be closed ten days later on Saturday, 27 December, just two days after Christmas Day. Neville Kahn, one of the three administrators from Deloittes said, 'we are now moving to the closing down sale period. It is a very difficult situation for a lot of people, particularly the staff, and we are trying to deal with it in as sensitive a way as possible.'[1] Some crumbs of comfort were offered to Woolworths' employees – the plan was for 300 of the stores to be sold and also the Woolworths brand name was up for sale. Woolworths had been trading in Britain for 99 years – and yet the game was up. Jenny's details as an employee (along with the other 22,000 permanent employees and the 5000 temporary employees) would be passed on to any buyer of the stores or the new owners of the brand name.

In total, some 27,000 Woolworths' staff were given ten days' notice, over the Christmas and the New Year period, of their redundancy. The mood of high street customers was odd. Across Britain there had been a significant drop (over 2 per cent) in 'foot fall' in the nation's high streets compared with the previous December; and retail experts were forecasting for 2009 a drop of 4 per cent in food, retail and internet sales generally.[2] However, against this general gloom, Woolworths (or 'Woolies' as it was affectionately known by generations of British shoppers) had seen a sharp increase in sales. Shoppers who had turned their backs on the store for years seem to flock back – in search of Christmas bargains and, perhaps, as a part of a collective experience of retail nostalgia.

No one needed credit to buy goods from Woolworths. They were selling at the value end of the market – so why did Woolworths collapse? Woolworths had been a large and successful company that set the retail style in the early 20th century. Before then, retailers kept their goods behind a counter and customers gave the clerk a list of the particular goods that they wanted. Woolworths started a retail revolution; its customers walked among the goods. It had introduced a fundamental shift in retailing. Just one hundred years ago, Woolworths had 600 stores in North America and it had branched out to, among other nations, Britain. In 1913, the Woolworth business was so dominant that it paid cash to build, at 57 stories high, the then tallest building in the world on Broadway in New York. The success of the business throughout the world was such that by 1979, Woolworths was the largest departmental store chain in the world.[3]

But from there it all seems to have gone down hill. Within the US, the company diversified its retail offer – it opened its discount chain Woolco; but it then faced stiff competition when Sam Walton started his Walmart stores. Walmart added a further twist to the retail revolution in the 20th century. Large discount stores that combined food and retail shopping became the norm. As a result of strong competition in its core markets, Woolworths went into decline in the US closing over half its stores and concentrating its business focus in the sportswear niche (where it now only trades in the US under the Foot Locker brand). Its extension to Australia in the 20th century saw it concentrate on food retailing there and it continues as a thriving presence in this market in the early 21st century.

The British Woolworths stores only became fully independent of their US parent in 1982. But becoming independent did not guarantee the continuing relevance of their brand or the sustainability of their business model. From there it took just 25 years for the stores to decline such that, as it was sliding into Administration, the BBC news story was entitled 'what is the point of Woolworths?' British shoppers had grown accustomed to niche retail shopping, then mall-based shopping and then at the end of the 20th century they began to enjoy the scale benefits of large 'one-stop' superstores. As a result of this trend, in 2008 nearly one-third of the nation's grocery market share was with Tesco alone. Tesco had developed a highly successful business model based on scale and value. And it spent over a decade moving aggressively into retail.

Perhaps it ought not to have been a surprise that shoppers had become confused about the incoherence of the offer and layout at Woolworths. Its core value items of CDs, DVDs and computer games could now all be bought much cheaper either online or at large supermarkets like Tesco. And much of the rest of the goods in the store were sourced, as with all other high street value stores in the UK, from China. Jenny's store was paying over £100,000 annually in business rates to the local council and in addition was paying roughly the same amount in ground rent to its landlord. It is not an easy task to finance overheads of this amount, the operating costs of the store, and the wages of Jenny and her colleagues, from a declining share of 'pick and mix' confectionary and Barbie pencils.

While it is true that Woolworths had lost its way and was in decline, the point of termination was actually caused because it was unable to finance its £385m of debt. In a final few painful days the directors of Woolworths had discussions with a range of potential buyers (mostly with Hilco UK) all of which ended in vain.[4] Trevor Bish-Jones, who had been running Woolworths since 2002, said at the previous annual meeting, 'making £3bn of sales for £30m of net profit is hard work this side of the fence.' According to the *Financial Times* in December 2008, sources close to Woolworths placed the cause of the collapse at the feet of the demerger from Kingfisher seven years earlier in 2001. At that time, 182 Woolworths stores were sold in a sale-and-leaseback deal in return for £614m that was paid back to Kingfisher shareholders as part of the demerger. In return, Woolworths was saddled with onerous leases that guaranteed landlords steadily rising income streams. From 2001, the rent bill for Woolworths rose from £70m to £160m – some five times more than the annual net profit for the whole chain.[5]

An outdated business model, more aggressive competition from Tesco, Sainsbury's and Asda (ironically now owned by Walmart) and the advent of a new style of online shopping, particularly for music and video, all played their part in the decline of Woolworths. The store that had started a revolution in the style of retail shopping had itself been swept away by fundamental shifts in retail shopping patterns four generations later. However, the reason Jenny got her redundancy letter from the administrators just before Christmas 2008 was because the company she worked for succumbed to a cash crisis. Its lease-adjusted debt was the highest in the high street and its cash flow could not finance its debt at a time when credit availability was getting scarcer by the day.

In a timely book on why some large and successful businesses fail, the management theorist Jim Collins argues that there are five inexorable stages in corporate decline. First, comes the hubris born of success.

Success in business is like success in life. It is based on the possession of
a disciplined set of competencies and capabilities; but it depends crucially
on confidence. But when confidence slips into overconfidence it becomes
all too easy to slip further into arrogance or hubris. Second, is the 'undis-
ciplined pursuit of more'. This is when organizations strive for growth
and expansion simply on the basis of replicating their past model for
success. If an approach, a strategy or a business model worked the first
time, why not simply try doing it all over again – only with bigger aims
and larger pay-offs? Third, is a stage when corporate leaders become
involved in a collective denial of risk and peril. A collective 'group-think'
can dominate even the most successful organization and the risks of
potential failure can be ignored or discounted. The fourth stage occurs
when leaders have woken up to the reality of their situation. They realize
that they have been overconfident, that their business strategy cannot
simply be replicated again and again, that they have discounted the risks
involved in operating in a dynamically changing environment and they
then start to acknowledge the corporate decline before them and begin
'grasping for salvation'.[6]

   Jim Collins points to how in the US, Walmart managed to avoid failure
and decline by ensuring a smooth transition of its organizational leadership when the founder, Sam Walton, retired. He contrasts Walmart's
successful strategy of disciplined growth with the 'arrogant neglect' of the
consumer by many other stores. At the conclusion of these four stages,
Collins argues that there is a fifth stage with two routes. One route leads
to a happy ending. The other route leads to failure. In this fifth stage,
businesses can find salvation and discover a route to recovery and renewal;
or instead they can simply capitulate to irrelevance and death. It is plain
what happened to Woolworths. And while the seeds of its decline could be
found in its neglect of its customers and its corresponding failure to adapt,
the timing of its death can be found in the ratio of its debt to its operating
profit and the consequent cash-flow crisis it faced just at the time when the
credit crunch in Britain was at its worst. This credit crunch foreshadowed
the most severe global economic recession for generations.

The source and the nature of the recession in 2008–9

No one single event triggered the global recession of 2008–9, although
several factors made matters worse. The four main sources of the recession are complexly intertwined:

1. A galloping global trade imbalance – largely between China and the rest of the world – which caused unsustainable deficits and credit bubbles in the US, Europe and Japan.[7]

2. Over-optimism on the part of people within the financial services sector that they had control of the system in which they worked such that the regulatory controls on investment banking were too 'light touch'; the personal incentives on senior executives in investment banking were overly focused on short-term measures of corporate performance;[8] the system placed over-reliance on inadequate assessments of corporate creditworthiness by ratings agencies; and the prevailing model of financial risk assumed that financial risk was linear and predictable. This resulted in a misapplication of quantitative techniques for modelling movements in equity markets and irrational exuberance and over-optimism about rising prices in asset and housing markets.[9]

3. An over-relaxation of lending for home purchase and credit purchase to unsustainable levels to sub-prime borrowers that resulted in 'toxic' loan portfolios in US lenders which, through contagion and uncertainty, led to the widespread contamination of the global financial system.

4. A synchronized global collapse in demand such that, 'for the first time in two generations, failures on the demand side of the economy – insufficient private spending to make use of available productive capacity – have become the clear and present limitation on prosperity for a large part of the world.'[10]

All recessions involve a collapse of demand in the economy. But in the recession of 2008–9 there was another aspect to low demand – pervasive and dramatic credit tightening. In November 2008, the scientific pretensions of economists had been punctured by a simple question from Her Majesty, the Queen of England. When opening a new building at the London School of Economics, she playfully asked those present, 'why did nobody notice the credit crunch coming?' Some eight months later her question was debated at a high-level forum convened by the British Academy. Professors Besley and Hennessy summarized the views of the forum in an open letter to the Queen that sought to answer her question.[11] They pointed out that one of the major banks, which had been brought into public ownership by the British government because it was 'too big to fail', had 4000 risk managers. Each of them had been focused on the risks of various different aspects of the bank's operations and yet none of them had foreseen the biggest risk to the banking and financial system as a whole.

The forum had concluded that the period before the credit crunch was one of the greatest examples 'of wishful thinking combined with hubris', conducted during a cycle 'fuelled, in significant measure, not by virtue but by delusion.' According to the considered views of most of those present, 'everyone seemed to be doing their own job properly on its own merit ... the failure was to see how collectively this added up to a series of interconnected imbalances over which no single authority had jurisdiction.' In summary, they said, the failure to foresee the crunch was 'a collective failure of imagination of many bright people ... to understand the risks to the system as a whole.' Bluntly, it seems that too many clever people in the global financial community could be excused dishonesty on the grounds that before they had deceived other people they had been at great pains to deceive themselves.[12] In relation to the timidity of regulators, Martin Taylor, the former Chief Executive of Barclays bank, argued that:

> We must not forget that regulators know no better, and usually a good deal worse, than the regulated. The melancholy truism will not change on the back of a couple of tough years. The failure of regulators to play any useful role in preventing the crisis can be no surprise to anyone who has observed their methods at work. We would not expect traffic wardens to bust drug dealing syndicates.[13]

In the whole sorry saga the only institutions, thankfully, that emerged with credit (literally as well as figuratively) were the various central banks and the treasury departments within governments. Their interventions sought first, to stabilize the financial sectors; second, to provide a fiscal stimulus to the wider economy; and third, to build a tougher regulatory framework. In the US, the Securities and Exchange Commission was still battling in mid-2010 to sustain a firm regulatory environment when it rocked the investment community further by charging Goldman Sachs with some £900m of securities fraud.[14]

The scale and speed of the fiscal stimulus provided by governments was the main factor that stopped the global financial system tipping the world economy into full-scale Depression. Those nations most affected by the global recession were all engaged in substantial fiscal stimulus measures in 2009. And those nations with the most exposed banking systems were spending vast sums to provide central bank liquidity, to offer treasury guarantees to banks and to provide equity injections into banks so as, effectively, to nationalize them.[15] In the US and UK in particular, hundreds of billions of dollars and pounds were committed by the respective governments to a massive programme of bank bailouts.

When those national economies most affected by the recession reached the turning point to recovery, their governments began moving from fiscal stimulus programmes to deficit reduction planning. Those economies that were affected for longer (such as the US and to a lesser extent the UK) therefore continued their fiscal stimulus into 2010. In comparison to the central banks, the regulators emerged much less favourably from the recession. With hindsight it seems that those regulating the financial system should have simply followed the homely advice of the longest serving chairman of the Federal Reserve, William McChesney Martin (1951–70), who said that main job of the regulator was 'to take away the punchbowl just as the party gets going'.[16]

Throughout history it seems that recessions that are accompanied by banking crises are different in character and longer in duration to those recessions that reflect the conventional business cycle (of rising and falling economic confidence among consumers, investors and businesses).[17] There can be little doubt that the global nature of capital flows and the dislocated geography of production, consumption and debt helped to convert what was a localized disruption in the US housing market into a global financial crisis. However, just three years after the Crunch officially began, the global economy, outside the US and Europe, was in recovery and the world's banking sector had returned to substantial profit. Quite how these developments will unfold is impossible to predict. Radical commentators suggest that new forms of global political response are required to deal with the inevitable crises in capitalism[18] whereas others suggest that, unlike in the 1930s, the integration of global financial markets has continued apace and that capital markets are the 'only show in town'[19] or that 'market fundamentalism' has demonstrated its weaknesses so severely that a new version of regulated capitalism is emerging.[20]

There is a downside risk that a large-scale fiscal stimulus involving quantitative easing might encourage too much saving rather than just enough spending. This is the warning that emerges from the decade-long recession in Japan according to the Nomura economist, Richard Koo. He argues that Japan experienced a highly specific 'balance sheet recession'. He suggests that after this form of recession it will take some time for households to repair their budgets, businesses to restore their balance sheets and banks to replenish their capital cushions. In such a balance sheet recession, businesses move from strategies that maximize their profits towards strategies that minimize their debts.[21] The collective effect of these household and business strategies (which are perfectly rational and understandable in their own terms) is to slow growth rather than speed it up.

Richard Koo's analysis may not apply in full measure to all economies but it suggests the adoption of, at best, a highly cautious approach. The lessons of the 'lost decade' in Japan weigh heavily upon all governments as well as their central banks.[22] For they have to choose between the path of fiscal stimulus to pump demand into their economies or the route of fiscal tightening that reduces public debt from their balance sheets. In 2010, the flagging nature of the US economy (with its high unemployment and fragile housing market) led Ben Bernanke the chairman of the Federal Reserve to hint at the need for further stimulus measures in the US, while at the same time and at the same conference, Jean-Claude Trichet, the president of the European Central Bank, argued that delaying cuts in public and private debts would be very dangerous and could stifle the recovery.[23]

A three-wave impact on governments and the public sector

The recession in the private economy presents enormous strains both on the process of governing and on government's ability to sustain its ambitions for the public sector. The economic recession of 2008 hit governments in three separate waves. The first came in the form of dramatic instability and uncertainty. Economic growth, stable during most of the past two decades, fell dramatically to minus 5 per cent for the whole of 2009. The severity of this decline caused settled ways of governing to be called into question. Conventional ways of acting, in the maelstrom of the new realities of the recession, could prove to be negligent or even reckless.

In the face of such extraordinary uncertainty, governmental strategies were reshaped. At the national level a profound change occurred in the very rules of engagement by governments. The scale of the bank bailouts alone created a new climate for 'intervention'. For example, in 2007 it would have been unthinkable for governments in liberal democracies to intervene, using taxpayer funds, to support domestic car manufacturers. And yet by early 2009, most governments had adopted a range of schemes to support this ailing sector (the so-called 'scrappage' schemes to encourage owners of old cars to trade them in at a discount for new and more energy efficient cars began in Germany in 2008 and quickly spread to a number of other countries).

The second wave impact of the recession on governments and public services is less direct. The second wave involves a reverberating effect of the recession as it ripples its way through the economy and wider society. This second wave effect is economic, social and psychological. It started in 2009 and will most probably persist for several years. It would be wrong to characterize the first wave as economic and the second as social – the difference is in the sequencing not the domains affected.[24] The second wave impact includes the economic effects of the recession on urban regeneration, on the viability of high streets as well as on business supply chains and public sector supply chains.

But it also includes the inevitable increase in demand in a range of social policy areas. Increased demands on social housing and social services are to be expected from those whose circumstances alter dramatically through unemployment. Spending on welfare benefits will rise and demands for primary services will also rise. But in a recession with a bursting property bubble, the demands for public services are affected by falls in equity prices. And even when asset prices recover, the near-term memory of their recent fall greatly influences consumer sentiment. For example, ageing homeowners who intended using a share of their equity in property to finance their personal care in retirement have to recalculate their plans; as do those people who intended to privately finance elements of their family's healthcare or education.

The third wave impact of the recession on governments and the public sector occurs in relation to falling public revenues and rising government debt. A decline in output reduces, among other things, corporation tax receipts, income tax receipts and sales tax receipts. It also increases the costs to government of servicing much higher levels of debt as well as higher volumes of welfare benefit payments. Advanced economies entered the recession with an average budget deficit of 1.1 per cent of national income. Three years later this figure had risen to 8.4 per cent as tax revenues plummeted and banks were bailed out. According to the International Monetary Fund, general government gross debt in these advanced economies is set to rise from 73 per cent of national income in 2007 to over 110 per cent by 2015.[25]

For example, in the UK in the year to April 2010, tax revenue fell by 10 per cent while public spending rose to some 48 per cent of GDP. Planned public expenditure was forecast to exceed income by £156bn – an improvement on the original forecast of £178bn by the Treasury but still an awesome figure that produced an enormous strain on public finances over the subsequent period. The fall in revenues combined with the need to bring down deficits creates this third wave that will wash across all areas of public spending. By 2010 this effect had driven virtually all democratic governments into some form of fiscal consolidation.

And most governments faced with reducing their deficits placed more emphasis on cuts in public spending than they did on overall levels in taxation. This was why at the end of the first decade of the 21st century most liberal democratic governments were focused intensely on how to retrench their public spending and how to make major budget savings in their welfare spending and across most areas of public spending.

When the financial crash started the first task of governments was to 'safeguard their economy'. Stimulating the economy to prevent recession became the second task; repairing the financial sector was an urgent, and global, third task. But the fourth task is likely to be the hardest in advanced economies – the aggressive downward adjustment to public spending and significant fiscal consolidation. Credible fiscal consolidation is needed if financial markets are to sustain their support of governments.[26] For while governments need the support of the electorate to attain power, they need a supportive financial sector to sustain them in power.

There is a strange symbiosis between governments and banks. In 2008, governments may have rescued several banks but, by 2010, they came to rely on banks to rescue them – by marketing and buying their debt.[27] And when there is a sharp imbalance in public finances, governments discover that the market for their sovereign debt is very volatile. In 2010, this problem beset Greece and the wider euro area, triggering a global drive to adjust public spending among advanced economies. This is why the dominant task for the post 2010 period became how to govern better for less.

In the US, the Office of Management and Budget of the White House introduced a 'Reduce Unnecessary Spending Act' to rein back duplicative, wasteful and unnecessary spending. By the end of September 2010, the US budget deficit stood at $1.3 trillion, at 9 per cent of GDP. The Congressional Budget Office in the US estimated that the federal debt would hit 87 per cent of GDP by 2020. With unemployment in the US flatlining at near 10 per cent, despite an enormous fiscal stimulus, it appeared in late 2010 that America was experiencing a jobless recovery of sorts. For over six million Americans had been out of work for more than six months in October 2010. Out of work benefits that normally last for just six months in the US were extended by the Congress to help the workless for up to 99 weeks. In response to the most severe recession, President Obama created a bipartisan 'deficit commission' to develop a plan to stabilize the deficit by 2015. The Commission proposed substantial cuts in spending alongside reductions in social security and tax reforms. The sweeping gains by the Republican Party (and strong sentiment supporting Tea Party reformers) in the US 'mid-term' elections to Congress in 2010 added further political pressure for cutbacks in public spending in the US.[28]

In Greece, Spain, Italy, Portugal and Ireland, governments of all different political hues began to lower public sector workers' salaries, reduce benefit entitlements and raise retirement ages. This led to a wave of protests across Europe. In May 2010, mostly women protestors gathered outside Italy's lower house of Parliament in the cobbled square of the Piazza di Montecitorio to denounce the Italian government's plan to shave 24bn euros off government spending over two years.[29] But the Italian government acted only after Greece had agreed to slash its budget by 30bn euros over three years; the Irish government had reduced government spending by 4bn euros; and the Spanish government had agreed a 15bn euro budget cuts package.

During 2010 a sovereign debt crisis occurred as a result of lack of market confidence in the economies of Greece, Ireland, Portugal and Spain. At first this appeared as investment squalls affecting individual countries but over a period of months the squalls seemed to develop into one systemic storm. The impact on individual countries threatened the coherence (even the future) of the euro itself and the German and French economies had to stand by to assist these smaller threatened nations. The financial pressures on Greece, Ireland and Portugal were substantial because their relatively small economies could not withstand the pressure of external investor shocks.

In Greece, the problem was not so much the scale of the public debt but the fact that three-quarters of it was held by foreign investors.[30] This over-reliance on foreign investment worsened Greece's problems. The crisis in Ireland had reached such a pitch that by the end of 2010 a leading bookmaker, Paddy Power, had overtaken the Bank of Ireland to become the eighth largest business in Ireland ahead of the country's main bank (which was established in 1783 and had been the official bank to the Irish government since the country gained independence from Britain in 1922). By late 2010, the Irish government had to negotiate a loan deal (of 85bn euros) with the IMF and the European Central Bank to prevent the nation sliding into bankruptcy, following a near collapse in its housing market – in return for which it had to initiate swingeing public spending cuts.

In a desperate attempt to prevent contagion from Greece and Ireland, the Portuguese government initiated its own programme of public spending cuts in late 2010. But in practice Greece, Ireland and Portugal were all effectively insolvent and were relying on the European Central

Bank to purchase their debt. While these three small countries were considered too big to let fail, the Spanish economy may be too big to rescue – it is twice the size of the combined economies of the other three nations. However, the Spanish economy itself has serious problems.

Not only did Spain have the highest levels of unemployment in the Eurozone area (over 20 per cent in the middle of 2010), but its system of governance with relatively high regional autonomy has a tendency to spook the financial markets. In late 2010 the rating agencies downgraded Spain's credit rating. One reason for the downgrading was the relative autonomy of Spain's 17 regions and the ability of the regions to issue bonds to raise finance to sustain their spending. In the 12 months to the end of the third quarter of 2010, the Spanish government's debt had risen by 15 per cent to 467bn euros, while the debts of the 17 regions had risen by 27 per cent to 108bn euros.[31] With a growing economy, regional autonomy can help to spread investment throughout a nation; whereas in a fiscal crisis, regional autonomy can serve to scare the international investment markets.

Elsewhere in Europe, the UK's newly formed Conservative–Liberal coalition government substantially increased the scope, scale and pace of the deficit reduction plan that had been instituted by its Labour predecessor. In its spending review published in October 2010, it set in train six years of consecutive public spending reductions – this was a remarkable ambition for a new government given that there had only ever been two consecutive years of public spending reductions in the previous sixty years (in 1976–7 and 1977–8).[32]

Tough austerity measures in public spending were not entirely confined to Europe. In Australia, the government moved from having a record surplus in 2008 to a record deficit in 2010 as it had borrowed billions of dollars to stimulate the economy during the global downturn. Australia's highly regulated banking sector and its strong export record meant that it largely escaped having a recession. Its debt levels remain low by international standards, and while the Australian economy benefits from the sustained demand for minerals and energy from China and India, nonetheless its government adopted a more cautious tone in its election year when instituting fresh curbs on public spending to lower the deficit. Notwithstanding this sheltered environment, there was a noticeable trend among state electorates towards support for deficit reducing political parties.

In 2010, governments in these advanced economies were each looking to implement plans of fiscal consolidation that were credible to the markets and that were also acceptable to their voters. However, most of the people involved in these governments (including those advising as well as those deciding) will not personally have dealt with a challenge as severe as this before in their careers. All they will have to draw upon is the lesson of previous approaches in their own countries or of previous approaches to similar situations in other countries. That is why the approach of the Canadian government in the 1990s to their fiscal deficit (at 9 per cent of GDP in 1992) has attracted attention from governments across the world.

In summary, the recession has had an enormous impact on private behaviour – of businesses and of consumers. Its shadow has altered the horizons of businesses and consumers alike. Many thousands of previously healthy companies have failed and many millions of previously productive people have lost their jobs. Unemployment in the US was still persistently at just below 9.5 per cent by the end of 2010 while the 16 countries in the Eurozone (at November 2010) were experiencing unemployment at just over 10 per cent – in the UK unemployment stood at 7.8 per cent at the year end; higher than Germany's 6.7 per cent but lower than France's 9.8 per cent. The recession has also dramatically changed the landscape for business and, as such, creates new opportunities for the agile and the adaptive.

The strain on public services is increasing just as the pain in the private economy begins to ease. The increased call on the public purse of both higher debt financing and higher welfare payments, inexorably leads to a decline in available public resources to finance public services more generally. The private sector crunch has produced a public sector squeeze. Private recession begets public retrenchment – and so very many Western governments have begun to apply the 'biggest squeeze' on the public purse for generations. This squeeze will test the mettle of those elected to govern public services as well as the imagination of those appointed to manage public services. Public services need to do better than be more efficient and provide better value for money; they need dramatically to lower their cost to the taxpayer.

The price of government

Each government has many citizens, and each citizen has several governments. For citizens have to pay taxes to several different layers of government – local, city/county, state and federal or national. And they pay taxes in different ways – through income tax, sales tax, property tax, asset tax and so on. For most democratic countries in the world, the total tax take of all layers of government amounts to about £4 in every £10 of citizens' aggregate income. The proportion of aggregate income in a country that people willingly commit to their governments could be termed the 'price of government'. But there is no right price for government – different people vary in what they consider to be acceptable in respect of the cost to them of their governments. Moreover, what is commonly viewed as 'acceptable' will vary from locality to locality.

Internationally the cost of different layers of government depends upon the distribution of functions to cities, counties, states and so on. One of the largest components of public spending in mature democracies is the cost of social protection (welfare entitlements); a function which is most usually the responsibility of central or federal government. Similarly another large cost of government is often the provision for (or social insurance for) healthcare services – again a function often the responsibility of central or federal governments. But the responsibility for education functions, policing and criminal justice functions, as well as social care functions, may each be held at city, county or state level. According to an assessment of the price of government in the US, there appeared to be no straightforward relationship between the resource base of each state, city or county government and the price of government. The three states with the highest price of government were Alaska, Wyoming and New Mexico; and the three largest cities with the highest price of government were Cleveland, Oakland and Atlanta.[33]

Through focusing on the cost of government – or more tellingly its price to its citizens – it may become possible to concentrate on those costs that are a problem and then set strategies for cost reduction that align with priorities. All governments that seek election want to demonstrate their prudence with public monies. And all governments are keen to promote an image that they are careful and caring stewards of public resources. Wantonly wasting taxpayers' money is no sensible route for re-election. Once broad choices have been made about the scope for increasing the take from the taxpayer and reducing the cost of welfare payments, the options then boil down to how best to reduce public spending. Minor reductions in public spending involve changes of degree; major reductions involve changes of kind. This is why all governments are struggling with a variety of system-wide and institutional approaches to reducing the cost of government services.

System-wide approaches include different types of public service reforms. These include extending the use of quasi-markets for public services (with users choosing between competing public service providers); widening the scope for privatization or outsourcing of public service provision; and the creation of special purpose public agencies that can focus intensely on a service, standardize its approach and leverage value from economies of scale. System-wide approaches lean towards 'crude percentage' solutions. High value consulting firms are usually engaged to decide which percentage should be applied to which large number. Public budgets of several billions are thereby reduced by 15 per cent or 25 per cent by fiat on the grounds that some new-fangled public service reform will deliver results over the medium term.

Institutional approaches to public service reform tend to adopt a more managerial focus on the waste, duplication and inefficiencies of government services. For example, consider the education system for children aged under 19 years. A system-wide approach would focus on the overall cost-effectiveness of all schools, the variance in costs among different types and sizes of schools, and the extent to which incentives for head teachers, in managing their schools, and incentives for parents, in choosing schools for their children, were aligned so as to increase overall system cost-effectiveness. Moreover, an institutional approach would focus on how schools could be more cost-effective in how they were led and managed and how they could deliver better outcomes at lower cost.

Efficiency, value for money and lowering cost

Most governments get elected to do new things. Usually this costs more money – and that money is taxpayers' money. During times of economic growth, governments reform their public services by delivering more for more. However, in times of fiscal consolidation governments need to reduce their costs – they need to deliver better for less. And to do so they choose between a blend of three main strategies: first, they can apply established management approaches to the task of cutting costs (by, say, changing targets for outcomes to targets for cuts); second, they can redesign services afresh to alter their cost base; and third, they can choose to stop or abandon particular services entirely.[34]

Internationally there are many examples of differing approaches to lowering public service costs. To project an approach based on thoughtfulness rather than crude cost cutting, governments generally tend to badge their spending reduction plans as 'efficiency' or 'value for money' drives. These commonly accepted phrases are slippery and therefore politically useful. Something is more efficient than something else if, for the same volume of inputs, it generates a higher volume or better quality of outputs. The notion of value for money is akin to the more precise idea of comparative cost-effectiveness. Something is better value for money than something else if its value is higher and its cost is lower. The phrase 'value for money' is used by audit professionals when they attempt to appraise the balance between comparative cost and comparative effectiveness. However, in common usage it stems neither from economics nor from accountancy but instead from consumer practice. It is a comparative term used either across a product or service range or in relation to change in value for money for the same product or service over time. On close examination the phrase 'value for money' is as ambiguous as the economic idea of efficiency – but nonetheless it has more currency with citizens and service users than the more technical notion of efficiency.

The key point to grasp in all this is that it is entirely possible to be more efficient, even to provide better value for money without lowering costs. Indeed it is possible to be more efficient and provide better value for money while actually increasing cost. After all it is perfectly reasonable to argue that a public service is more efficient if it increases service activity levels, outputs or outcomes by, say, 10 per cent while doing so at the same cost. Indeed it is also correct to argue that a service is becoming more efficient if it increases service activity levels, outputs or outcomes by, say, 20 per cent if while so doing its costs actually rise by, say, 10 per cent. The challenge for democratic governments over the coming decade is to reduce the cost of public services and not just increase their efficiency and value for money. To do this they will need to reorganize these public services. But all reorganizations have a 'cost of change', including the cost of transition to a lower cost platform. A focus on efficiency and value for money doesn't guarantee that overall costs will be lower. And therefore it is cost reduction strategies that are the key to lowering public spending and not just technical requirements to improve efficiency or value for money.

Governments across the world have adopted very many business techniques to reduce public spending. The most significant phase of this business oriented approach (particularly that which included the privatization or outsourcing of many public services) begun in the 1980s with the Thatcher government in the UK and with the Reagan presidency in the US. Under the Clinton administration in the 1990s, the US federal government adopted many business techniques with alacrity. Following this they were adopted throughout the 1990s among the governments in New Zealand, Australia and the UK. But the privatization of public utilities, assets and services was not simply a federal or national government strategy – it was implemented in states as well as in city and county government. During the eight-year tenure (1999–2007) of Jeb Bush as

Republican governor of Florida, privatization and competitive sourcing was used over 130 times to save $500m. During the same time, Richard Daley, the Democrat mayor of Chicago privatized more than 40 city services generating $3bn in upfront payments from private sector leases of city assets including the Chicago Skyway toll. By early 2010, the use of privatization as a means of lowering costs was being advanced simultaneously in New Jersey (at the request of Republican Governor Chris Christie) and in the Queensland state of Australia (at the request of Labor Premier Anna Bligh).[35]

The UK has been a particular laboratory for public service reform over the past three decades. It has implemented a battery of institutional and managerial reforms to improve public services and to inject business management into the public sector. In the 1980s and 1990s, the UK government under Margaret Thatcher developed a string of related initiatives to reform public services and control public spending. Together these approaches were said to herald a 'new public management'. The first of these initiatives was developed under the direction of Derek Rayner, the former chief executive of the British retailer Marks & Spencer. Derek Rayner was arguably Whitehall's first 'efficiency expert'. He concluded that too small a share of Whitehall spending was directed at delivery and that too many senior civil servants focused on policy advice rather than managerial efficiency. As a result, a Whitehall-based efficiency scrutiny programme commenced in 1982 with a focus on corporate planning, goal setting and clarity over personal responsibility for delivery.

Some years later Robin Ibbs, the former chief executive of ICI, was recruited to run the Efficiency Unit at No. 10 Downing Street. In 1988, the Efficiency Unit published a report on 'Improving Management in Government', which proposed that service delivery be the responsibility of Next Steps agencies. Over the following ten years, some 375,000 staff, amounting to three-quarters of all centrally employed civil servants, were transferred to over 130 such agencies or 'arms-length bodies'. Although they operated within departmental framework agreements, they were given freedom to manage their activities with the aim of improving efficiency and delivery.

By 1997, the incoming Labour government had accepted the essence of the next steps approach and attempted to improve upon it through a variety of managerial reforms. The focus on delivering national policy priorities through more detailed targets moved Whitehall from broad goal setting to more detailed performance targets – of activities, outputs, processes and then service outcomes. In 2000, the Blair government recruited Peter Gershon, from being a board director at GEC, to run the Office of Government Commerce with responsibility for procurement across Whitehall. And in 2003 he was asked by both the prime minister and the chancellor of the exchequer to report on how to apply efficiencies across public services. Peter Gershon's report was published alongside the 2004 comprehensive spending review and seeded the terrain for work on efficiency in the UK for the following six years.[36]

Peter Gershon suggested that overall some £20bn could be saved by way of efficiency measures across all public services – and of this total he suggested that at least £12bn would be cash savings that could be recycled to improve front-line delivery. In essence he had concluded that some £8bn of efficiency measures were by way of productivity improvements that improved services without releasing cash. Peter Gershon defined as 'efficiencies' changes to delivery processes and resource usage that achieved one of five different results:

- reduced numbers of inputs (for example people or assets), while maintaining the same level of service provision; or
- lower prices for the resources needed to provide public services; or
- additional outputs, such as enhanced quality or quantity of service, for the same level of inputs; or
- improved ratios output per unit cost of input; or
- changing the balance between different outputs aimed at delivering a similar overall objective in a way which achieves a greater overall output for the same inputs ('allocative efficiency')

To give effect to his proposals he recommended that government departments and devolved public agencies (including local government) focused on four main work-streams. These were: 'back office' support functions; procurement and purchasing; the efficiency of transactional services to citizens and customers; and the scale of policy, funding and regulatory functions. The twofold categories of 'cash' (actual savings) and 'non-cash' (productivity improvements) efficiencies, together with the four main work-streams set the framework for efficiency across public services in the UK from 2004 to 2010.

In 2010, the coalition government in the UK refocused the efforts of Whitehall. It created a new Office of Budget Responsibility to give an independent element to forecasts of economic growth; it abolished many of the 'arms-length bodies' that had developed under its predecessor; and it created an 'efficiency and reform group' within the Cabinet Office.

The efficiency ethic generated within the British public sector by Peter Gershon and his predecessors was both necessary and useful. It bore significant fruits in orienting public servants towards the better management of their business and towards the better use of smart metrics to generate cash-releasing efficiencies. Peter Gershon's approach (predicated on generating efficiency gains of about 3 per cent per year) did suggest significant changes were needed in the British public sector in terms of both supply management and demand management – and some significant changes ensued from his approach. But as with all other regimes of public service reform, Gershon's programme suffered from the problem of diminishing returns. Efficiencies arising from incremental approaches do not generate sufficiently transformational change. The scale of the challenge to reduce costs over the coming period cannot be met by aggregating small-scale efficiency measures.

This truth was recognized by another private sector expert brought into advise on making government more efficient, when the coalition government asked Sir Philip Green of the fashion retailer Topshop to look into government costs. His report lacked the depth of analysis of Sir Peter Gershon's earlier work but it drew similar conclusions. His report restated the truism that if all supply purchasing by government is aggregated it could benefit from economies of scale.[37] His focus was on property, energy costs and utilities. Although his report contains little added insight to the earlier studies by external private sector expert managers, it has added impetus to the UK government's resolve to make savings through centralized procurement and to strengthen its approach to departmental budget management.

It is fairly easy to draft a high level analysis of government inefficiencies and public sector waste so as to point to what should be done. However, the craft of public management involves actually delivering – through changing services so as to lower their costs. It is easy to cut services; it is harder to lower their cost and preserve if not enhance their service outcomes. And yet across most of the developed democracies it is probably the central challenge to those involved in reshaping government and public organizations for the coming decade. And so this is the focus of the next chapter. The practice of reducing costs in the delivery of public services – the art of delivering services better, quicker and cheaper.

Chapter 10

Better, Quicker, Cheaper
How to reduce the cost of public services

The prevailing perception of government services in much of the developed world is that they are less than best, slow to arrive and yet costly to the taxpayer. To reverse this perception it is essential for public leaders (whether elected or appointed) to focus on how they can redesign public services and public organizations to make them more customer centred. They need to be better, quicker and cheaper. Better and quicker to meet the urgent needs of public service users; cheaper to meet the pressing needs of taxpayers.

In government, there is too much attention paid to budgets and to spending and too little attention paid to costs. Government focuses on its budget – its size and scope – and conventionally public officials are held to account mainly for not overspending in relation to their budgets. This can often produce a mentality where public institutions spend up to their agreed budget because public officials have slipped into a false belief that good management is synonymous with not overspending. In the delivery of public services, few officials receive opprobrium when they underspend their budgets (despite the fact that taxpayers have surrendered their hard earned money to finance some desperately needed service programme). Even fewer get sacked for underspending their budgets. But considerable attention is paid when projects overrun or service budget allocations are overspent. When there has been a casual disregard of budgetary control this is understandable – but not always. The concern about variance of spend to budget may be displaced and those commentators focused on overspends may be unaware of the realities of managing resources and may instead be entranced by policy discussions about resource allocation, budgetary controls and spending patterns.

As a result, scant attention is paid to cost management in the public sector. Too few public institutions or public managers have a detailed knowledge of their costs and in particular the factors that drive changes in their costs. What's more, there is insufficient attention paid to the various dimensions of cost control and management. Cost metrics dominate private sector enterprises and yet they are fairly underdeveloped in the public sector. Instead there has been an over-reliance on quantitative performance indicators. Even the most comprehensive texts on public management avoid the issue of cost control. They tend to deal with strategy, performance improvement, public agency collaboration, audit and inspection as well as outsourcing.[1] The purpose of this chapter is to show how costs can be reduced in the design and delivery of public services and to offer practical suggestions for the development of cost reduction strategies across a range of different services.

The character of public sector services varies immensely; as does the cost base for these public services. They include resource transfers (such as vouchers given directly to service users for them to purchase services themselves). They include services delivered through personal contact and professional intervention (such as child protection or health visiting). They include general good services to everyone (street lighting, parks and recreation) and, finally, they include facility-based services (schools, libraries and so on). To control and lower the costs involved in each of these different services, it is vital to first know how the costs are established – and this will vary from service to service. Once the cost base is clear, it is then important to establish a system for measuring changes in the underlying costs. And while measurement should never be confused with management, it is not possible to manage without measuring. Performance metrics are an important aspect of management ('are we doing things better and quicker?') but so too are cost metrics ('are we doing things cheaper?'). Cost metrics include activity-based costs, whole service or whole life costs, unit costs, and institutional costs and whole system costs.

At its broadest, the cost of the state is structured in four main ways. The cost of welfare; the cost of the design and delivery of public services; the cost of collecting taxes and other income to support government activity; and the cost of governance and regulation involved in securing public services. Each of these needs attention if the cost of the state is to be lowered – but here in this chapter I shall focus specifically on the cost of the design and delivery of public services.

Reducing cost in the design and delivery of public services sounds straightforward. But in practice it often raises complex political problems about fairness and cross-subsidy. Imagine the case of a city that has twenty libraries. Let's say that it employs 120 library staff to work in these libraries. And now let's assume that to save money it has decided to reduce its libraries by eight, and divert some resource (in terms of staffing and money) to marketing the remaining twelve libraries to try to maintain service user coverage. Those users of the libraries that are proposed for closure will now have to attend different libraries (probably further away from their homes) and incur some additional marginal costs to themselves. Transferring some of the demand for physical access to books by promoting the take up of books over the internet will serve to reduce cost but it may not reduce the political heat that will inevitably arise from strategies to close libraries. In the public sector, reducing levels of service in this way can have complex and pressing consequences for elected politicians. But helping citizens to gain value out of the public sector at lower cost to taxpayers is important politics in itself because it often involves changing the respective responsibilities of citizens and the state in relation to public services. Any public service that is offered at less than full cost to its users results in a transfer of value from the general taxpayer to the specific service user and therefore any change in the level of subsidy (up to complete removal by charging full cost or by simply ceasing the service) is bound to generate some political contest.

Four levels of cost analysis and four sources of economies

A starting point in any approach to reduce costs in the public sector is to understand that there are four different levels in which costs are crystallized into the design and delivery of public services.[2] These levels are (1) the system; (2) the institution or public agency; (3) the service activity; and (4) the individual transaction between customer and service.

1. Consider the case of the secondary school system. First, there are whole system costs. In a city of one million people there may be up to 80 schools for pupils aged 11–18. The cost of the system includes the whole cost of the schools but it also includes the costs of transport, of special education, of external support and regulation of the schools and of all other system-related costs (like insurance, audit, fire and safety protection costs and so on). The cost of this school system depends crucially upon the size of the schools and the extent to which there is consistency or variety across the schools. For example, does each school have to replicate the offerings of all the other schools?

2. Second, is the cost of the individual schools themselves. This includes property-related costs (including repair and maintenance) and utility costs, facilities management costs (including ICT and media), staffing costs, supplies and services costs and so on. The cost of staff includes

the salaries and wages of teaching and non-teaching staff but also their oncosts (such as pension-related costs and payroll taxes where relevant) and their overheads such as the leadership and governance costs of the school. The total pay and pension costs of the staff in each school is probably the biggest single item of spending and so the way in which staff are organized and deployed is usually the most critical for determining the overall cost of school provision generally.

3. Third, is the cost of any individual aspect of the school's activities. Sports, for example, could include the cost of retaining and maintaining gyms and games pitches as well as the cost of transporting pupils to play matches against other schools and other associated costs (like specialist insurance, and special training costs). Some costs may be incurred in hiring specialist facilities for training or in using facilities that are not available onsite – such as swimming pools.

4. Finally, it is possible to construct costs for each school pupil individually. Costs may vary by age (older pupils may cost more as they are usually taught in smaller classes than the younger pupils – they therefore require lower, and hence more expensive, teacher–pupil ratios). And costs may vary by subject studied or by the degree to which pupils are more easily 'teachable'. In many countries, schools are funded on a per capita basis but it is not unusual for pupils with higher needs (say, because their prior assessed ability was lower than average or because of their relatively poor family circumstances) to be funded at a higher rate to compensate for their educational disadvantages. In public or state school systems this funding comes from the central or local state but in private systems it comes from individual parents. There are few 'user charges' in school systems, although with increasing austerity measures this may change: current examples include charging for home–school transport, charging for meals and refreshments, charging for extra-curricular activities (such as music lessons, sporting trips and so on).

And so in the case of city with one million people and 80 secondary schools, the costs need to be examined at the level of the whole system; at the level of the individual school; at the level of specific school activities or agreed spending lines; and finally at the level of the individual pupil. Cost reductions at one level do not automatically flow into cost reductions at all other levels. Forty schools may work hard to reduce their costs but the other forty may increase their costs by a greater amount. Similarly, reductions in costs of, say, sports at any one school may be dwarfed by increasing costs in drama and science at the same school. And increased charges to parents for discretionary activity may not result in lower costs if this is simply used to finance higher expenditure.

Just as there are four levels to costs so there are four different sources for achieving economies in these costs. These are: (1) economies of scale; (2) economies of scope; (3) economies of flow; and (4) economies of penetration. Of course it is possible to reduce costs by minor incremental changes such as stopping, trimming and delaying expenditure. Costs can be reduced by stopping things. For example, it would be possible to stop sending the pupils to a swimming pool and save the costs of transport and the cost of the fees for using the pool. Costs can also be reduced by trimming back on things. Rather than sending the pupils swimming each week, this could be altered to every alternate week, thereby saving one-half of the relevant costs. Finally, costs can be delayed. Rather than purchase some necessary educational equipment this year, let's delay it for a few months and incur the cost next year. Delaying spending is a classic false economy in that it does not reduce spending but rather simply shifts the accounting period for the spending. And indeed, in the case of spending on assets, delaying spending may make future spending costs higher. This is precisely what happens when schools delay spending on the repairs and maintenance of their buildings – higher investment costs occur as a direct result. The key point is that these three tactics (stopping, trimming and delaying) are just that – tactics. They do not comprise a strategy for achieving economies. For that we have to examine economies of scale, scope, flow and penetration.

1. **Economies of scale** arise in the production of private goods by extending the use of plant and technology to produce ever greater volumes. And in different sectors (from manufacturing to retail), the management task is to discover the optimal scale. In manufacturing, economies of scale arise from the dynamics of production; in retail they arise from the dynamics of consumption. While there are production scale economies possible in the public sector, it is likely that, as the sector is principally concerned with delivering services, most of the scale economies will arise from how the service is consumed. This is why techniques of mass customization can usefully help to reduce costs and yet meet customer needs for public services.

2. **Economies of scope** arise, in the private sector, from the opportunity of using the same process for producing similar products. In the service sector, a strategy for achieving 'scope economies' would see private companies parcelling different service offerings to the same

group of consumers. At its simplest, local government is an attempt to achieve economies of scope in public services in that different services are provided under one common management to a given local population. Essentially, local governments are attempting to bundle a series of services under one management (from child protection to environmental maintenance). Services that, from a customer perspective, are best delivered complementarily to each other can be either designed to be delivered together or organized through coordinated commissioning (where service purchasers source suppliers to provide complementary services to the same group of customers). This drive to achieve economies of scope locally is why there is a real challenge in getting local governments to share services and find economies of scale bigger than themselves – by disposition they are focused on how best to produce economies of scope.

3. **Economies of flow** arise in the private sector through the application of lean techniques and process improvement strategies. Flow approaches stem from systems thinking applied to the production of goods and services. The emphasis in this approach is on eliminating waste and duplication and establishing a rhythm of production that optimises resource deployment and keeps it in tune with the changing rhythms of demand. Its core ideas stemmed originally from the work of the management theorist W E Deming who was concerned to manage variation so as to improve cost-effectiveness.[3] It was then developed further in Japan and particularly in the car industry (notably Toyota)[4] from whence it has spread throughout the world as 'lean process' management into financial services and more latterly into public services.[5] In the public sector, flow economies can be achieved by applying lean or 'six sigma' techniques (essentially operational management and statistical control measures) to any complex process.[6]

    However, in the public sector one of the most fundamental issues involves how demand can be better managed. For twenty years private sector advice into the public sector has concentrated on how supply ought to be better managed. And undoubtedly improvements in procurement and supply management can produce significant economies. But the key to lowering cost in the public sector is to manage demand better. Improved management of failure demand (where customers keep returning to the provider, again and again, to get errors and mistakes fixed) will reduce the overall cost of providing services by making sure that service is provided right first time. But the biggest cost reductions will come in those services where it is feasible to divert and deflect demand – so that users learn how best to serve themselves rather than require public services in the first place.

4. **Economies of penetration** occur in the provision of goods and services in the private sector where the producer or retailer has gained intimate knowledge of their customers' purchasing habits and preferences such that they are able, at lower cost, to sell different goods and services to them. This strategy has become enabled by smart card technologies and the development of web-based purchasing. It is best exemplified by the Amazon reference, 'people who bought this book, also bought these other books'. Detailed knowledge of customer preferences enables companies to eliminate marketing costs, establish new lines of business and new partnerships with other complementary companies. Other examples include web-based travel companies that link customers with flights, hotels, car hire and restaurants, all based on revealed preferences. In the public sector, a considerable amount of customer information is collected but few public agencies have sufficiently sophisticated 'customer relationship management' systems that enable effective cross-selling. Of course in the public sector, there are ethical and other considerations to bring to bear on this particular strategy – but that does not mean that economies of penetration offer little prospect for lowering costs in public service delivery.

The key to the adoption of any cost reduction strategy based upon any of the approaches set out above is that it needs to be considered and implemented in a disciplined way. The discipline of management includes a variety of practices and processes; but these practices and processes need to be directed specifically to the service in question.[7] A disciplined approach to public service management will include the management of both supply and demand;[8] and the effective management of programmes and projects. It will also include value chain analysis and related process improvement techniques.

However, above all these practices, two others stand out for particular mention as they are absolutely crucial to realizing cost reductions. The first is the way in which management practice links changes in work cultures with investments in technology. Technological investment of itself does not heighten productivity or lower costs. But the adoption of new practices allied to the introduction of technologies does generate real benefits.[9] The second is the simple but often neglected art of execution – of implementing and getting things done. One of the main reasons why sensible cost reduction strategies fail is because managers lack the resolve, resilience and determination to follow through and implement them. The emotional demands of cutting people's jobs or reducing their terms and conditions or simply asking them to work differently in the future are sometimes more easily avoided.[10]

Loaning a book, preventing a crime

To consider how costs can be reduced in the provision of public services, it is best to think through some concrete and simple examples. Here are two such examples – library services and crime prevention services. These are both long established public services with strong traditions in communities. Everyone knows their local public library and everyone has a view about the effectiveness of their local police in reducing crimes locally.

We tend to use the public library service at particular stages in our life cycle – when we are young and studying, when we have young children, and when we are retired. Of course, people at work without children may be very active library users but generally life-cycle stages describe the main drivers of consumer use. Libraries play a key role in local communities. Not only can they inspire a love of reading, they can also help people acquire new skills, promote community development, and bridge the digital divide. By contrast we do not 'use' the crime prevention service – we simply expect it to function effectively and efficiently. We may think that the police service is the crime prevention service but on reflection it is clear that several other public sector staff in other public agencies work closely with the police to prevent crime. These include community wardens, youth service staff, probation service staff, those engaged in prosecution services and those working in local prisons.

Let us consider the case of these two services in one nation – in England. Throughout England some £970m is spent on 3500 public libraries, employing 21,000 staff. The cost to the taxpayer per active library user is £91.50 or about £3.70 each time they borrow a book (as they borrow an average of 24 books each per year).[11] This means that the average sized local authority will spend about £5m on its public library service. Although in each local area, there will also be a range of other libraries that are available to specific users. School libraries and college and university libraries exist in localities but very few of these are generally available to the public or contain a range of books and materials for general users rather than their specialized student users. For the average library service in England, the cost of the books and all the materials in the library is some 12 per cent of the overall cost of the library service. The use of consortia purchasing arrangements, among library authorities, has served to drive down the cost of book buying generally. Indeed if publishers provided their books to public libraries free of charge, the overall cost of the library service in England would reduce by just 8 per cent.

The trend increase in children's book reading together with service innovation among library professionals has served to increase the productivity of library services. This has been achieved by better marketing, more targeted opening hours, and by the introduction of 'self service' terminals. Each library service knows its detailed activity rates, its most marketable products and the cost per issue of each book in each library. But knowing this doesn't reduce the costs. For the bulk of the cost of the service is factored into its design – the number of libraries and their opening hours. With overall income, from fees and charges, recovering less than 10 per cent of gross revenue costs (one-fifth of which comes from overdue charges), the scope for reducing net costs by raising income is very restricted. And the demand for borrowing books has changed dramatically with generational changes in the pattern of reading, with the growth of online information and the rise of school-based and home-based internet usage, and with the reducing cost and rising accessibility of ebooks and so on.

Examined coldly, the costs of this service seem barely able to justify the benefits. However, libraries are more than places for loaning books – so many other creative, civilizing, social and learning experiences are available in libraries. They remain a publicly sponsored place where those without access to the internet at home can quench their thirst for learning. But the main option for altering the cost base of the service rests in changing the number of service points and reducing staffing levels – or put simply, reducing the number of libraries in a locality. Presented in this way, reducing costs is simply cutting services. The alternative is to redesign the library service, completely changing the nature of the service, its offer to its users and perhaps the distance they travel to visit a library. Two ways forward are feasible. First, it may be sensible to develop fewer, better libraries that are better marketed and that may therefore have a bigger social and economic impact upon a local area than a larger number of smaller libraries. Second, it may be sensible to integrate small local libraries into other locally based facilities thus helping to reduce the cost of premises or staffing overheads.

Let's now consider our other example. Crime prevention is the role we expect from our local police. That is why there is often so much public discussion and comment on front-line police numbers. There are 43 police forces in England employing over 228,000 personnel. This includes over 141,000 police officers, nearly 76,000 police staff and over 15,000 police community support officers. The police service also makes use of 14,000 volunteer police officers known as special constables.[12] Police efforts and energies are usually directed at 'crime types' (burglary, robbery and so on) as well as towards offering general reassurance by foot patrolling. Public confidence in the police rests upon their effective engagement with communities in preventing crime as well as their specific effectiveness in catching criminals. Available evidence suggests that three out of the top four strategies for improving public confidence in the police all included an element of communicating and engaging with the community.[13]

But actual crime is prevented in very many different ways. Improved design of homes, businesses, cars and even mobile phones make them less open to crime. Designing out the opportunity for crime helps to prevent crime. Diverting specific groups of people away from criminal behaviour is also effective in preventing crime. But so too is the vigilant safeguarding of the public realm. However, police officers are not employed simply to meander along the streets randomly in case crimes happen. They are deployed in a targeted fashion to give visible reassurance to the community in known 'hotspots'; to identify and detect alleged criminals; as well as to catch and convict those who are perpetrating crimes. The police service is not a service that is used by people; it is a service that serves the public generally.

In any one locality there are a range of public service staff and public agencies focused on preventing crime. For example, the reconviction rate for ex-offenders is some 65 per cent. This means that targeted work with ex-offenders to reduce their rate of reoffending may greatly impact on the overall levels of crime committed in an area (but only if this targeted work is actually effective). Similarly, very many crimes arise from behaviour that is triggered by compulsive addiction to drugs and alcohol. Working to reduce levels of addiction may (again, if it is effective) also help to reduce levels of criminal behaviour.

For every twenty police officers engaged in the average local area in England to prevent crime (in a variety of ways), there are two probation staff working with ex-offenders, one local-authority-employed community safety worker, one youth worker organizing diversionary activity, one specialist drugs and alcohol worker, one mental health specialist, and one member of the crown prosecution service trying to convict those who are caught. The way in which all these workers blend their activities together is central to the efficacy and efficiency of their collective efforts in preventing crime in an area. But even if they all work well together the overall system may be inefficient. If, say, a local prison releases people on Friday afternoons without effective liaison with the community services charged with resettling offenders, these released prisoners are highly likely to reoffend. This simple illustration shows how public service redesign often requires system redesign across a number of agencies. Cost reductions can be found when like services have linked processes about the same clients. Better integration enables costs to be reduced. Examined alone, each service can be redesigned to lower its costs and improve its effectiveness. It is only when they are examined together that the whole system can improve its efficiency.

These two simple examples show how reducing the cost of public services to the taxpayer requires a detailed understanding of individual public services – how they are designed and how their costs are built up. Overall costs need to be reduced by a repertoire of managerial economics. These include smarter supply management; defter demand management; better collaborative working; more focused management of functions and activities; shifting costs onto the customer; and better use of private sector suppliers as well as third sector agencies in the outsourcing of services.

Service redesign: focus change on the user's needs

Traditionally, public service reforms have focused squarely on service improvement. A great deal of this improvement has resulted from a focus on the gaps between policies, services or institutions. To this end, frontline professionals have collaborated to better align their activities around the needs of service users. Examples of this include the multi-agency work for children and families and the multi-professional work with people leaving hospital. But a focus on increased collaborative working (with, say, different professionals working with the same client albeit on differing dimensions of their needs) tends to address problems of service effectiveness; it does not tend to lower costs. Of course it may lead to costs being lowered – through, say, common assessment processes. But the usual outcome is that front-line professionals discover gaps between services in order to fill them. If anything, this drives up costs.

By contrast, a focus on overlaps explicitly focuses on potential duplication, waste and inefficiency. Overlaps can occur across policies, services and institutions. Some overlaps are inevitable but some are sites of unnecessary costs that can be eliminated. Service redesign involves addressing the fundamentals of a service – identifying unnecessary steps in the service so that waste and duplication can be eliminated and the overall process simplified for the customer. These fundamentals are most likely to be addressed by the customers themselves and by the front-line staff working with these users. The British creative entrepreneur Charles Leadbeater has written powerfully of the value of 'leading edge users' in service innovation and he has also suggested that public agencies ought to adopt more emergent approaches to innovation to redesign public services and reduce overall cost to the taxpayer.[14] His approach rests upon web-enabled mass involvement – and is suggestive of a new form of 'user generated state'.

Allied to this approach at harnessing innovative techniques to improve public services are the developments encouraged by the Design Council in the UK. The Design Council has developed a 'public services by design' approach that works with service users to envision different designs and modes of delivery for public services. Their approach has been used in services as varied as sexual health screening in Gateshead, in worklessness projects in Sunderland and in diabetes self-management in Bolton.[15]

At its broadest, the service redesign approach to reducing costs has two further component steps. The first step involves considering the best way to change the boundary of the service between the service provider and the service user. Shifting power and responsibility to the service user is a powerful means of service change. Across developed economies, this approach is being adopted in the field of adult social care through the adoption of a direct payment route to achieving more personalized social care. Consumers who help themselves can do so at lower overall cost to the taxpayer if the incentive structure is right. The second step involves focusing on those aspects of the public service that are high cost but that provide only modest or low value to the customer. In analysing their cost base, service providers rarely examine the value of each costed service component to the customer, instead they focus their attention on what is costly to them as a provider. Eliminating high cost but low value elements of the service is a crucially important step in the process of service redesign.

Figure 10.1 differentiates between the costs that stem principally from how a service is designed; the costs that stem from how work is organized; and the costs that flow from adopting different organizational models. For example, some services are delivered from a facility that service users have to attend to gain any benefit. Other services may not be delivered from a facility and instead may rely on deploying field staff.

How work is organized is another important consideration in revising costs. In the average public service, labour costs comprise about two-thirds of all costs. And so the direct cost of staff, their oncosts (that is, their pension entitlements and other conditions of employment) as well as how they are organized, is central to how total costs are built up. It is rarely feasible to reduce the cost of public services without reducing the numbers of people employed by the state, or without reducing their pay or reducing their other benefits. Changing how they are organized may assist in cost reduction by flattening structures and reducing management ratios. Moreover, there are different opportunities to lower staffing costs by reorganizing work depending upon the nature of how work is organized – for example, field staff working in single professional teams will produce different costs from, say, office-based staff working in multidisciplinary teams. Finally, limiting senior executive pay to a clear multiple of average (or lowest) pay may also act as a ceiling on the trend for rising executive pay.[16]

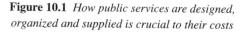

Figure 10.1 *How public services are designed,
organized and supplied is crucial to their costs*

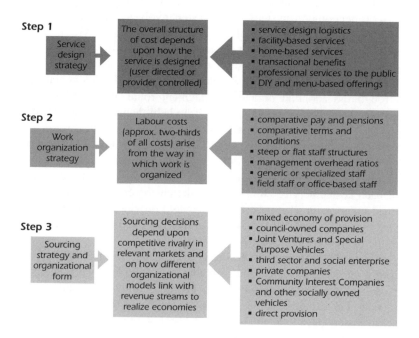

The 'sourcing strategy' for service delivery is also crucial to costs. For there is an issue about how to reduce costs by engaging companies and not-for-profit agencies to deliver services through service contracts rather than directly engaging staff through employment contracts. There has been a great deal of research on the merits and demerits of outsourcing. Unfortunately much of this research is smothered in bias and tends to be insufficiently objective and rigorous. Looked at objectively, an analysis of outsourcing advantages and disadvantages should be informed by the principles and practices of transaction cost economics whereby the 'make-or-buy' decision pivots on the comparison between production costs (when producing internally) and transaction costs (when using the market). The opportunities for outsourcing to the market depend critically on the nature of the supply market for any given service. Some markets have multiple suppliers in dynamic competition while others are composed of a small number of suppliers, each with a weak capacity to grow and compete.[17] Understanding this 'supply ecology' is crucial to managing the market well and gaining the best from competition, innovation and private sector practice.

Generally, an average of some 10 per cent of costs can be saved through outsourcing (usually through the process of specialization and standardization), although account has then to be made of the costs of contract management and the inevitable cost of dispute handling which eats into a little of that 10 per cent saving.[18] However, this needs to be balanced against the fact that in the absence of a fully competitive supply market for public services the best option is to retain some form of 'mixed economy' of provision.

To reconfigure public services to reduce costs dramatically requires the abandonment of some services or whole system redesign that reshapes services rather than simply revamps them. Whole system redesign requires changes in service design, changes in work organization; and changes in organizational form. But whole system change is extraordinarily difficult to achieve – it often seems so much easier to stick with tinkering with one dimension of the redesign problem. And in many instances that may be a sensible if tactical option to pursue. However, whole system change offers the most prospects for both the taxpayer and the service user as it enables costs to be lowered and services to be improved. After all, at the current time we are trying to recast very many public services that are simply too ineffective, too slow and too high cost. Citizens demand public services that are better, quicker and cheaper. That is achieved by lowering costs while raising productivity. Public service productivity is notoriously lower than in the private sector but in practice it is more difficult to improve. Why should this be? Consider the following by way of example.

Haircuts, hip replacements and improving productivity

In large cities throughout the developed world the average haircut costs about £30 and takes about forty minutes. There is an obvious gender difference at play in respect of haircuts but personality trait is also important – with the self-regarding vain being more inclined to part with more money than those who care less about how they appear to others (the vain might argue that this latter group are themselves too careless about their appearance). Hairdressers and barbers know how many haircuts they can complete in a usual working day and those who own the hairdresser's or barber shops know the seating capacity of their shops – in fact they increasingly just rent seats on a weekly basis to self-employed hairdressers. It is very likely that today the average hairdresser spends the same amount of time cutting someone's hair as they did ten years ago – and what's more, they are likely to spend roughly the same amount of time doing so in ten years' time. The way that hairdressers can charge their customers more is by adding value at lower cost (per minute) through the embellishment of colouring and affixing hair extensions. But the scope for this is limited and the opportunity to cut people's hair more quickly so that volumes can increase is also limited. It is very likely that there are steep diminishing returns in this process – unless everyone agrees to have the same very short haircut; in which case they might as well get their partners to do it or just do it for themselves!

By contrast, the average hip replacement costs £8000 and takes four hours. A hip replacement will be undertaken by a medical team working to the highest standards of clinical practice. However, it is likely that this clinical team will be undertaking the operation very differently than they did ten years ago and it is probable, given the speed of change in technical innovation and in clinical practice, that the way in which they do the operation will be different again in ten years' time. This offers opportunities to those performing hip replacements to improve their productivity and offer an improved service. Hairdressers and barbers with a comb, scissors and a hair dryer have far fewer options for productivity gains of the same order.

The question is whether specific public services are more of the character of haircuts or more of the character of hip replacements? Very many personal social care services, for example, are 'haircut type' services. Few are 'hip replacement type' services. The argument about the 'productivity gap' between the private and the public sector places a veil over these crucial economic distinctions. The production of goods that are sold in the private sector is capable of high order gains in productivity through technical innovation and other techniques. The delivery of services in the private sector is less capable of such high productivity gains, although if the service is built around a good, then it is possible to leak productivity gains from the good to the service. Consider the case of the car. Cars can be built ever more cheaply because of technical innovation. And companies that specialize in car servicing can improve their productivity as a result of design changes in cars themselves. The same applies with companies that build homes and companies that repair and maintain homes. But personal service companies in the private sector are much less able to capture productivity gains from altering the nature of their service provision. They will be focused on innovation and productivity improvements because they operate in a competitive market but they suffer very many of the constraints that public agencies face when they deliver personal services.

This point is not made here simply to make a case against raising productivity in the public sector. Indeed the absence of market pressures means that much more attention needs to be paid to productivity improvement in public services. Teachers, social workers, police officers, planners and health visitors may feel that their work is not amenable to productivity improvement – they would be wrong. But they are right if they argue that comparing their productivity to those working in the manufacture of private sector goods is both a bald and a false comparison.[19]

Summary

Across the developed world, governments are waist deep in debt and deficits. The private recession that swept the globe sucked taxpayers' money into most governments and into many banks simply to sustain the global economy. When the time for fiscal stimulus gave way to a time for fiscal consolidation the age of enforced austerity began. In this way, private recession has given way to public retrenchment. Politicians and public managers are searching for new ways actively to cut the cost of the state. Increasing taxes and lowering the cost of social welfare payments offers two viable paths forward. But the most fruitful path forward is that which dramatically reduces the cost of public services. The precise balance between cuts in public spending, cuts in welfare entitlements and raising taxation is a matter for democratic governments to make given the pressures on them from the investor markets, voters' acceptability of public spending reductions and broader public sentiments.

The scale of reductions in public spending being planned across Western democratic governments for the coming period is very significant. In the US, large-scale fiscal retrenchment at the federal level is likely to follow the cutting of huge public programmes in 2010 among state and local governments (as every state, except Vermont, is required by law to balance its budget every year – a fiscal straightjacket that does not bind the federal government). European governments face particular challenges with their ageing and growing populations but all governments face a squeeze between service users and taxpayers. For when citizens are service users, their expectations for quality of service rise unremittingly upward while at the same time citizens as taxpayers make equally relentless demands for lower cost public services.

The traditional initiatives on efficiency and value for money have been useful preliminaries to the major task that confronts governments in their drive to dramatically reduce the cost of public service provision. The past decade has seen significant improvements in the accessibility of public services across many governments. Digital era governance has made many public services more accessible. It is so much easier, convenient and quicker to engage with the state in 2010 compared with ten years ago. Improvements to public service management, more effective service strategies and smarter service design have each improved service outcomes. Important transactions (like being treated in hospital, and having a hip replacement) have also greatly improved. But these improvements have tended to cost the taxpayer more.

The coming period is a much more challenging test for political leaders and public managers. It is easy to improve services at greater cost. It is also easy to cut budgets and cut services. The difficult task is to reduce costs while not making the same commensurate cuts in service standards, levels and coverage. Greater use of new technologies is bound to offer tools to reduce costs further; and improvements to public service productivity (although more limited in potential than the private sector) also play a part. It is entirely feasible to reduce costs and deliver improvements. The critical issues are the depth of reductions required, the pace at which change can be properly delivered in differing service domains and the sustainability of the new, lower cost, service platforms that are to be developed. Budget reduction strategies that reduce costs too arbitrarily will render public services, and those who desperately need them, at risk. Delivering appropriate reductions will require talented and innovative managers to take measured risks in changing services to lower their cost.

Chapter 11

Conclusion

The late American theologian and political commentator Reinhold Niebuhr wrote: 'Man's capacity for justice makes democracy possible; but man's inclination to injustice makes democracy necessary.'[1] Democratic governments have such ancient foundations that we tend to forget their first imaginings – what they were designed to achieve and how they were designed to operate. Thankfully the reformers and revolutionaries of the late 18th century set out some clear designs for government that rested on these foundations. These designs offer us a strong framework for government even now. The ideas of effective representation, of transparency of public decision-making, of disinterested advice combined with political conviction, of constitutional checks and balances – these all have value in today's world. But these ideas were sharpened before universal suffrage, before the creation of political parties, before the rise of the welfare state (let alone the responsive state), and before the socially dynamic, hyper-connected and media-rich environment in which democratic governments now function. After the collapse of communism, some believed that liberal democracies had won through and that history had ended: that the challenges to democratic government were over. What hubris. Democratic government continues to be challenged from without and from within. That is why it needs to be re-imagined. So that it can begin to meet the needs of tomorrow's citizens today.

Very many citizens are suspicious of their government and of those who govern them. These citizens may have become disenchanted with the prospects of government doing good or they may have grown despondent about the potential of democratic politics to solve the problems they see around them. They may be buoyed in their belief by periodic examples of abuse of power and authority by those they elect and those who are appointed to serve at their pleasure. It should therefore come as no surprise that these citizens tend to vote against incumbents, to punish those in power and give 'the other guy a chance'. And there is some force and justice to their disaffection. Democratic politics can let us

197

down and democratic governments can disappoint us. But as Reinhold Niebuhr suggests, democracy is necessary because of our inclination to inflict injustice on each other.

Good government relies on good people determined to do good things and do them well for the public good. But in a highly plural and geographically diverse society people will differ markedly as to their interpretation of what constitutes 'the public good'. People will always have their own special and particular interests that differ from, and may conflict with, the wider public interest. Democratic governments need to be careful that they don't simply subsume these special interests within the broader public interest. But they also need to give due regard and respect to these special interests. That is because when democratic governments exercise public choice on behalf of their citizens, they need to seek as much popular consent as is feasible (or at least they need to attain the public's acquiescence in what they, the government, plan to implement). In the challenging times of the early 21st century, very many democratic governments are changing the shape of the state, reducing the scope of public services, and altering the bases of welfare entitlements. But they are unwise if they simply impose these changes on their citizens. For we know that public discussion, open deliberation and public reason are at the heart of good government.

It has been a central contention of this book that government and public services are improved through moral purpose combined with practical reasoning rather than through the pursuit of some freshly minted ideology. Governments solve problems that we cannot solve alone – they have to take account of competing claims and they have to balance differing interests. But they cannot solve our problems by ideological fiat. With the increasing scale, complexity and diversity of human relations, our collective problems are getting knottier as every year passes. Solving life's problems by peaceful and open dialogue beats any of the alternatives. James Madison's truism that, 'men are not angels' reminds us that however open and peaceful our dialogue is, it will always be flawed. But the fundamental flaws of human nature should not absolve us from trying to solve problems through democratic dialogue and through the medium of representative government.

Through a mix of stories and theories I have tried to show the richness of government and the complexities of public policy. And I hope this richness demonstrates why, among every generation, so many people are drawn to serve the public. For those of us living in mature democracies, we live in comparative safety and security because of the resilience of our military and the fabric of our security and police services. And the quality of our lives and the quality of our life-chances depend in no small measure on the quality of the public services in the areas where we were born, grew up and now live.

Government helps create the conditions for our success but we succeed if it doesn't get in our way, preventing progress and the achievement of ambition. Governments must first do no harm before they then try to do good. In this way our homes, schools, roads, hospitals, buses, trains, and places of work depend upon an enabling public sector that in turn requires effective government at national and local level. In short, government matters: not in the quantity of what it does but in the quality of what it does. In the decade after the 2008 Crash, it is likely that many liberal democratic governments will get sidetracked into a politics about the size of the state. They will be right to question and revise the size of the tax burden, the breadth and depth of established welfare entitlements and the scope of the public sector. But reducing the scale of public deficits is not the same as deciding what government in the 21st century should be for.

What's more, while technical progress and economic growth will continue into the future, new public problems will inevitably present themselves. For in the governance of nations, one generation solves the problems set it by its predecessor but in so doing creates new sets of problems for its succeeding generation. The key point that flows from this is that elected politicians and appointed public servants need to focus less narrowly on the fashionable policy instrument of the moment and more broadly on betterment – on making things better from one generation to the next.

In this book I have attempted to explore the issues of politics, government and the management of public service from a number of different perspectives. Of course, it is not possible to encompass the full art of governing in such a short book. But I hope to have addressed some of the most important issues that confront democratic governments. These include how to expand public value, how to help people find common cause, how to arrive at decisions in the public interest, how to cope with geographical variety and social diversity, how to handle risk and uncertainty, and how to manage retrenchment in public spending. The depth and breadth of public spending cuts across many nations will itself impact upon how democratic governments operate. For if we are to reduce public spending so significantly, governments will not only need to reshape the nature of service delivery they will also need to stimulate innovation in the social and private economy so that a clearer and more sustainable path is found to future economic prosperity and growth.

In a democracy, elected politicians and appointed public servants are two sides of the same coin. They need each other: one is the path to democratic legitimacy, the other the path to objective advice and committed execution. The tense and complex issues involved in offering advice or counsel to those who govern have been known for millennia. These issues include the personal dynamics of fealty and enmity as much as they involve rational analytical advice giving. But politicians do not simply ask others for advice on what to do; they also ask others to implement and execute their decisions.

That is why political strategies about the future of the state are empty if they lack managerial expression. And it is also why public sector managers need to move beyond a measured detachment in the execution of political goals. Distant and uninvolved managers will find it hard to achieve the goals set them by their political masters because they are unlikely to carry others with them. For public agencies to achieve their goals they need dedicated, resourceful and well-motivated staff – for which they require effective managerial leaders. These leaders need to be impartial in respect of the policy being pursued but wholly emotionally engaged with its implementation. If they are not, their prospects of achieving public goals are slim.

What's more, political strategies that seek to rewire the relationship between citizens and their state will fail if they rely entirely on a lazy managerialism. For managerial solutions can only take us so far. The deepest change in a nation or a community involves political and social change – it involves much more than the redrawing of institutional or organizational boundaries. Of course, it is vital that public institutions are continually challenged from without. Open public institutions provide the essential bedrock for effective government. But the most significant challenge involves new cultures of expectation, ambition and hope among citizens and across wider civil society. For service users are able to generate change on their own, citizens are able to self-organize solutions for themselves, and very many communities are willing to meet communal needs and are capable of fostering civic innovation locally.

Changing democratic government, reforming public services

Democratic government is framed through the principle of representation but is challenged by the pervasive demands of responsiveness. In truth, all elected politicians rely on a fragile democratic legitimacy. They should never over-rely on the fact of their election (however large or slender the margin of their victory) but instead they should focus, as John Locke argued, on what they are doing to improve the good of the people. In a networked world of ubiquitous media access, politicians are incredibly pressured to keep ahead of the growing number of 'crowd-sourced' social movements and the invasive demands upon them of 24-hour rolling television news channels. What's more, the demands of public reason stretch politicians' convictions to their limits (as they seek to justify a consistent stance towards issues while circumstances change with bewildering pace). Added to which the highly personal demands of emotional connection stretch politicians' psychological capacity to reveal themselves as balanced and rounded individuals (as 'angels' even) to an enquiring electorate.

In the early 21st century, mass populism and niche social movements mingle awkwardly with direct and representative democracy to develop a 360-degree democracy where everyone seems accountable to everyone else on a 24/7 basis. Despite this, elected politicians retain a privileged position – they are elected to represent us all and, when we are unable to do so ourselves, it falls to them to take collective choices. And so systems of representation are important – we want good systems that enable us to vote out governments we don't like and we want these same systems to offer us a fair chance of being able to vote for representatives who share some of our approaches to collective issues. But we also want our government to be conducted in an open manner with as much disclosure and transparency as is feasible.

Furthermore, in the context of the information-rich and socially networked world in which we now live, we know that there are many new ways in which we can solve problems for ourselves. We gather our own information and we can garner our own support. And we are now able to act through emergent social networks to discover common cause among ourselves – joining and leaving social movements through web connections as much as through real connections. And because we know that the connected and linked world of the 21st century affords us better tools to govern ourselves we demand from those who are elected to govern us that they do so lightly and with more humility.

Governments are founded on collective action. As such they usually involve the build-up of collective liabilities – either moral or financial. What we owe to each other may be by way of attachment or loyalty. But what we also owe may be by way of collective financial debt. Public debt has accompanied the purposes of government for hundreds of years. And for the foreseeable future, public debt will cast a long shadow over many democratic governments across the globe. These governments not only seek to reduce their costs; they also seek to reduce their citizens' expectations of what their government should do for them. In consequence many governments have developed, as an explicit aim of public policy, the aggressive downward adjustment of citizen expectations.[2] Over a short and shallow period of public spending cutbacks it may be feasible for governments to adopt a 'business as usual' approach (implementing cutbacks incrementally). But a prolonged period of deep austerity requires a different approach – more fundamental managerial change and a deeper style of democratic engagement between elected politicians and service users. Linking new forms of public spending to new paths for economic growth is the fresh challenge for early 21st-century democracies as they rein back welfare entitlements, increase taxation, reduce substantially their public spending and try to stimulate private sector growth. Just as democratic governments will need to change, so too will the public services they seek to deliver.

Across the globe too many confusions litter the landscape of public service reform. The conventional approaches to reforming public services seem to involve little more than different forms of privatization and substantial reductions in public service costs (including public sector pay and pensions, and so on). These approaches continue to have general merit but they do not describe the full scope of what can be done and in some instances may contribute more problems than solutions. Now and then some clarity emerges in how to reform public services. During the second term Blair government, a coherent theoretical framework for public service reform was developed in the UK. This approach has been described in a number of texts[3] but its clearest expression is found in the work of Julian Le Grand, an academic who worked briefly for the Blair government.

Julian Le Grand rightly charges that all approaches to public service reform rest on underlying assumptions about what motivates public servants (whether elected or appointed). His approach was heavily influenced by Hume's dictum that, 'in contriving any system of government every man should be supposed to be a knave and to have no other end, in all his actions, than private interest.' Le Grand suggested that traditional approaches to public service reform presumed 'knightly' behaviour on the part of public service professionals (such as doctors and head teachers) and failed to recognize their own intrinsic drive to serve their own interests. In a separate strand of argument he suggested that different approaches to public service reform placed 'agency' (the power to act) with either public service institutions or with service users themselves.[4] His model suggests a fourfold approach to public service reform – each of which was pursued by the then Blair government, although without the coherence of the ideas that energized it.

The first of these four approaches is built on the prospects of improved service through 'knightly' behaviour of professional service networks. This approach, among other examples, underlay the attempt to encourage joint-agency working – collaborative service partnerships that stimulate greater integration between front-line professionals. In this approach, the agent of service improvement is the local service provider. What matters is the quality of their leadership, their strategic direction setting, the quality of their performance management, their specific competencies and their overall capabilities. The second approach is based on the opposite style of thinking. In this approach, front-line professionals are assumed to be motivated by 'knavish' concerns (that is, to serve their own interests) and, as a result, they require top-down direction from government. This direction comes in the form of targets, close performance management and even closer regulation and inspection.

This tightly focused approach to delivering results in a narrow field (such as reducing street robbery levels, increasing the literacy of 11 year olds, reducing the time waiting to be seen on attending a hospital) was, for a time, elevated to the status of a pseudoscience among some policymakers. Indeed, in his account of his time as head of Tony Blair's delivery unit, Michael Barber referred to it as 'deliverology'.[5] Some commentators have described this, in respect of how the system worked in the management of hospitals, as the 'targets and terror' approach.[6] But whatever generalized criticism is applied to this approach, it does seem that, in the UK at least, it resulted in significant improvements in performance in specific service areas in the eight-year period to 2008.

The third approach identified by Le Grand is one based on 'voice' – where service users, their advocates or politicians are afforded more opportunities to have a stronger input into the design and delivery of services. This approach includes reforms as varied as service user surveys, customer redress, and user involvement in service governance. The idea behind the 'voice' approach is that citizens hold public institutions to account through direct customer sovereignty, indirect user advocacy or political representation. Le Grand's fourth approach is one based on more market-based techniques to expand service user 'choice'. Here Le Grand suggests that public service users should have greater choice between different professionals, different service standards, and different service providers. However, for choice to be exercised it requires some surplus capacity (in what is being chosen) and it requires a degree of competition between providers operating in some form of quasi-market for public services.

Le Grand's fourfold approach remains the most coherent framework for understanding the options (and the underlying theoretical bases) for public service reform, although within the context of the British welfare state, he clearly favours the choice and competition route as offering the best chance of shaking up entrenched provider interests in public service delivery.[7] The British coalition government that took office in 2010 built upon this model by adding greater emphasis to diversifying the supply of public services, breaking up 'public sector provider monopolies' and making public spending more transparent (through web-based expenditure reporting).[8]

Managerial solutions to public service reforms seem sensible when the problem that needs fixing is underperforming public services. But what if the problem that needs fixing is more the character of a social problem – let's say, what is needed are changes in the behaviour of some group of citizens? If the aim of policy is to, say, reduce crime, reduce health inequalities, improve employability, or encourage people to reduce their carbon footprint, then the goal of policy is some form of behaviour change among citizens (or a sub-group of them). Managerial solutions that seek to improve organizational effectiveness are less relevant here. Instead, policymakers may be looking for prompts, triggers or nudges that encourage some form of 'pro-social' behaviour among citizens generally or among a smaller group of citizens.

This is one of the reasons why there has been a growing interest across governments in behavioural economics, social psychology and social marketing. In this general field of enquiry, perhaps the most influential text has been *Nudge* by Richard Thaler and Cass Sunstein. In their book they set out how policymakers should design a 'choice architecture' for the public and encourage citizens, through a mix of small signals and 'touch points', to improve among other things their own health and welfare. They called their approach a form of libertarian paternalism.[9] But their work does not stand alone, the growth of behavioural economics and the related discipline of social psychology has had a real impact on public policy across many governments.[10]

Lowering costs and improving effectiveness

The cost of government includes the cost of welfare, the cost of spending on public services and the cost of failure in meeting social demands. Service users (who generally do not pay for the full cost of the public services they receive) want higher quality and more effective services, while taxpayers want services to be ever more cost-efficient. Following the biggest and most severe global recession, most advanced democracies are entering a period of austerity in respect of public spending.

Public sector retrenchment involves reducing the scope of public services. But if public services are to remain effective in delivering their core purposes, they will need to change their shape and not just their scope. Substantial service redesign is needed to reduce costs dramatically and, where feasible, to improve service effectiveness. Invoking big change is simple. Those politicians in government can simply pick a percentage – let's say, 25 per cent. This percentage reduction can then be applied to a very large service budget and those responsible for the service (the local political leaders or the relevant public sector managers) can simply get on with it as best they can. In some instances this crude invocation will reveal managerial entrepreneurship. For some public managers will redesign services, redeploy effort and marshal resources differently to achieve the same if not better outcomes. They can chase 'best practices' and seek innovative solutions.

But achieving changes that lower cost while sustaining service standards will not be easy. Many politicians and public managers will be seduced by the allure of investing in technology as a quick route to lowering costs and raising productivity. Technological change is an important ingredient in any attempt to lower costs but implemented poorly it may simply raise the cost of service delivery. In truth, innovation stems less from investment in technology and more from the diffusion of better business processes. Moreover, productivity growth is driven more by enhancing organizational capital through more focused business models, improved management practices and slicker operational processes.[11]

In terms of whole system redesign, there are three main ways forward to the reform of public services. The first involves smarter strategic collaboration between public agencies; the second is based upon on 'user directed change'; and the third is found in different forms of 'sponsored disruptive innovation'. Each of these three different ways forward can be used to lower costs; keep services relevant to dynamically changing needs; and ensure that they are responsive and valuable to their users. It is not a case of choosing between these three paths – they each offer promise in the differing and varied service domains that make up the public sector.

Smarter strategic collaboration

In this approach, all public agencies working within the same programme area (say across waste collection and waste disposal; or the whole criminal justice system) or public agencies within the same locality agree to align their strategies and their budgets to maximize their collective effectiveness and reduce overall costs to the taxpayer. This approach builds on two aspects of managerial economics. First, is the idea that services need to be organized at the right scale. Second, is the general sense that specialisms need to be better coordinated if costs are to be lowered and service outcomes improved. When the degree of coordination applied is strong, the tendency is for services to be integrated into a single management or within a combined system of management. When the degree of coordination applied is weak, the tendency is for services to operate within a self-regulated network under separate managements. The grouping or federating of schools, GP practices, further education colleges, hospitals and so on are all examples of different forms of strong or weak styles of coordination across organizational boundaries.

In trying to lower costs across agencies it is often suggested that, 'we need to get everyone involved in the same room redesigning everything together'. However this is rarely practicable. The combinatorial challenges involved in coordinating multiple goals and strategies across several agencies present enormous practical difficulties to achieving change quickly. Moreover, there is a problem in that costs are crystallized within the boundaries of public agencies whereas combined savings often occur across these agencies. This means that each public agency needs assurance that any savings accrued as a result of their combined action will sediment within the agencies commensurate to their efforts in achieving the aggregate savings.

User directed change

In this approach, the agent of change is the individual users purchasing services through direct payments, vouchers or some other form of direct involvement. In Britain, user directed change in personal social care (such as for people with learning disabilities) has successfully empowered thousands of otherwise highly dependent people and has also enabled the modernization of service delivery. And relative success in this ethically difficult and complex area suggests that user directed change offers wider promise in many other areas of public service delivery. It places a premium on relevant, responsive and reliable services to individuals in their use of public services. But it may also be beneficial in the delivery of services to larger groups of people. Leading-edge service users may well relish the notion of taking responsibility for directing change in a given service – enabling it to be delivered more efficiently and more effectively to all its users. Moreover, transferring public assets or facilities to community use groups (such as parks or community centres) may enable their cost to be lowered and their usage to be increased.

The difficulties in this approach are twofold. First, user directed change makes sense in areas where public services to individuals are relatively high cost and when public budgets can be offered directly to users for them to purchase service for themselves. It makes less sense when the cost of use is low or when it is more difficult to unpack the service for individual users. Second, the pace of change required by users is often faster than the capacity of service providers to change their organization. This means that while it offers the real prospect of being empowering to service users, it may result in high transition costs arising from the medium-term costs of service redundancy.

Sponsored disruptive innovation

This approach to public service reform is based on the idea that innovation is the fundamental key to major change in service delivery and that in some areas there is a real prospect of 'game changing' innovation. It is also based on the idea that the prevailing ecology of service provision (say, in the school system, or in the healthcare system) is a problem of itself. In some instances innovation stems from technological change; in other instances it is prompted by changes from existing ways of working (by front-line professionals, leading-edge service users and the like); whereas in yet other instances innovation is best sourced from outside the system: by new entrants or by substitute or replacement services.

Innovation is central to the reform of public services. In the private sector, innovation arises from competitive rivalry in the marketplace. Competition acts to lower the cost of products and services as well as to raise the productivity of service providers. But innovation in the public sector does not arise simply from competition. Instead, a range of different factors feed into the innovation process among public services. This deeply affects the character of innovation in the public sector. First, the dynamics of innovation differ between product innovation and service innovation. The public sector delivers few tangible products; hence process innovation is more relevant in the design and delivery of public services.[12] Second, it is widely acknowledged that the competencies that enable organizations to innovate successfully in one era often serve to hold them back from implementing new value propositions in the following era – this effect is termed the 'innovator's dilemma'.[13]

Third, if organizations are to be innovative they need to avoid organizational cultures of blame and instead develop cultures that foster creativity.[14] This can be difficult in the public sector as the requirements of political accountability often produce a personalized and captious approach to fault-finding that is not conducive to organizational learning. However, and fourthly, it remains the case that public service innovations can be based upon adopting many private sector practices that encourage user-centred innovation.[15] Importantly, innovation is not the application of a few new ideas. Above all it is a social process that relies on the gradual collision of ideas between people who are combining and recombining different approaches to solving practical problems. In both the private and the public sectors, multidisciplinary project teams used to be the crucible of innovation; the internet now serves as a worldwide crucible for innovation – powering innovation across organizational and disciplinary boundaries.[16]

In most advanced economies there is considerable scope for private sector companies and third sector organizations to take part in a more open ecology of public service provision. This would accelerate the pace of innovation in the supply market for any given service. For while there is a strong tradition of innovation within public sector agencies, this tradition is not as wide and deep as it ought to be – particularly given the pace of innovative change in the commercial world and in civic life generally. The application of social media models for service delivery, for example, is barely developed within the public sector. Again, the pace of change in this form of innovation may well be faster than that arising from smarter collaboration but, as with user directed change, the cost of transition may well be higher.

Public service reform is an exercise of perpetual motion; of discovering ever more effective ways of modernizing services and ever better approaches to achieving value for money and lowering costs. For much of the past four decades public services in mature democracies have innovated to be more effective – they now need to innovate to be more efficient, to lower their costs and raise their productivity. Ambitious governments start boldly but they often underestimate the institutional impediments to change and the professional protectionism and vested interests involved. They may start by working against one set of powerful vested interests but the changes they institute inevitably create another set of vested interests. Governments need to learn much more from international experience about how to reduce public spending,[17] how to reshape public sector organizations[18] and how to design public service systems that work for service users as well as for taxpayers.

Thimbles and forks

Over the past thirty years the politics of statecraft has, in very many democratic governments, become reduced to the craft of managing public services. To be fair, this has had positive effects. It has restrained the producer bias of many public services and it has sharpened their focus on achieving real service outcomes in health, education, social care, crime reduction and so on. But it could be said that politics, expressed as the collective values through which we govern ourselves, has shrivelled as a consequence.

There are two separate dangers posed by the scale of the public spending cuts currently being implemented by many democratic governments. First, some may argue that in making their states smaller they should also become more passive – only responding to cries of help. This would be wrong. Smaller states can be just as active as larger states – and, in fact, because they may be less tied to dealing day by day with the necessities of large-scale service provision, they may be more able to change how they help citizens. The second danger is that severe cutbacks may result in a redoubling of managerial approaches. Of course, good management is required to reduce the cost of the state but with substantial cutbacks in public spending the close involvement of elected politicians is unavoidable: their skills will be needed to orchestrate and stimulate public debates about the future of public services. Indeed, given the scale of the challenge, the existing tools and techniques for governing and managing are likely to be inappropriate for the 21st century.

In 1874, Lewis Carroll wrote the nonsense poem *The Hunting of the Snark*. The poem describes 'the impossible voyage of an improbable crew to find an inconceivable creature' by seeking it with thimbles, forks, railway-shares, smiles and soap.[19] After crossing a sea guided by a blank sheet of paper the hunting party of ten set off in all directions to find the Snark, although they had been warned that if the Snark turned out to be a Boojum they would softly and suddenly vanish away. In a foretaste of modern dilemmas the banker, who is one of the party, goes insane.

The poem ends in the discovery that after all the thrills and spills of the hunt, the Snark was a Boojum after all – as the baker who claims briefly to have found the Snark, disappears on finding it. There is little doubt that the hunting of the Snark was energizing and entertaining for those involved. Various implements and tools were used by the pursuers – although none seemed suitable for the quarry being pursued. The poem reminds us, among other things, of the truth that the pursuit of something doesn't of itself make the thing exist. It also reminds us that it is far easier to order a search for ideal solutions than it is practically feasible to discover them. The elaborate and costly chase of an elusive quarry may be worth the effort of the hunt. But if the quarry proves to be non-existent (from the Yeti to Big Foot and the Loch Ness monster) the whole exercise is rendered pointless.

The restless pursuit of the reform of government and public services may seem a bit like hunting the Snark. We seem forever tantalized by the prospect of discovering some 'best solution' to government and public service delivery. But just before we grasp at the solution it dissolves into thin air and more complex problems seem to appear. If we are pursuing some ideal form of government or public service then we are mistaken. Ideal forms cannot exist in the real world. We can simply create better ones than we have now. In this way we are pursuing an elusive quarry, we are not in pursuit of something that doesn't exist. Instead, our error is in our mistaken use of tools, particularly the tool of quantification.

In using the wrong tools we have missed the quarry completely and failed to reform government and public services. Instead, the tools that are needed to make our reforms a success include the concepts and ideas contained in this book. We should certainly not rely exclusively on measures; on so-called 'outcome indicators'; or on the 'evidence base'. We have become over-reliant on quantification, we have become over-impressed by aggregating uninformed opinion, we have become over-optimistic about the capacity of our measures to capture what is important in the government of our society, and we have become overconfident that the available evidence supports our prior beliefs. A disciplined approach to applying the wrong ideas will get us nowhere. The best tools we have are in our heads not in our hands. And the best of our efforts stem from our concern for others rather than our concern for things.

In a marvellous review of the impact of science on human progress, Peter Medawar wrote of the importance of always trying to 'effect all things possible'. Medawar was a self-styled 'meliorist' – a simple and practical philosophy that attempts at nothing more elaborate than making things better. He argued that Hobbes was right when in *Leviathan* he suggested that life was like a race which had no finishing post and that, 'the great thing about the race was to be in it, to be a contestant in the attempt to make the world a better place.'[20]

Not even wrong!

Trying to solve persistent public problems requires fresh policy and new initiatives. This usually results in attempts to influence, intervene or otherwise alter the fabric of social reality. This is the case whether it involves cycles of disadvantage within families or communities, or widespread criminal or anti-social behaviour among, say, young people. The impulse to speculate about what causes change in the social fabric of the world is a crucial component of what makes us human. As is the impulse to suggest how the social fabric of our world can be improved; how cycles of disadvantage can be broken; or how levels of youth crime can be dramatically reduced. However, this impulse to speculate can just as easily take the form of mysticism as rationalism.

I may be able to give reasons why I believe some government policy will work – and my reasoning may be plausible; but it may still be wrong. The web of probabilistic causation that underlies the social fabric of life renders most of our ideas hopelessly simplistic. They may even be mystical. In posing solutions to society's problems, politicians and policy professionals are equally prone to adopting approaches that suit their own prejudices rather than trial approaches based on open conjecture and reasoned experiment. This blinkered mentality has a powerful impact in the natural sciences. In the social sciences it is endemic.

The physicist Wolfgang Pauli was renowned for being a tough audience. He was one of the pioneers of quantum mechanics and his perfectionism as a thinker was legendary. He would regularly disclaim during lectures if he felt the speaker had made errors. He had three levels of criticism. First, he would say that an assertion was *falsch* – wrong. Second, he would claim it was *ganz falsch* – completely wrong. Finally, he would say it was *nicht einmal falsch* – not even wrong. An idea is 'not even wrong' if it is sufficiently incomplete that it cannot be used to explain something adequately or even make predictions that could be compared with observations to see if the idea is wrong. In science a 'theory' that makes no predictions, not even wrong ones, which explains nothing and which avoids the test of falsifiability is closer to mysticism than real science. Theories are powerful if they help us understand the world so as to predict it and change it. Theories that excite the mind but have no practical utility are best avoided. And yet so much of social policy falls into this trap – it is not even wrong.

In social policy, good intentions, in the form of political motive and professional zeal, can often overpower the careful exercise of reason. People often search for policy solutions that fit their view of humanity and their sense of the correct role of the state and of government. And when they do so, they often look for evidence to support the case for their preferred policy. It is understandable that those closest to the problem find it hardest to attain the necessary detachment and objectivity that is needed to test ideas in social policy. But rather than rely on assertions about 'common sense', it is preferable to develop testable social innovations and then to appraise them thoroughly and independently.

Persistent social problems are seldom solved by simple public policy interventions. Of course, it is easy to speculate about the causes of these social problems. And it may also be easy to speculate on the multiple causes of these causes. However, it is extraordinarily difficult to devise testable ideas about how best to alter the web of causation so as to solve these social problems. And yet that is why people are drawn to public life – to assure positive social results, to make positive social impact on the world and to achieve positive social goals.

We devise our best ideas, marshal the smartest resources available, craft our best policy instruments and shape our cleverest approaches to doing good in the world – and more often than not we find that we are 'not even wrong'. This is why it is enormously complex and intrinsically difficult to achieve real progress in solving important and urgent public problems. And it is also why solving these problems provides both the abiding attraction and the palpable reward for those pursuing a life of public service.

'Is everyone all right?'

The last words spoken by Bobby Kennedy soon after he was shot on the night of 4 June 1968 in the Ambassador Hotel ballroom in Los Angeles were, 'is everyone all right?' Through these four words Bobby Kennedy offers an evocative example of the public leader's deepest concern for the welfare of others. The selfless regard of and respect for our fellow human beings is the pinnacle of values-based public leadership. We know that this is so, for we recognize this trait in a few exceptional public leaders.

At the start of the 21st century we need to re-imagine government in the context of a hyper-connected and fast changing world. But we must do so in the context of known aspects of human frailty and error. We need to renew public service but we do so in the knowledge that service users seek active empowerment not passive dependency. The contours of government may be changing because the character of our time is changing. But the fundamentals of good government remain. It is so easy to get sidetracked away from achieving long-term goals by the urgent necessities of the moment. It is also so easy to be diverted from doing what is right but unpopular by the desire to be liked and admired.

Sustaining a stable moral reasoning when the world is changing fast may be difficult, but it is also vitally important. Moral reasoning helps to establish direction; it does not stop at measuring utility. Moral reasoning gives us a basis to define what we mean in practical terms when we talk about 'fairness'.

Eleven weeks before Bobby Kennedy uttered these fateful four words, he gave a brilliant speech to a university audience in Lawrence, Kansas, in which he said:

> We seem to have surrendered community excellence and community values in the mere accumulation of material things. ... if we should judge America by our gross national product we would count the special locks for our doors and the jails for those who break them. ... yet it does not allow for the health of our children, the quality of their education, or the joy of their play. It does not include the beauty of our poetry or the strength of our marriages, the intelligence of our public debate or the integrity of our public officials. It measures neither our wit nor our courage; neither our wisdom nor our learning; neither our compassion nor our devotion to our country; it measures everything, in short, except that which makes life worthwhile.[21]

This is a reminder that we should measure our progress with less certainty – for our happiness stems from our relationships with others and not from just the material well-being we have for ourselves. It also reminds us that we need to be clear about the difference between tools and goals. Too often our attempts at governmental and public sector reform have been to chase ideal goals. Pursuing ideal goals to governing and delivering public services is pointless when we need to attend to practical problems now. We need to focus on the urgent and important public problems of today and then set out to fix them.

We need to recognize that whereas competition is the discipline of the private sector, in the public sector the key discipline is public accountability – where public servants 'give an account' of how they have spent public money for best effect; and where they are 'held to account' for the overall performance of the public services they design and deliver. What's more, we need to go beyond simply refashioning the state, we need to revitalize the public realm. To do this we need to help communities develop both their civility and their civic literacy so that people may live more tolerably with each other and make their democracies function in a more open and healthy way.[22] Governing is a risky business in an uncertain world. To govern well requires detailed attention to the continual reform of public services and of democracy itself. But governing involves much more than dealing with the demands of the state. Governing is not just doing things fairly – it involves doing good for the public overall.

There is grandeur to the practice of democratic government. For despite their many flaws, democratic governments can achieve great things (at the national, city and local level). They are able to institute quite minor changes that nonetheless can have a major impact on society. They do so by extending freedoms, building capabilities and helping people to live peacefully together.[23] Open and plural democracies work best when they involve their citizens in their own governance and when they routinely hold their governments to account. Healthy democracies need critically enquiring media that seek the truth. They need politicians imbued with a sense of conviction, of reason and of proportion; they need public managers who are fuelled by a desire to solve a community's worst problems; and they need citizens to be engaged with each other on a voyage of civic discovery, finding common cause and shaping the future of their nations and communities together. But there is also a great simplicity to government – for the goal of good government is nothing more than public betterment. This simple grandeur of government needs to be re-imagined by new generations of public activists to shape a new public realm in the swirl and connectedness of the 21st century. Public service is a journey where we try to do no harm while trying to make things appreciably better. A practical journey yes, but a moral and noble one nonetheless.

Notes

Chapter 1

1 Lloyd, J. (2004) *What the Media are Doing to Our Politics*, London: Cotable and Robinson

2 There are many accounts of international democratic politics. Of these, Fareed Zakaria's *The Future of Freedom* is the most accessible. It describes the differing paths to democracy that different countries have taken. His main point is that illiberal democracy is more prevalent in the world than liberal democracy and that liberal nations need to recognize that other nations cannot have liberalism naively pasted onto them. Rather they need effective government, healthy political institutions and cultural conditions of pluralism and challenge. Zakaria, F. (2007) *The Future of Freedom*, New York: Norton

3 The connection between politics and capitalism is complex. It could well be the case that capitalism prompts political openness and democracy with a growing middle class demanding political change (bourgeois democracy to use Marx's somewhat pejorative term). After all, if you are free to buy what you want, why can't you be free to think and argue what you want?

4 Dunn, J. (2005) *Setting The People Free*, London: Atlantic, p. 16

5 Hind, D. (2010) *The Return of the Public*, London: Verso, p. 19

6 Pharr, S. and Putnam, R. (2000) *Disaffected Democracies*, Princeton: Princeton University Press

7 Duffy, B. et al. (2010) *One World, Many Places: Citizens' views of municipal government and local areas across the world*, London: Ipsos-Mori

8 Hayward, B. et al. (2008) *Survey of Public Attitudes towards Conduct in Public Life*, published by the Committee on Standards in Public Life, UK House of Commons

9 Bobbit, P. (2002) *The Shield of Achilles*, New York: Knopf

10 Duggan, W. (2007) *Strategic Intuition*, New York: Columbia Business School

11 Goldsmith, S. (2010) *The Power of Social Innovation*, San Francisco: Jossey-Bass

12 Hood, C. (1998) *The Art of the State*, Oxford: Oxford University Press

13 Christakis, N. and Fowler, J. (2010) *Connected*, London: Harper Press

14 Dunleavy, P. (2010) *The Future of Joined-up Public Services*, London: 2020 Public Services Trust

15 Jerome Kagan writes of the different ways of thinking between natural scientists, social scientists and those pursuing humanities. He refers to their different approaches to establishing 'truth' and the differing mental models they use. Those in humanities tend to use semantics; those in social science seek to use schematic models; while those in the natural sciences use mathematical models. Kagan, J. (2010) *The Three Cultures*, Cambridge: Cambridge University Press

16 Different approaches exist between the style and content of analysis of, say, biographers, constitutional historians and political journalists. In relation to two

different periods in US politics, see Sheshol, J. (1997) *Mutual Contempt*, New York: Norton; and Woodward, B. (2010) *The Obama Wars*, New York: Simon & Schuster. In relation to British politics in the Blair era, see Powell, J. (2010) *The New Machiavelli*, London: Bodley Head; Hennessey, P. (1988) *Whitehall*, London: Secker &Warburg; and Rawnsley, A. (2010) *The End of The Party*, London: Penguin

17 A nuanced and complex account of public servants acting as as 'principled agents', balancing their private interests with the broader interests of the public, was set out by Besley, T. (2006) *Principled Agents?* Oxford: Oxford UP. The more cynical perspective of public servants as motivated principally by self-interest stems largely from the 'public choice' school of political economy and was initially outlined in the work of Buchanan, J. and Tullock, G. (1962) *The Calculus of Consent*, Michigan: Ann Arbor

18 Michael Sandel, the American moral philosopher, quotes Kant on scepticism as follows: 'Scepticism is a resting place for human reason where it can reflect upon its dogmatic wanderings but it is no dwelling place for permanent settlement. Simply to acquiesce in scepticism can never suffice to overcome the restlessness of reason.' From Michael Sandel on TedTalks.com

19 The idea of 'requisite variety' stems from systems thinking – developed by W. Ross Ashby in 1956 in his *Introduction to Cybernetics*. In this he argued that if a system is to be stable, the number of states of its control mechanism must be greater than or equal to the number of states in the system being controlled. Put simply, he said, 'variety absorbs variety'. Its original conception by Ashby as a 'law' is an overstatement – but as a metaphor it is useful in explanatory terms

20 New Economics Foundation (2009) *National Accounts of Well-being*, available at www.nationalaccountsofwellbeing.org

21 Ingelhart, R. et al. (2008) 'Development, freedom, and rising happiness', *Perspectives on Psychological Science*, 3(4): 264–85

22 Westen, D. (2007) *The Political Brain*, New York: Public Affairs

23 Zajonc, D. (2004) *The Politics of Hope*, Austin: Synergy Books

24 Arguments between optimists and pessimists pervade political culture. Some of the most insightful accounts from the perspective of a cultural pessimist can be found in the work of John Gray. Gray, J. (2002) *Straw Dogs*, London: Grant Books

25 Seligman, M. (1990) *Learned Optimism*, New York: Knopf

Chapter 2

1 James Madison (1788) *Federalist No. 51*

2 Ellis, J. (1998) *American Sphinx*, New York: Vintage

3 Ellis, J. (2000) *Founding Brothers*, New York: Random House. There are very many sources on Madison, Hamilton and Jefferson. Ellis's account offers a marvellously accessible sketch of the deal struck between the three men; it also offers a compelling summary of the life of those at the heart of the American Revolutionary generation

4 IMF (2010) *World Economic Outlook: Rebalancing Growth*, April, International Monetary Fund

5   *Federalist No. 51* (1788) Madison was deeply influenced by European Enlight-enment thinkers. His rhetoric draws heavily on Voltaire's satire of uncritical optimism (in *Candide*); on Immanuel Kant's contention that humanity is composed of 'crooked timber'; and on David Hume's suggestion that those constitutionalists who design governments should consider those who seek power to be energized more by 'knavish' motives than 'knightly' intentions

6   Ackerlof, G. and Shiller, R. (2009) *Animal Spirits*, Princeton: Princeton University Press

7   Cicero (1993) *On Government*, London: Penguin Classics, p. 196. The transla-tion by Michael Grant combines two of Cicero's major works *On the State* and *On Laws* – the *salus populi* reference is found in the section from *On Laws* and refers to what ought to be the dominant preoccupations of those with civic lead-ership responsibilities

8   Moots, G. and Forster, G. (2010) '*Salus Populi Suprema Lex Esto*: John Locke versus contemporary democratic theory', *Perspectives on Political Science*, January–March, 39(1): 35–45

9   The '*salus populi*' motto was adopted by, among others, the City of Salford in Manchester and the London Borough of Lewisham

10   Bacon, N. et al. (2010) *The State of Happiness*, London: Young Foundation

11   Miller, P. (1994) *Defining the Common Good*, Cambridge: Cambridge University Press (quote on p. 421)

12   Nye, J. (2004) *Soft Power*, New York: Public Affairs

13   Garfinkel, I. et al. (2010) *Wealth and Welfare States: Is America a laggard or a leader?* Oxford: Oxford University Press

14   United Nations (2008) *World Population Prospects*, the 2008 revision medium forecast

15   Brooks, D. (2011) 'The achievement test', *New York Times*, 3 January 2011

16   Zürn, M. and Leibfried, S. (2005) 'Reconfiguring the national constellation', in S. Leibfried and M. Zürn (eds) *Transformations of the State?* Cambridge: Cambridge UP. Zurn and Leibfried comment on the transformation of TRUDI – the Territorial state, the Rule of law state, the Democratic state; and the Interven-tionist state

17   It is a measure of health inequalities in the world that, among others, sub-Saharan African countries are still concerned on an annual basis with the prevention of famine, while humans in the West simply get fatter. For a graphic explanation of these global disparities, visit Hans Rausling's work on variations in international life expectancy on TedTalks.com

18   Thaler, R. and Sunstein, C. (2008) *Nudge: Improving decisions about health, wealth, and happiness*, Boston, MA: Yale University Press

19   In 2000, the United Nations agreed Millennium Development Goals that among other things tried to halve the proportion of people living on less than $1.25 a day (at purchasing power parity). By 2008, progress had been made towards this target but the numbers of people at risk of falling into poverty had doubled. World Bank (2010) *Poverty Reduction and Equity*, worldbank.org

20   Fukuyama, F. (2004) *State Building: Governance and world order in the 21st century*, New York: Cornell University

21 Lijphart, A. (1977) *Democracy in Plural Societies: A comparative exploration*, New Haven: Yale University Press. Building from the case of the Netherlands and comparative political studies, Lijphart suggests that socially and culturally segmented societies will tend to eschew 'majoritarian' democratic approaches and instead develop consensus-based democracy through forms of power-sharing and veto arrangements

22 Weber, M. (1922) *Economy and Society*, Berkeley: University of California Press

23 Samuels, D. and Shugart, M. (2010) *Presidents, Prime Ministers and Parties*, Cambridge: Cambridge University Press

24 The 'reverse dominance hierarchy' stems from the groundbreaking work of social anthropologist Christopher Boehm who, from in-depth studies of primates, suggests that through evolution, egalitarianism developed as a collective group reaction to anyone's attempt to dominate his fellows. Boehm, C. (2001) *Hierarchy in the Forest: The evolution of egalitarian behavior,* Cambridge, MA: Harvard University Press

25 Stoker, G. (2006) *Politics Matters*, Basingstoke: Palgrave Macmillan, p. 202

26 Norris, P. (2002) *Democratic Phoenix: Reinventing political activism*, Cambridge: Cambridge University Press, p. 222

27 Prior, M. (2007) *Post-Broadcast Democracy*, Cambridge: Cambridge UP. Prior argues, among other things, that the media-rich environment in which elections are conducted serves to alter the extent and degree of involvement by voters in the electoral system, such that those who are engaged and participate have less moderate views than the electorate as a whole

28 Runciman, D. (2008) *Political Hypocrisy*, Woodstock, Oxfordshire: Princeton University Press

29 Lijphart, A. (1994) *Electoral Systems and Party Systems*, Oxford: Oxford University Press

30 Popper, K. (1999) *All Life is Problem Solving*, London: Routledge. This book contains an earlier paper (Chapter 8, pp. 93–8) written by Karl Popper that argues in favour of the US and UK two-party systems and against an electoral system of party-based proportional representation. Popper's case centres on the importance of the negative power of getting rid of a ruling government and sustaining a healthy opposition to its rule

31 Soroka, S. and Wlezian, C. (2010) *Degrees of Democracy*, Cambridge: Cambridge University Press

32 Mulgan, G. (2006) *Good and Bad Power*, London: Penguin/Allen Lane

33 *The Economist* (2010) 'A world of connections', 28 January

34 Stengel, R. (2010) 'Only connect', *Time*, 27 December, p. 37

35 Popper, K. (2003) *The Open Society and its Enemies: Volume 1 Plato*, London: Routledge (quote from the Preface to the 1950 edition, pp. xii–xiii)

36 Morozov, E. (2011) *The Net Delusion*, London: Allen Lane

37 Granovetter, M. (1983) 'The strength of weak ties: a network theory revisited', *Sociological Theory*, 1: 201–30

38 Wilson, J.Q. (1997) *The Moral Sense*, New York: Free Press Paperbacks

39 Purdy, J. (2000) *For Common Things*, New York: Vintage, pp. 84–5

40 Senge, P. et al. (1999) *The Dance of Change*, New York: Currency Doubleday

41 Mintzberg, H. (1994) *The Rise and Fall of Strategic Planning*, New York: Free Press
42 The phrase 'the art of the soluble' was used in relation to scientific research by Peter Medawar in (1967) *The Art of The Soluble*, London: Methuen
43 This quote is from Cleveland, H. (1972) *The Future Executive*, New York: Harper & Row. An appreciation of the contemporary import of Cleveland's work is found in Frederickson, G. (2005) 'Whatever Happened to Public Administration?', in E. Ferlie et al. (2005) *Oxford Handbook of Public Management,* Oxford: Oxford UP. Frederickson builds on the earlier work of Cleveland, who first coined the term 'governance' by describing 'plural, inter-jurisdictional, and inter-organizational mediated decision making networks of public executives operating in the context of blurred distinctions between public and private organizations'

Chapter 3

1 Kevin Hines' personal story is summarized on YouTube.com where a nine-minute shortened feature of the documentary *The Bridge* is available
2 For details of Golden Gate Bridge's governance, management and budget, visit www.goldengatebridge.org
3 Best, J. (2008) *Social Problems*, New York: Norton
4 Bryson, J. and Crosby, B. (1992) *Leadership for the Common Good: Tackling problems in a shared-power world*, San Francisco: Jossey-Bass (quote on p. xi)
5 The term 'wicked issues' or 'wicked problems' has been used for several years – its uses stem from an academic paper by Rittel, H. and Webber, M. (1973) 'Dilemmas in a general theory of planning', *Policy Sciences*, 4: 155–69, Elsevier Scientific Publishing Company, Amsterdam
6 Johansson, F. (2006) *The Medici Effect*, Boston: Harvard Business School Press
7 Goodin, R. et al. (2008) 'The public and its policies', in M. Moran et al., *The Oxford Handbook of Public Policy*, Oxford University Press (quote on p. 28)
8 Moore, M. (1995) *Creating Public Value*, Cambridge, MA: Harvard University Press
9 Osborne, D. and Gaebler, T. (1993) *Reinventing Government*, New York: Plume
10 Cole, M. and Parston, G. (2006) *Unlocking Public Value*, Hoboken, NJ: John Wiley & Sons
11 Kelly, G. et al. (2002) *Creating Public Value*, Cabinet Office Strategy Unit, UK Government
12 This public value approach was used by the BBC in 2004 as an element in its campaign to renew its Charter from the British government. It was also used by both the Metropolitan Police and the Royal Opera House to devise metrics about citizen satisfaction and confidence. It was subsequently developed by the Work Foundation in a paper in 2006, *Deliberative Democracy and the Role of Public Managers,* based on its research across a number of public agencies on how public managers seek to reveal public policy preferences. The centre for management education on public value in the UK (which complements the work being undertaken at the JFK School of Government at Harvard) is at Warwick University

13   Rawls, J. (2000) *The Law of Peoples with The Idea of Public Reason Revisited*, Cambridge, MA: Harvard University Press

14   Clifford, W.K. (1999) *The Ethics of Belief and Other Essays*, Prometheus Books (originally published 1877)

15   James, W. (1956) *The Will to Believe and other essays in popular philosophy*, Mineola, NY: Dover Publications (originally published 1897)

16   Blackburn, S. (2006) *Truth*, London: Penguin

17   The most developed argument for public consent as a prime aim of rational public discourse is found in the work of Jurgen Habermas (1984) *The Theory of Communicative Action*. Vol I: *Reason and the Rationalization of Society*, T. McCarthy (trans.) Boston: Beacon

18   Reschler, N. (1992) *Pluralism: Against the demands for consensus*, Oxford: Oxford University Press

19   Sen, A. (2009) *The Idea of Justice*, London: Allen Lane (quote from p. xviii)

20   Ibid. (quote from p. 16)

Chapter 4

1   Quirk, B. (2007a) *Making Assets Work*, Dept for Communities and Local Government, London: TSO

2   Blond, P. (2010) *The Ownership State*, London: Nesta

3   Phillips, A. and Taylor, B. (2010) *On Kindness*, London: Penguin

4   Smith, A. (2009) *The Theory of Moral Sentiments*, London: Penguin, see Section I, Chapter II on the 'pleasure of mutual sympathy'; and Section II, Chapter IV on the 'social passions'

5   Cooperation stems from kin-based concerns. It then develops into self-interested reciprocal altruism – where cheaters are punished and cooperation arises from sustained relationships with people whom you grow to trust. These ideas derive from theoretical work in biology and evolutionary psychology. Trivers, R. (2002) *Natural Selection and Social Theory*, Oxford: Oxford University Press; Sober, E. and Wilson, D. (1999) *Unto Others: The evolution and psychology of unselfish behavior*, Cambridge, MA: Harvard University Press; Dugatkin, L. (2006) *The Altruism Equation*, Princeton: Princeton University Press. For an account of the tragic life and brilliant work of George Price, who devised an algorithm of altruism, see Harman, O. (2010) *The Price of Altruism*, London: The Bodley Head

6   Neuroscientists have discovered that cells in the brain that fire when you poke the patient with a needle ('pain neurons'), will also fire when the patient watches *another* patient being poked. These 'mirror neurons' would seem to dissolve the barrier between self and others and offer a biological explanation of empathy and fellow feeling. Ramachandran, V.S. (2003) *The Emerging Mind*, London: Profile Books

7   The evolutionary anthropologist and primatologist Robin Dunbar has computed a fascinating inference from the relative ratio of the neocortex and the social group size of primates that the optimum groups size for humans is about 150 people. He then supports this with a series of empirical observations about functioning group size among modern humans. Dunbar, R. (1996) *Grooming, Gossip*

and the Evolution of Language, London, Faber & Faber; Dunbar, R. (2010) 'The magic number', *RSA Journal*, Spring 2010, pp. 16–19

8   The argument that reciprocity is not simply a positive predisposition to cooperate with others but also requires the appropriate punishment of those who violate the norms of cooperation was made in the 1980s by Robert Trivers, the evolutionary biologist. Trivers, R.L. (1985) *Social Evolution*, Menlow Park, CA: Benjamin/Cummings. These ideas are developed in full in Hauser, M. (2006) *Moral Minds*, London: Abacus

9   Arrow, K. (1974) *The Limits of Organization*, New York: Norton

10 Seabright, P. (2004) *The Company of Strangers: A natural history of economic life*, Princeton, NJ: Princeton University Press

11 Quirk, B. (2007b) 'Roots of cooperation and routes to collaboration', in S. Parker and N. Gallagher (eds) *Our Collaborative Future*, London: Demos, pp. 48–60

12 Schelling, T. (1978) *Micromotives and Macrobehavior*, New York: Norton

13 Putnam, R. (1993) *Making Democracy Work: Civic traditions in modern Italy*, Princeton, NJ: Princeton University Press

14 Portes, A. (2000) 'The two meanings of social capital', *Sociological Forum*, 15: 1–12

15 Burke, E. (1790) *Reflections on the Revolution in France*, Boston, MA: The Harvard Classics, para. 75

16 Thaler, R. and Sunstein, C. (2008) *Nudge: Improving decisions about health, wealth, and happiness*, Boston: Yale University Press. This book stimulated considerable coverage on libertarian paternalism and behaviour change techniques for public service purposes, although there are very many other excellent examples of 'how to' advice from think tanks. These included: Prendergrast, J. et al. (2008) *Creatures of Habit: The art of behaviour change,* The Social Market Foundation; and *The Capital Ambition Guide to Behaviour Change* (2010) The Young Foundation.org.uk

17 Ridley, M. (2002) *The Origins of Virtue*, London: Penguin; Olson, M. (1965) *The Logic of Collective Action*, Cambridge, MA: Harvard University Press; Hardin, G. (1968) 'The tragedy of the commons', *Science*, 162: 1234–8; Platt, J. (1973) 'Social traps', *American Psychologist*, 28: 641–51

18 If you do go for a meal with strangers, it's perhaps best if you first read Uri Gneezy et al. (2004) 'The inefficiency of splitting the bill', *Economic Journal*, 114(495): 265–80 … an economics study of a restaurant setting in which groups of diners are faced with different ways of paying the bill. The two options are splitting the bill between the diners and having each pay individually. Gneezy et al. found that subjects consume more when the cost is split, resulting in a substantial loss of efficiency. Diners prefer the individual pays to the split-bill method. When forced to play according to a less preferred set of rules, they minimize their individual losses by taking advantage of others

19 Olson, M. (1965), op. cit.

20 Hardin, G. (1968), op. cit.

21 Tomasselo, M. (2009) *Why We Cooperate*, Boston: Massachusetts Institute of Technology, p. 21

22 Axelrod, R. (1984) *The Evolution of Cooperation*, New York: Basic Books

23 Ostrom, E. (1990) *Governing the Commons*, New York: Cambridge University Press

24 Putnam, R. (1993) *Making Democracy Work: Civic traditions in modern Italy*, Princeton: Princeton UP; and Putnam, R. (2002) *Democracy in Flux: Social capital in contemporary societies*, Princeton: Princeton UP

25 Rothstein, B. (2005) *Social Traps and the Problem of Trust*, Cambridge: Cambridge University Press

26 Riesman, D., Glazer, N. and Denney, R. (1950) *The Lonely Crowd*, New Haven: Yale University Press

27 Sennett, R. (2003) *Respect*, London: Allen Lane, p. 3

28 Buonfino, A. and Mulgan, G. (2009) *Civility Lost and Found*, London: Young Foundation

29 Bauman, Z. (2001) *Community*, Oxford: Blackwell, p. 71

30 *Financial Times*, 23 December 2010, 'Blow to Cameron's vision of Big Society'

31 Blackburn, R. (1998) *Ruling Passions*, Oxford: Clarendon

32 Bandura, A. (1997) *Self-Efficacy*, New York: WW Freeman, p. 489

33 Hamilton, A. (2008) *The Revolutionary Writings of Alexander Hamilton*, Indianapolis: Liberty Fund, p. 11

34 Sacks, J. (2007) *The Home We Build Together*, London: Continuum

Chapter 5

1 White, J. (2007) *London in the Nineteenth Century*, London: Jonathon Cape

2 Comte-Sponville, A. (2002) *A Short Treatise on the Great Virtues*, London: Vintage

3 John Stuart Mill did more than follow in Bentham's footsteps; he was rigorously educated by his father to lead a life based on strict adherence to Benthamite principles. Reeves, R. (2009) *John Stuart Mill: Victorian firebrand*, London: Atlantic Books

4 Sandel, M. (2009) *Justice*, London: Allen Lane

5 This list of five principles draws on, King, I. (2008) *How to Make Good Decisions and Be Right All the Time*, London: Continuum

6 Damasio, A. (2000) *The Feeling of What Happens*, London: Vintage

7 Kahneman, D. and Tervsky, A. (1979) 'Prospect Theory: An analysis of decision under risk', *Econometrica*, 47: 263–91; Kahneman, D., Slovic, P., and Tversky, A. (eds) (1982) *Judgment Under Uncertainty: Heuristics and Biases*, New York: Cambridge University Press; Piatelli-Palmarini, M. (1994) *Inevitable Illusions: How mistakes of reason rule our minds*, New York: John Wiley & Sons

8 Finkelstein, S., Whitehead, J. and Campbell, A. (2008) *Think Again: How good leaders make bad decisions and how to keep it from happening to you*, Boston, MA: Harvard Business Press

9 Gerstein, M. and Ellsberg, M. (2008) *Flirting with Disaster: Why accidents are rarely accidental*, New York: Union Square

10 Although this disaster attracted much comment and attention, the causes of the BP Deepwater Horizon blowout have yet to be fully explained. The well is located in 5000 ft of water some 50 miles from the coast of Louisiana, although the depth of the well was a further 13,000 below the sea floor (not unusually

deep). The ultimate cause may prove to be that the well plan did not have suffi-cient cement between its casings – a technical design failing more than a case of incaution on the part of the BP, who created a £20bn fund to pay for damages caused by the oil spill. *Financial Times*, 13 August 2010; for technical analysis see www.oildrum.com

11   Simon, H. (1957) 'A behavioral model of rational choice', in his *Models of Man, Social and Rational*, New York: Wiley
12   Lehrer, J. (2009) *The Decisive Moment*, Edinburgh: Canongate
13   Schwartz, B. (2004) *The Paradox of Choice*, New York: HarperCollins
14   Schofield, P. (2006) *Utility and Democracy: The political thought of Jeremy Bentham*, Oxford: Oxford University Press
15   Bachrach, P. and Baratz, M. (1962) 'Two faces of power', *The American Political Science Review* (December) 56(4): 947–52
16   Sen, A. (2010) *The Idea of Justice*, London: Allen Lane
17   Skinner, Q. (2008) *Hobbes and Republican Liberty*, Cambridge: Cambridge University Press
18   James Fishkin is professor at the Center for Deliberative Democracy at Stanford University
19   Dunn, J. (2005) *Setting The People Free*, London: Atlantic, pp. 62–3
20   The ideas behind these examples and the reference to Borda, Condorcet and Kenneth Arrow's work stems from Sen, A. (2002) *Rationality and Freedom*, London: Belknapp/Harvard
21   Isaacs, W. (1999) *Dialogue and the Art of Thinking Together*, New York: Currency
22   Hibbing, J. and Theiss-Morse, E. (2002) *Stealth Democracy*, Cambridge: Cambridge University Press
23   Popper, K. (1945) *The Open Society and its Enemies Vol II*, London: Routledge & Kegan Paul, p. 225
24   Quirk, B. (2008) *The Art of Advice Giving*, London: Solace at www.solace.org.uk

Chapter 6

1   For national and urban population statistics see www.citypopulation.de; UN Habitat (2008) *State of the World's Cities 2008/9*, United Nations, Nairobi: Earthscan
2   Schama, S. (1995) *Landscape and Memory*, London: HarperCollins
3   Information on the cultural offer of the conurbation is available at www.newcastlegateshead.com
4   *Financial Times,* 18 March 2010, 'Nissan to build plug-in car in UK'
5   Information on the economic and labour market trends in the north-east of England can be found on the regional development agency website: www.onenortheast.co.uk
6   Ackroyd, P. (2008) *Thames: Sacred River*, London: Vintage
7   Friedman, T. (2000) *The Lexus and the Olive Tree*, New York: Anchor Books
8   Hudson-Smith, A. et al. (2008) *Mapping for the Masses: Accessing web2.0 through Crowdsourcing*, Working Paper Series 143, Centre for Advanced Spatial Analysis, UCL: London

9   Fukuyama, F. (1992) *The End of History and the Last Man*, New York: Avon Books

10   Huntington, S. (1997) *The Clash of Civilizations and the Remaking of the World Order*, London: Simon & Schuster

11   Möisi, D. (2008) *The Geopolitics of Emotion*, New York: Doubleday

12   Quirk, B. (2006) 'The three 'Rs': respect, reason and rights', London: Solace Foundation Imprint, *Complexity and Cohesion*, December, pp. 21–34

13   Besley, T. and Coate, S. (2003) 'Centralized versus decentralized provision of local public goods: a political economy approach', *Journal of Public Economics*, 87: 2611–37

14   'Occam's razor' is the principle that the simplest explanation is usually the correct one. Simplest is not defined by the time or number of words it takes to express the theory; it is referring to the theory with the fewest new assumptions

15   Barrow, J. (1992) *Theories of Everything*, London: Vintage, pp. 194–5

16   De Blij, H. (2009) *The Power of Place*, Oxford: Oxford University Press, p. 3

17   Jacobs, J. (1969) *The Economy of Cities*, New York: Random House

18   Glaeser, E. et al. (2001) 'Consumer city', *Journal of Economic Geography*, 1: 27–50

19   Florida, R. (2002) *The Rise of the Creative Class*, New York: Basic Books

20   Storper, M. and Scott, A. (2009) 'Rethinking human capital, creativity and urban growth', *Journal of Economic Geography*, 9: 147–67

21   Glaeser, E. (2011) *The Triumph of the City*, London: Penguin

22   Florida, R. (2007) *Who's Your City*, New York: Basic Books

23   Bacon, N. et al. (2010) *The State of Happiness*, London: Young Foundation

24   Duffy, B. and Chan, D. (2009) *People, Perceptions and Place*, London: Ipsos-Mori

25   Duffy, B. et al. (2010) *One World, Many Places: Citizens' views of municipal government and local areas across the world*, London: Ipsos-Mori

26   The radical human geographer Danny Dorling suggests that there are five myths used by the powerful to propagate injustice and to foster its passive acceptance. These are: elitism is efficient; exclusion is necessary; prejudice is natural; greed is good; and despair is inevitable. Dorling, D. (2010) *Injustice: Why social inequalities persist*, Bristol: Policy Press

27   Dobbs, R. et al. (2011) *Urban World: Mapping the economic power of cities*, McKinsey Global Institute, available at www.mckinsey.com

28   Rentfrow, P., Gosling, S. and Potter, J. (2008) 'A theory of the emergence, persistence, and expression of geographic variation in personality traits', *Perspectives on Psychological Science*, 3: 339–69

29   Oguz, S. and Knight, J. (2010) 'Regional economic indicators', *Economic & Labour Market Review*, (4)2: 31–50, available at www.statistics.gov.uk

30   Harvey, D. (2010) *The Enigma of Capital*, London: Profile Books, p. 148

Chapter 7

1   DCSF statistical returns on referrals, assessments and child protection plans for each local authority are available at the DCSF website (reference SFR22/2009).

The figures used for the East Midlands city are those reported for Leicester City Council in the year 2008–9

2   Deming, W.E. (2000) *The New Economics for Industry, Government, Education* (2nd edn), Cambridge, MA: MIT Press; Collins, J. (2001) *Good to Great*, New York: HarperCollins

3   Kolb, D. (1984) *Experiential Learning: Experience as the source of learning and development*, Englewood Cliffs, NJ: Prentice Hall

4   Honey, P. and Mumford, A. (1986) Learning Styles Questionnaire, available at www.peterhoney.com

5   Senge, P. et al. (2005) *Presence: An exploration of profound change in people, organisations and society*, London: Nicholas Brearly

6   Fermi's lesson about random chance and the power of retrospective bias is told in Carl Sagan's (1995) *The Demon-Haunted World*, London: Headline, p. 201

7   Kelman, S. et al. (2009) *Successfully Executing Ambitious Strategies in Government: An empirical analysis*, Faculty Research Working Paper 09-009, Harvard Kennedy School

8   The seminal works on management written from within a managerial perspective are by Drucker, P. (1954) *The Practice of Management*, New York: Harper Business; and Handy, C. (1976) *Understanding Organisations*, Harmondsworth: Penguin

9   Quirk, B. (2003) 'Local government: The adaptive tier of governance', in T. Bentley and J. Wilsdon (eds) *The Adaptive State*, London: Demos

10   Dive, B. (2008) *The Accountable Leader*, London: Kogan Page

11   Grint, K. (2005) *Leadership: Limits and possibilities*, London: Palgrave Macmillan

12   Mintzberg, H. (2009) *Managing*, Harlow: Pearson

13   Giuliani, R. (2002) *Leadership*, London: Time Warner

14   Heifetz, R. and Linsky, M. (2002) *Leadership on the Line*, Boston, MA: Harvard Business School Press

15   Adapted from the work of Beckhard, R. and Pritchard, W. (1992) *Changing the Essence*, San Francisco: Jossey-Bass

16   Lawrence, P. and Nohria, N. (2002) *Driven: How human nature shapes our choices*, San Francisco: Jossey-Bass

17   Thomas, K. (2000) *Intrinsic Motivation at Work*, San Francisco: Berrett-Koehler

18   Pearce, T. (2003) *Leading Out Loud: Inspiring change through authentic communication*, San Francisco: Jossey-Bass

19   Kanter, R.M. (2004) *Confidence*, New York: Random House

20   Bandura, A. (1997) *Self-Efficacy: The exercise of control*, New York: W H Freeman & Co

21   Kouzes, J. and Posner, B. (1993) *Credibility*, San Francisco: Jossey-Bass; Kouzes, J. and Posner, B. (1995) *The Leadership Challenge*, San Francisco: Jossey-Bass; and Kouzes, J. and Posner, B. (1999) *Encouraging the Heart*, San Francisco: Jossey-Bass

22   Zohar, D. and Marshall, I. (2004) *Spiritual Capital*, San Francisco: Berrett-Koehler

23   Goleman, D. (1995) *Emotional Intelligence*, New York: Random House

24 Mulgan, G. (2009) *The Art of Public Strategy*, Oxford: Oxford University Press, p. 13

25 Rainey, H. (2009) *Understanding and Managing Public Organizations*, San Francisco: Jossey-Bass

26 Quirk, B. (2005b) 'The welfare of the people above all', in *What is Public Management For?*, London: Public Policy & Management Association

27 Collins, J. (2005) *Good to Great and the Social Sectors*, Boulder, CO: Jim Collins

28 Gardner, H. (2007) *Five Minds for the Future*, Boston, MA: Harvard Business Press

29 Pimlott, B. and Rao, N. (2002) *Governing London*, Oxford: Oxford University Press, p. 16, referencing Yates, D. (1977) *The Ungovernable City: The politics of urban problems and policy-making*, Cambridge, MA: MIT Press

30 Frederickson, H.G. (2005) *The Adaptive City*, New York: ME Sharpe; and Svara, J. and Associates (1994) *Facilitative Leadership in Local Government: Lessons from successful mayors and chairpersons*, San Francisco: Jossey-Bass

31 Hale, S.J. (1996) 'Achieving high performance in public organizations', in J. Perry (ed.) *Handbook of Public Administration* (2nd edn) San Francisco: Jossey-Bass

32 Barsh, J. et al. (2008) *Centred Leaders: How talented women thrive*, available at www.mckinsey.com

33 According to British economist and 'happiness guru' Richard Layard, people's reported happiness scores are lower when they are with their boss than when they are with anyone else. They are even happier being alone than when they spend their time with their boss! Layard, R. (2005) *Happiness: Lessons from a new science*, London: Allen Lane, p. 16

34 Ghoshal, S. and Moran, P. (2005) 'Towards a good theory of management', in J. Birkinshaw and G. Piramal (eds) *Sumantra Ghoshal on Management*, Harlow: Pearson

Chapter 8

1 'Mexican schools shut as epidemic hits critical point', *Washington Post*, 28 April 2009

2 'La Gloria at centre of "cover up claims" over cause of swine flu', *The Times*, 3 May 2009

3 Ibsen, H. (1882) *Enemy of the People*, www.bibliobazaar/opensource

4 'Flu outbreak raises a set of questions', *New York Times*, 26 April 2009

5 'Swine flu: country by country', *BBC News*, data from the World Health Organization and the European Centre for Disease Prevention and Control

6 '"Lucky break" in swine flu fight', *BBC News*, Thursday 8 October 2009

7 Laurence, J. (2010) 'A Little Knowledge', *The Independent*, 3 May 2010, pp. 16–17

8 BBC news website (12 January 2010) 'World Health Organization to review swine flu response'

9 *The Guardian* (28 March 2010) 'WHO accused of losing public confidence over flu pandemic'

10   *The Economist* (2010) 'Chins Up, Hopes High', 26 August, London print edition
11   Teague, B. et al. (2010) *Final Report 2009 Victorian Bushfires Royal Commission*, Victoria, July 2010
12   Beck, U. (1992) *The Risk Society: Towards a new modernity*, London: Sage
13   Sparrow, M.K. (2008) *The Character of Harms: Operational challenges in control*, Cambridge: Cambridge UP. Malcolm Sparrow makes a strong case that the nature of the control task in 'sabotaging' harms as well as controlling and mitigating harms and hazards presents particular challenges to public sector managers
14   HM Government (2009) *Pursue, Prevent, Protect, Prepare: The UK strategy for countering international terrorism*, London: TSO
15   Fox, J. and Zawitz, M. (2010) *Homicide Trends in the United States*, Washington, DC: Dept of Justice, Bureau of Justice Statistics
16   Reason, J. (2000) 'Human Error: Models and management', *BMJ Digest*, 172(June): 393–6
17   Gardner, H. (2009) *Risk: The science and politics of fear*, London: Virgin Books
18   Gigerenzer, G. (2002) *Reckoning with Risk*, London: Penguin
19   Mandelbrot, B. and Hudson, R. (2008) *The (Mis)Behaviour of Markets*, London: Profile, p. 124
20   Mintzberg, H. (1994) *The Rise and Fall of Strategic Planning*, New York: Free Press
21   Clausewitz, C. (1997) *On War*, Ware, Hertfordshire: Wordsworth Editions Ltd
22   Jomini, Baron A. (1836) *The Art of War*, special edition, translated in 2005 by G. Mendell and W. Craighill, El Paso Texas: El Paso Norte Press
23   Duggan, W. (2007) *Strategic Intuition*, Columbia Business School
24   Taleb, N.N. (2007) *Black Swan: The impact of the highly improbable*, London: Allen Lane
25   Hood, C., Rothstein, H. and Baldwin, R. (2004) *The Government of Risk: Understanding risk regulation regimes*, Oxford: Oxford University Press
26   Sparrow, M.K. (2008) *The Character of Harms*, op. cit., pp. 67–8
27   National Audit Office (2000) *Supporting Innovation: Managing risk in government departments*, London: TSO

Chapter 9

1   *The Times*, 'Woolworths to close all stores by January', 17 December 2008
2   *The Economist*, 'Hard Sell, Hard Times', 11 December 2008
3   Plunkett-Powell, K. (1999) *Remembering Woolworths: A nostalgic history of the world's most famous five-and-dime*, New York: St Martins Press
4   *Financial Times*, 'Woolworths left to wonder what went wrong', 26 November 2008, Tom Braithwaite
5   *Financial Times*, 'Seeds of Woolworths demise sown long ago', 29 November 2008, Elizabeth Rigby
6   Collins, J. (2009) *How the Mighty Fall*, New York: Random House
7   Blanchard, O. and Milesi-Ferretti, M. (2009) *Global Imbalances: in midstream?* IMF Staff Position Note, 22 December, International Monetary Fund
8   Augar, P. (2009), *Chasing Alpha*, London: Bodley Head

9   Mandelbrot, B. and Hudson, R. (2008) *The (mis)Behaviour of Markets*, London: Profile Books

10   Krugman, P. (2008) *The Return of Depression Economics and the Crisis of 2008*, London: Penguin (quote from p. 182)

11   Besley, T. and Hennessy, P. (2009) *Open Letter to HM Queen*, 22 July, British Academy

12   This phrase was used by Sir Peter Medawar in his devastating critique of *The Phenomenon of Man* by the theologian and geologist, Pierre Teilhard de Chardin; it seems highly applicable to the investment banking sector in the circumstances of 2008–9

13   Taylor, M. (2009) 'Reflections on the Crunch', *Prospect*, 23 July, issue 161

14   *Financial Times*, 'Goldman versus the regulators', 18 April 2010, P. Jenkins and F. Guerrera

15   National Audit Office (2009) *Maintaining Financial Stability across the United Kingdom's Banking System*, London: TSO

16   *Financial Times*, 'Ditch theory and take away the punchbowl', 6 August 2009, John Plender

17   The most comprehensive account of the history of financial collapse following excessive debt accumulation is found in Reinhart, C. and Rogoff, K. (2009) *This Time is Different*, Princeton: Princeton UP; a shorter summary of the argument set out in this book is available online at Reinhart, C. and Rogoff, K. (2008) *The Aftermath of Financial Crises*, available at www.economics.harvard.edu/files/faculty/51_Aftermath.pdf

18   Perhaps the most radical interpretation of the causes and consequences of the Crunch is found in the work of the British geographer David Harvey. Harvey, D. (2010) *The Enigma of Capital*, London: Profile Books

19   John Gieve, the former deputy governor of the Bank of England, was quoted in *The Observer* (8 August 2010) saying that, 'Of course the credit crunch is leading to lots of changes and we haven't seen them all yet. But in two big respects, I don't think it changed the world. First, the speed of globalization, the integration of the global economy, including finance, is continuing; and second, it is continuing around broadly a free-market model. … Capitalism is still the only game in town.'

20   Kaletsky, A. (2010) *Capitalism 4.0*, London: Bloomsbury

21   Koo, R. (2009) *The Age of Balance Sheet Recessions*, Tokyo: Nomura Research Institute

22   In Japan, some 60 per cent of public spending is through local government and an IMF study of the Japanese experience of fiscal stimulus in the 1990s concluded that the public investment multipliers for local government were higher than those of the central government: Brückner, M. and Tuladhar. A. (2010) *Public Spending as a Fiscal Stimulus: Evidence from Japan's regional spending during the 1990s*, IMF Working Paper 10,110, IMF.org

23   Reports from the Jackson Hole conference in Kansas, *Financial Times*, 28 August 2010

24   The Audit Commission report, *When it Comes to the Crunch* (August, 2009) describes three waves of impact on public services: economic, social, longer term and unequal recovery

25   'Public finances, daunted by deficits', *Financial Times*, 22 June 2010

26 McCrae, J. et al. (2009) *Undertaking a Fiscal Consolidation*, London: Institute for Government

27 *The Economist*, 'Rescuing the Rescuers', 29 May 2010, pp. 76–9

28 *The Economist*, 'The President's Deficit Commission', 13 November 2010, p. 56

29 *Daily Telegraph*, 'Advance guard of angry women lead Italians into European protests over austerity cuts', 29 May 2010

30 Blommestein, H. et al. (2010) 'Debt Markets: policy challenges in the post-crisis landscape', *OECD Journal Financial Market Trends*, 1: 1–27

31 *Financial Times*, 'Spanish deficit falls as austerity bites', 21 December 2010

32 Institute for Fiscal Studies, special report on public spending, November 2010, available on www.solace.org.uk

33 Osborne, D. and Hutchinson, P. (2004) *The Price of Government*, New York: Basic Books, pp. 56–7

34 Hood, C. (2010) *Reflections on Public Service Reform in a Cold Fiscal Climate*, London: 2020 Public Services Trust

35 Zimmer, R. et al. (2010) *Report of the New Jersey Privatization Task Force*, State of New Jersey

36 Gershon, P. (2004) *Releasing Resources to the Front Line*, HM Treasury, London: TSO

37 Green, P. (2010) *Efficiency Review*, HM Treasury, London: TSO

Chapter 10

1 Flynn, N. (2007) *Public Sector Management* (5th edn) London: Sage

2 Quirk, B. (2005a) 'Localising efficiency – more than just saving money, *Local Government Studies*, 31(5): 615–25

3 Deming, W.E. (2000) *The New Economics for Industry, Government, Education* (2nd edn) Cambridge, MA: MIT Press

4 Womack, J. et al. (2007) *The Machine that Changed the World*, London: Simon & Schuster; Womack, J. and Jones, D. (2003) *Lean Thinking*, London: Simon & Schuster

5 Seddon, J. (2008) *Systems Thinking in the Public Sector*, Axminster: Triarchy Press; and Seddon, J. (2010) *Delivering Public Services that Work*, Axminster: Triarchy Press

6 Six Sigma originated in the Motorola company; it is focused on minimizing variability in manufacturing and business processes through statistical control measures. Although heavily marketed as a business management strategy, it is more simply a quality improvement process

7 Collins, J. (2001) *Good to Great*, New York: HarperCollins; Collins, J. (2005) *Good to Great and the Social Sectors*, Monograph, Boulder, CO: Jim Collins

8 Lysons, K. and Farrington, B. (2005) *Purchasing and Supply Chain Management* (7th edn) London: FT Pearson

9 Brynjolfsson, E. and Saunders, A. (2009) *Wired: How information technology is reshaping the economy*, Cambridge, MA: MIT Press

10 Bossidy, L. and Charan, R. (2002) *Execution: The discipline of getting things done*, New York: Random House

11 CIPFA (2009) *Public Library Statistics: 2008–9 estimates and 2007–8 actuals*, London: CIPFA
12 Home Office (2010) *Police Service Strength*, HO Statistical Bulletin, 28 January, London
13 Rix, A. et al. (2009) *Improving Public Confidence in the Police: A review of available evidence*, Research Report 28 (2nd edn) London: Home Office
14 Leadbeater, C. (2008) *We-Think*, London: Profile Books
15 Design Council (2009) *The Role of Design in Public Services*, http://www.designcouncil.org.uk
16 Hutton, W. (2010) *Fair Pay in the Public Sector*, Interim Report, HM Treasury: TSO
17 Porter, M. (1980) *Competitive Strategy*, New York: Free Press
18 Hodge, G. (2000) *Privatization: An international review of performance*, Boulder, CO: Westview
19 The case for a more sophisticated approach to productivity measurement in the public sector was outlined in Aldred, J. (2009) *The Skeptical Economist*, London: Earthscan

Chapter 11

1 Niebuhr, R. (1944) *Children of Light and the Children of Darkness*, New Jersey: Prentice Hall
2 Ipsos Mori (2010) *What do People Want, Need and Expect from Public Services*, London: 2020 Public Services Trust at the RSA
3 Halpern, D. (2010) *The Hidden Wealth of Societies*, London: Polity Press
4 Le Grand, J. (2003) *Motivation, Agency and Public Policy: Of knights, knaves, pawns and queens*, Oxford: Oxford University Press
5 Barber, M. (2007) *Instruction to Deliver*, London: Politico's
6 Propper, C. et al. (2008) 'Did "targets and terror" reduce waiting times in England for hospital care?', *The BE Journal of Economic Analysis and Policy*, 8(2), Article 5
7 Le Grand, J. (2007) *The Other Invisible Hand: Delivering public services through choice and competition*, Oxford: Princeton University Press
8 HM Government (2010) *Decentralisation and Localism Bill: An essential guide*, London: TSO
9 Thaler, R. and Sunstein, C. (2008) *Nudge: Improving decisions about health, wealth, and happiness*, New Haven: Yale University Press
10 Among the 'think tanks' who have drawn upon behavioural economics and other related disciplines are Dawnay, E. and Shah, H. (2005) *Behavioural Economics: Seven principles for policy makers*, London: New Economics Foundation, available at www.nef.org.uk ; Prendergrast, J. et al. (2008) *Creatures of Habit? The art of behavioural change*, London: Social Market Foundation, available at www.smf.co.uk ; *The Capital Ambition guide to behaviour change*, London: Young Foundation and the Office for Public Management (2010), available at www.youngfoundation.org.uk ; Dolan, P. et al. (2010) *Mindspace: Influencing behaviour through public policy*, London: Institute for Government

11   Brynjolfson, E. and Saunders, A. (2009) *Wired for Innovation: How information technology is reshaping the economy*, Cambridge, MA: MIT Press

12   Utterbuck, J. (1994) *Mastering the Dynamics of Innovation*, Boston, MA: HBS Press

13   Christensen, C. (1997) *The Innovator's Dilemma*, New York: Harper Business

14   Syrett, M. and Lammiman, J. (2002) *Successful Innovation*, London: Profile Books

15   Von Hippel, E. (2003) *Democratizing Innovation*, Cambridge, MA: MIT Press

16   Johnson, S. (2010) *Where Good Ideas Come From: The natural history of innovation*, London: Riverhead Books

17   Bourgon, J. (2009) *The Government of Canada's Experience Eliminating the Deficit 1994-9: A Canadian case study*, London: Institute for Government

18   Parker, S. et al. (2010) *Shaping Up: A Whitehall for the future*, London: Institute for Government

19   Gardner, M. (1974) *The Annotated Snark*, London: Penguin

20   Medawar, P. (1982) *Pluto's Republic*, Oxford: Oxford University Press, p. 339

21   MacAfee, N. (ed.) (2004) *The Gospel According to RFK*, Boulder, CO: Westview, p. 41

22   Milner, H. (2002) *Civic Literacy: How informed citizens make democracy work*, Hanover, NH: University Press of New England

23   US President Bill Clinton used regularly to say that the purpose of democratic government was 'to extend the reach of freedom, widen the circle of opportunity; and strengthen the bonds of community.' The elegant simplicity of his rhetoric is seductive but, following Nussbaum and Sen (1993), a 'capabilities' approach may be more useful than one based on 'opportunities'; and as Sen (2006) separately argues, the bonds of community can sometimes be too strong – enabling communities to live peacefully together despite their fundamental differences may be a more important goal of government. Nussbaum, M. and Sen, A. (1993) *The Quality of Life*, Oxford: Oxford University Press; Sen, A. (2006) *Identity and Violence: The illusion of destiny*, London: Allen Lane

Bibliography

Ackerlof, G. and Shiller, R. (2009) *Animal Spirits*, Princeton: Princeton University Press.

Ackroyd, P. (2008) *Thames: Sacred River*, London: Vintage.

Aldred, J. (2009) *The Skeptical Economist*, London: Earthscan.

Arrow, K. (1974) *The Limits of Organization*, New York: WW Norton & Co.

Ashby, W.R. (1956) *Introduction to Cybernetics*, London: Chapman & Hall.

Audit Commission (2009) *Financial Management in a Glacial Age*, www.audit.commission.gov.uk.

Augar, P. (2009) *Chasing Alpha*, London: Bodley Head.

Axelrod, R. (1984) *The Evolution of Cooperation*, New York: Basic Books.

Bachrach, P. and Baratz, M. (1962) 'Two Faces of Power', *The American Political Science Review*, 56(4): 947–52.

Bacon, N. et al. (2010) *The State of Happiness*, London: Young Foundation.

Bandura, A. (1997) *Self-Efficacy*, New York: WW Freeman & Co.

Barber, M. (20097) *Instruction to Deliver*, London: Politico's.

Barrow, J. (1992) *Theories of Everything*, London: Vintage.

Barsh, J. et al. (2008) *Centred Leaders: How Talented Women Thrive*, available at www.mckinsey.com.

Bauman, Z. (2001) *Community*, Oxford: Blackwell.

Beck, U. (1992) *The Risk Society: Towards a New Modernity*, London: Sage.

Beckhard, R. and Pritchard, W. (1992) *Changing the Essence*, San Francisco: Jossey-Bass.

Besley, T. (2006) *Principled Agents?* Oxford: Oxford UP.

Besley, T. and Coate, S. (2003) 'Centralized Versus Decentralized Provision of Local Public Goods: A Political Economy Approach', *Journal of Public Economics*, 87: 2611–37.

Besley, T. and Hennessy, P. (2009) *Open Letter to HM Queen*, 22 July, British Academy.

Best, J. (2008) *Social Problems*, New York: WW Norton & Co.

Blackburn, R. (1998) *Ruling Passions*, Oxford: Clarendon.

Blackburn, S. (2006) *Truth*, London: Penguin.

Blanchard, O. and Milesi-Ferretti, M. (2009) *Global Imbalances: In Midstream?* IMF Staff Position Note, December 22, International Monetary Fund.

Blommestein, H. et al. (2010) 'Debt Markets: Policy Challenges in the Post-crisis Landscape', *OECD Journal Financial Markets*, 1: 1–27.

Blond, P. (2010) *The Ownership State*, London: Nesta.

Bobbit, P. (2002) *The Shield of Achilles*, New York: Knopf.

Boehm, C. (2001) *Hierarchy in the Forest: The Evolution of Egalitarian Behavior*, Cambridge, MA: Harvard University Press.

Bossidy, L. and Charan, R. (2002) *Execution: The Discipline of Getting Things Done*, London: Random House.

Bourgon, J. (2009) *The Government of Canada's Experience Eliminating the Deficit 1994–9: A Canadian Case Study*, London: Institute for Government.

Brückner, M. and Tuladhar, A. (2010) *Public Spending as a Fiscal Stimulus: Evidence from Japan's regional spending during the 1990s*, IMF Working Paper 10,110, IMF.org.

Brynjolfsson, E. and Saunders, A. (2009) *Wired: How Information Technology is Reshaping the Economy*, Cambridge, MA: MIT Press.

Bryson, J. and Crosby, B. (1992) *Leadership for the Common Good*, San Francisco: Jossey-Bass.

Buchanan, J. and Tullock, G. (1962) *The Calculus of Consent*, Michigan: Ann Arbor.

Buonfino, A. and Mulgan, G. (2009) *Civility Lost and Found*, London: Young Foundation.

Burke, E. (1790) *Reflections on the Revolution in France*, Boston, MA: The Harvard Classics.

Christakis, N. and Fowler, J. (2010) *Connected*, London: Harper Press.

Christensen, C. (1997) *The Innovator's Dilemma*, New York: Harper Business.

Cicero (1993) *On Government*, London: Penguin Classics.

CIPFA (2009) *Public Library Statistics: 2008–9 Estimates and 2007–8 Actuals*, London: CIPFA.

Clausewitz, C. (1997) *On War*, Ware, Hertfordshire: Wordsworth Editions Ltd.

Cleveland, H. (1972) *The Future Executive*, New York: Harper & Row.

Cole, M. and Parston, G. (2006) *Unlocking Public Value*, Hoboken, NJ: John Wiley & Sons.

Collins, J. (2001) *Good to Great*, New York: Harper Collins.

Collins, J. (2005) *Good to Great and the Social Sectors*, Boulder, CO: Jim Collins.

Collins, J. (2009) *How the Mighty Fall*, New York: Random House.

Comte-Sponville, A. (2002) *A Short Treatise on the Great Virtues*, London: Vintage.

Damasio, A. (2000) *The Feeling of What Happens*, London: Vintage.

Dawnay, E. and Shah, H. (2005) *Behavioural Economics: Seven Principles for Policy Makers*, London: New Economics Foundation, available at www.nef. org.uk.

De Blij, H. (2009) *The Power of Place*, Oxford: Oxford University Press.

Deming, W.E. (2000) *The New Economics for Industry, Government, Education* (2nd edn) Boston: MIT Press.

Design Council (2009) *The Role of Design in Public Services*, http://www. designcouncil.org.uk.

Dive, B. (2008) *The Accountable Leader*, London: Kogan Page.

Dobbs, R. et al. (2011) *Urban World: Mapping the Power of Cities*, McKinsey Global Institute, available at www.mckinsey.com.

Dolan, P. et al. (2010) *Mindspace: Influencing Behaviour Through Public Policy*, London: Institute for Government.

Dorling, D. (2010) *Injustice: Why Social Inequalities Persist*, Bristol: Policy Press.

Drucker, P. (1954) *The Practice of Management*, New York: Harper Business.

Duffy, B. and Chan, D. (2009) *People, Perceptions and Place*, London: Ipsos-Mori.

Duffy, B. et al. (2010) *One World, Many Places: Citizens' Views of Municipal Government and Local Areas Across the World*, London: Ipsos-Mori.

Dugatkin, L. (2006) *The Altruism Equation*, Princeton: Princeton University Press.

Duggan, W. (2007) *Strategic Intuition*, New York: Columbia Business School.

Dunbar, R. (1996) *Grooming, Gossip and the Evolution of Language*, London: Faber & Faber.

Dunbar, R. (2010) 'The Magic Number', *RSA Journal*, Spring, pp. 16–19.

Dunleavy, P. (2010) *The Future of Joined-up Public Services*, London: 2020 Public Services Trust.

Dunn, J. (2005) *Setting The People Free*, London: Atlantic,

Ellis, J. (1998) *American Sphinx*, New York: Vintage.

Ellis, J. (2000) *Founding Brothers*, New York: Random House.

Finkelstein, S., Whitehead, J. and Campbell, A. (2008) *Think Again: How Good Leaders Make Bad Decisions and How to Keep It From Happening to You*, Boston MA: Harvard Business Press.

Florida, R. (2002) *The Rise of the Creative Class*, New York: Basic Books.

Florida, R. (2007) *Who's Your City*, New York: Basic Books.

Flynn, N. (2007) *Public Sector Management* (5th edn) London: Sage.

Fox, J. and Zawitz, M. (2010) *Homicide Trends in the United States*, Washington, DC: US Dept of Justice, Bureau of Justice Statistics.

Frederickson, G. (2005) 'Whatever Happened to Public Administration?,' in E. Ferlie et al. *Oxford Handbook of Public Management*, Oxford: Oxford University Press.

Frederickson, H.G. (2005) *The Adaptive City*, Armonk, New York: M E Sharpe.

Friedman, T. (2000) *The Lexus and the Olive Tree*, New York: Anchor Books.

Fukuyama, F. (1992) *The End of History and the Last Man*, New York: Avon Books.

Fukuyama, F. (2004) *State Building: Governance and World Order in the 21st Century*, New York: Cornell University.

Gardner, H. (2007) *Five Minds for the Future*, Boston, MA: Harvard Business Press.

Gardner, H. (2009) *Risk: The Science and Politics of Fear*, London: Virgin Books.

Gardner, M. (1974) *The Annotated Snark*, London: Penguin.

Garfinkel, I. et al. (2010) *Wealth and Welfare States: Is America a Laggard or a Leader?* Oxford: Oxford University Press.

Gershon, P. (2004) *Releasing Resources to the Front Line*, HM Treasury, London: TSO.

Gerstein, M. and Ellsberg, M. (2008) *Flirting with Disaster: Why Accidents are Rarely Accidental*, New York: Union Square.

Ghoshal, S. and Moran, P. (2005) 'Towards a Good Theory of Management', in J. Birkinshaw and G. Piramal (eds) *Sumantra Ghoshal on Management*, Harlow: Pearson.

Gigerenzer, G. (2002) *Reckoning with Risk*, London: Penguin.

Giuliani, R. (2002) *Leadership*, London: Time Warner.

Glaeser, E. (2011) *The Triumph of the City*, London: Penguin.

Glaeser, E. et al. (2001) 'Consumer City', *Journal of Economic Geography*, 1: 27–50.

Gneezy, U. et al. (2004) 'The Inefficiency of Splitting the Bill', *Economic Journal*, 114(495): 265–80.

Goldsmith, S. (2010) *The Power of Social Innovation*, San Francisco: Jossey-Bass.

Goleman, D. (1995) *Emotional Intelligence*, New York: Random House.

Goodin, R. et al. (2008) 'The Public and its Policies', in M. Moran et al., *The Oxford Handbook of Public Policy*, Oxford: Oxford University Press.

Granovetter, M. (1983) 'The Strength of Weak Ties: A Network Theory Revisited', *Sociological Theory*, 1: 201–30.

Gray, J. (2002) *Straw Dogs*, London: Grant Books.

Green, P. (2010) *Efficiency Review*, HM Treasury, London: TSO.

Grint, K. (2005) *Leadership: Limits and Possibilities*, London: Palgrave Macmillan.

Habermas, J. (1984) *The Theory of Communicative Action*. Vol I: *Reason and the Rationalization of Society*, T. McCarthy (trans.) Boston: Beacon.

Hale, S.J. (1996) 'Achieving High Performance in Public Organizations', in J. Perry (ed.) *Handbook of Public Administration* (2nd edn) San Francisco: Jossey-Bass.

Halpern, D. (2010) *The Hidden Wealth of Societies*, London: Polity Press.

Hamilton, A. (2008) *The Revolutionary Writings of Alexander Hamilton*, Indianapolis: Liberty Fund.

Handy, C. (1976) *Understanding Organisations*, Harmondsworth: Penguin.

Hardin, G. (1968) 'The Tragedy of the Commons', *Science*, 162: 1234–8.

Harman, O. (2010) *The Price of Altruism*, London: Bodley Head.

Harvey, D. (2010) *The Enigma of Capital*, London: Profile Books.

Hauser, M. (2006) *Moral Minds*, London: Abacus.

Hayward, B. et al. (2008) *Survey of Public Attitudes Towards Conduct in Public Life*, published by the Committee on Standards in Public Life, UK House of Commons.

Heifetz, R. and Linsky, M. (2002) *Leadership on the Line*, Boston, MA: Harvard Business School Press.

Hennessey, P. (1988) *Whitehall*, London: Secker & Warburg.

Hibbing, J. and Theiss-Morse, E. (2002) *Stealth Democracy*, Cambridge: Cambridge University Press.

Hind, D. (2010) *The Return of the Public*, London: Verso.

HM Government (2009) *Pursue, Prevent, Protect, Prepare: The UK Strategy for Countering International Terrorism*, London: TSO.

HM Government (2010) *Decentralisation and Localism Bill: An Essential Guide*, London: TSO.

Hodge, G. (2000) *Privatization: An International Review of Performance*, Boulder, CO: Westview.

Home Office (2010) *Police Service Strength*, HO Statistical Bulletin, 28 January, London.

Honey, P. and Mumford, A. (1996) *Learning Styles Questionnaire*, www. peter-honey.com.

Hood, C. (1998) *The Art of the State*, Oxford: Oxford University Press.

Hood, C. (2010) *Reflections on Public Service Reform in a Cold Fiscal Climate*, London: 2020 Public Services Trust.

Hood, C., Rothstein, H. and Baldwin, R. (2004) *The Government of Risk: Understanding Risk Regulation Regimes*, Oxford: Oxford University Press.

Hudson-Smith, A. et al. (2008) *Mapping for the Masses: Accessing web2.0 through Crowdsourcing*, Working Paper Series 143, Centre for Advanced Spatial Analysis, London: UCL.

Huntington, S. (1997) *The Clash of Civilisations and the Remaking of the World Order*, London: Simon & Schuster.

Hutton, W. (2010) *Fair Pay in the Public Sector*, Interim Report, HM Treasury, London: TSO.

Ibsen, H. (1882) *Enemy of the People*, www.bibliobazaar/opensource.

IMF (2010) *World Economic Outlook: Rebalancing Growth*, April 2010, International Monetary Fund.

Ingelhart, R. et al. (2008) 'Development, Freedom, and Rising Happiness', *Perspectives on Psychological Science*, 3(4): 264–85.

Institute for Fiscal Studies (2010) Special report on public spending, November 2010, available on www.solace.org.uk

Ipsos Mori (2010) *What Do People Want, Need and Expect from Public Services?* London: 2020 Public Services Trust at the RSA.

Isaacs, W. (1999) *Dialogue and the Art of Thinking Together*, New York: Currency.

Jacobs, J. (1969) *The Economy of Cities*, New York: Random House.

Johansson, F. (2006) *The Medici Effect*, Boston: Harvard Business Press.

Johnson, S. (2010) *Where Good Ideas Come From: The natural history of innovation*, London: Riverhead Books.

Jomini, A. (1836) *The Art of War*, special edition, G. Mendell and W. Craighill (trans) (2005) El Paso, Texas: El Paso Norte Press.

Kagan, J. (2010) *The Three Cultures*, Cambridge: Cambridge University Press.

Kahneman, D. and Tervsky, A. (1979) 'Prospect Theory: An Analysis of Decision Under Risk', *Econometrica*, 47: 263–91.

Kahneman, D., Slovic, P. and Tversky, A. (eds) (1982) *Judgment Under Uncertainty: Heuristics and Biases*, New York: Cambridge University Press.

Kaletsky, A. (2010) *Capitalism 4.0*, London: Bloomsbury.

Kanter, R.M. (2004) *Confidence*, London: Random House.

Kelly, G. et al. (2002) *Creating Public Value*, Cabinet Office Strategy Unit: UK Government.

Kelman, S. et al. (2009) *Successfully Executing Ambitious Strategies in Government: An Empirical Enalysis;* Faculty Research Working Paper 09-009, Harvard Kennedy School.

King, I. (2008) *How to Make Good Decisions and Be Right All the Time*, London: Continuum.

Kolb, D. (1984) *Experiential Learning: Experience as the Source of Learning and Development*, Englewood Cliffs, NJ: Prentice Hall.

Koo, R. (2009) *The Age of Balance Sheet Recessions*, Tokyo: Nomura Research Institute.

Kouzes, J. and Posner, B. (1993) *Credibility*, San Francisco: Jossey-Bass.

Kouzes, J. and Posner, B. (1995) *The Leadership Challenge*, San Francisco: Jossey-Bass.

Kouzes, J. and Posner, B. (1999) *Encouraging The Heart*, San Francisco: Jossey-Bass.

Krugman, P. (2008) *The Return of Depression Economics and the Crisis of 2008*, London: Penguin.

Lawrence, P. and Nohria, N. (2002) *Driven: How Human Nature Shapes Our Choices*, San Francisco: Jossey-Bass.

Layard, R. (2005) *Happiness*, London: Allen Lane.

Leadbeater, C. (2008) *We-Think*, London: Profile Books.

Le Grand, J. (2003) *Motivation, Agency and Public Policy: Of Knights, Knaves, Pawns and Queens,* Oxford: Oxford University Press.

Le Grand, J. (2007) *The Other Invisible Hand: Delivering Public Services Through Choice and Competition,* Oxford: Princeton University Press.

Lehrer, J. (2009) *The Decisive Moment*, Edinburgh: Canongate.

Lijphart, A. (1977) *Democracy in Plural Societies: A Comparative Exploration*, New Haven: Yale University Press.

Lijphart, A. (1994) *Electoral Systems and Party Systems*, Oxford: Oxford University Press.

Lloyd, J. (2004) *What the Media are Doing to Our Politics*, London: Constable and Robinson.

Lysons, K. and Farrington, B. (2005) *Purchasing and Supply Chain Management* (7th edn) London: FT Pearson.

MacAfee, N. (ed.) (2004) *The Gospel According to RFK*, Boulder, CO: Westview.

James Madison (1788) *Federalist No. 51.*

Mandelbrot, B. and Hudson, R. (2008) *The (mis)Behaviour of Markets*, London: Profile Books.

McCrae, J. et al. (2009) *Undertaking a Fiscal Consolidation*, London: Institute for Government.

Medawar, P. (1967) *The Art of The Soluble*, London: Methuen.

Medawar, P. (1982) *Pluto's Republic*, Oxford: Oxford University Press.

Miller, P. (1994) *Defining the Common Good*, Cambridge: Cambridge University Press.

Milner, H. (2002) *Civic Literacy: How Informed Citizens Make Democracy Work*, Hanover: University Press of New England.

Mintzberg, H. (1994) *The Rise and Fall of Strategic Planning*, New York: Free Press.

Mintzberg, H. (2009) *Managing*, Harlow: Pearson.

Möisi, D. (2008) *The Geopolitics of Emotion*, New York: Doubleday.

Moore, M. (1995) *Creating Public Value*, Cambridge, MA: Harvard University Press.

Moots, G. and Forster, G. (2010) '*Salus Populi Suprema Lex Esto*: John Locke versus Contemporary Democratic Theory', *Perspectives on Political Science*, Jan–Mar, 39(1): 35–45.

Morozov, E. (2010) *The Net Delusion*, London: Allen Lane.

Mulgan, G. (2006) *Good and Bad Power*, London: Penguin/Allen Lane.

Mulgan, G. (2009) *The Art of Public Strategy*, Oxford: Oxford University Press.

National Audit Office (2000) *Supporting Innovation: Managing Risk in Government Departments*, London: TSO.

National Audit Office (2009) *Maintaining Financial Stability Across the United Kingdom's Banking System*, London: TSO.

New Economics Foundation (2009) *National Accounts of Well-being*, available at www.nationalaccountsofwellbeing.org.

Niebuhr, R. (1944) *Children of Light and the Children of Darkness*, New Jersey: Prentice Hall.

Norris, P. (2002) *Democratic Phoenix: Reinventing Political Activism*, Cambridge: Cambridge University Press.

Nussbaum, M. and Sen, A. (1993) *The Quality of Life*, Oxford: Oxford University Press.

Nye, J. (2004) *Soft Power*, New York: Public Affairs.

Oguz, S. and Knight, J. (2010) 'Regional Economic Indicators', *Economic & Labour Market Review*, 4(2): 31–50, available at www.statistics.gov.uk.

Olson, M. (1965) *The Logic of Collective Action*, Cambridge, MA: Harvard University Press.

Osborne, D. and Gaebler, T. (1993) *Reinventing Government*, New York: Plume.

Osborne, D. and Hutchinson, P. (2004) *The Price of Government*, New York: Basic Books.

Ostrom, E. (1990) *Governing the Commons*, New York: Cambridge University Press.

Parker, S. et al. (2010) *Shaping Up: A Whitehall for the Future*, London: Institute for Government.

Pearce, T. (2003) *Leading Out Loud: Inspiring Change Through Authentic Communication*, San Francisco: Jossey-Bass.

Pharr, S. and Putnam, R. (2000) *Disaffected Democracies*, Princeton: Princeton University Press.

Phillips, A. and Taylor, B. (2010) *On Kindness*, London: Penguin.

Piatelli-Palmarini, M. (1994) *Inevitable Illusions: How Mistakes of Reason Rule Our Minds*, New York: John Wiley & Sons.

Pimlott, B. and Rao, N. (2002) *Governing London:* Oxford: Oxford University Press.

Platt, J. (1973) 'Social Traps', *American Psychologist*, 28: 641–51.

Plunkett-Powell, K. (1999) *Remembering Woolworths: A Nostalgic History of the World's Most Famous Five-and-dime*, New York: St Martins Press.

Popper, K. (2003) *The Open Society and its Enemies: Vol I, Plato*, London: Routledge.

Popper, K. (1945) *The Open Society and its Enemies Vol II*, London: Routledge & Kegan Paul.

Popper, K. (1999) *All Life is Problem Solving*, London: Routledge.

Porter, M. (1980) *Competitive Strategy*, New York: Free Press.

Portes, A. (2000) 'The Two Meanings of Social Capital', *Sociological Forum*, 15: 1–12.

Powell, J. (2010) *The New Machiavelli*, London: Bodley Head.

Prendergrast, J. et al. (2008) *Creatures of Habit? The Art of Behavioural Change*, London: Social Market Foundation, available at www.smf.co.uk.

Prior, M. (2007) *Post-Broadcast Democracy*, Cambridge: Cambridge University Press.

Propper, C. et al. (2008) 'Did "Targets and Terror" Reduce Waiting Times in England for Hospital Care?', *The BE Journal of Economic Analysis and Policy*, 8(2), Article 5.

Purdy, J. (2000) *For Common Things*, New York: Vintage.

Putnam, R. (1993) *Making Democracy Work: Civic Traditions in Modern Italy*, Princeton: Princeton UP.

Putnam, R. (2002) *Democracy in Flux: Social Capital in Contemporary Societies*, Princeton: Princeton UP.

Quirk, B. (2003) 'Local Government: The Adaptive Tier of Governance', in T. Bentley and J. Wilsdon (eds) *The Adaptive State*, London: Demos.

Quirk, B. (2005a) 'Localising Efficiency – More Than Just Saving Money', *Local Government Studies,* 31(5): 615–25 November.

Quirk, B. (2005b) 'The Welfare of the People Above All', in *What is Public Management For?*, London: Public Policy & Management Association.

Quirk, B. (2006) 'The Three 'Rs': Respect, Reason and Rights', London: Solace Foundation Imprint, *Complexity and Cohesion*, December, pp. 21–34.

Quirk, B. (2007a) *Making Assets Work*, Dept for Communities and Local Government, London: TSO.

Quirk, B. (2007b) 'Roots of Cooperation and Routes to Collaboration', in S. Parker and N. Gallagher (eds), *Our Collaborative Future*, London: Demos pp. 48–60.

Quirk, B. (2008) *The Art of Advice Giving*, London: Solace at www.solace.org. uk.

Rainey, H. (2009) *Understanding and Managing Public Organizations*, San Francisco: Jossey-Bass.

Ramachandran, V.S. (2003) *The Emerging Mind*, London: Profile Books.

Rawls, J. (2000) *The Law of Peoples with The Idea of Public Reason Revisited*, Cambridge, MA: Harvard University Press.

Rawnsley, A. (2010) *The End of The Party*, London: Penguin.

Reason, J. (2000) 'Human Error: Models and Management', *BMJ Digest*, 172: 393–6, June.

Reeves, R. (2009) *John Stuart Mill: Victorian Firebran*d, London: Atlantic Books.

Reinhart, C. and Rogoff, K. (2008) *The Aftermath of Financial Crises*, available at www.economics.harvard.edu/files/faculty/51_Aftermath.pdf

Reinhart, C. and Rogoff, K. (2009) *This Time is Different*, Princeton: Princeton UP.

Rentfrow, P., Gosling, S. and Potter, J. (2008) 'A Theory of the Emergence, Persistence, and Expression of Geographic Variation in Personality Traits', *Perspectives on Psychological Science*, 3: 339–69.

Reschler, N. (1992) *Pluralism: Against the Demands for Consensus*, Oxford: Clarendon Press.

Ridley, M. (2002) *The Origins of Virtue,* London: Penguin.

Riesman, D., Glazer, N. and Denney, R. (1950) *The Lonely Crowd*, New Haven: Yale University Press.

Rittel, H. and Webber, M. (1973) 'Dilemmas in a General Theory of Planning', *Policy Sciences*, 4: 155–69, Elsevier Scientific Publishing Company, Amsterdam.

Rix, A. et al. (2009) *Improving Public Confidence in the Police: A Review of Available Evidence*, Research Report 28 (2nd edn) London: Home Office.

Rothstein, B. (2005) *Social Traps and the Problem of Trust*, Cambridge: Cambridge University Press.

Runciman, D. (2008) *Political Hypocrisy*, Woodstock, Oxfordshire: Princeton University Press.

Sacks, J. (2007) *The Home We Build Together*, London: Continuum.

Sagan, C. (1995) *The Demon-Haunted World*, London: Headline.

Samuels, D. and Shugart, M. (2010) *Presidents, Prime Ministers and Parties*, Cambridge: Cambridge University Press.

Sandel, M. (2009) *Justice*, London: Allen Lane.

Schama, S. (1995) *Landscape and Memory*, London: HarperCollins.

Schelling, T. (1978) *Micromotives and Macrobehavior*, New York: WW Norton & Co.

Schofield, P. (2006) *Utility & Democracy: The Political Thought of Jeremy Bentham*, Oxford: Oxford University Press.

Schwartz, B. (2004) *The Paradox of Choice*, New York: HarperCollins.

Seabright, P. (2004) *The Company of Strangers: A Natural History of Economic Life*, Princeton, NJ: Princeton University Press.

Seddon, J. (2008) *Systems Thinking in the Public Sector*, Axminster: Triarchy Press.

Seddon, J. (2010) *Delivering Public Services that Work*, Axminster: Triarchy Press.

Seligman, M. (1990) *Learned Optimism*, New York: Knopf.

Sen, A. (2002) *Rationality and Freedom*, London: Belknapp/Harvard.

Sen, A. (2006) *Identity and Violence: The Illusion of Destiny*, London: Allen Lane.

Sen, A. (2009) *The Idea of Justice*, London: Allen Lane.

Senge, P. et al. (1999) *The Dance of Change*, New York, Currency Doubleday

Senge, P. et al. (2005) *Presence: An Exploration of Profound Change in People, Organisations and Sciety*, London: Nicholas Brearly.

Sennett, R. (2003) *Respect*, London: Allen Lane.

Sheshol, J. (1997) *Mutual Contempt*, New York: WW Norton.

Simon, H. (1957) 'A Behavioral Model of Rational Choice', in his *Models of Man, Social and Rational*, New York: Wiley.

Skinner, Q. (2008) *Hobbes and Republican Liberty*, Cambridge: Cambridge University Press.

Smith, A. (2009) *The Theory of Moral Sentiments*, London: Penguin.

Sober, E. and Wilson, D. (1999) *Unto Others: The Evolution and Psychology of Unselfish Behavior*, Cambridge, MA: Harvard University Press.

Soroka, S. and Wlezian, C. (2010) *Degrees of Democracy*, Cambridge: Cambridge University Press.

Sparrow, M.K. (2008) *The Character of Harms: Operational Challenges in Control,* Cambridge: Cambridge University Press.

Stengel, R. (2010) 'Only Connect', *Time*, 27 December.

Stoker, G. (2006) *Politics Matters*, Basingstoke: Palgrave Macmillan.

Storper, M. and Scott, A. (2009) 'Rethinking human capital, creativity and urban growth', *Journal of Economic Geography*, 9: 147–67

Svara, J. and Associates (1994) *Facilitative Leadership in Local Government: Lessons from Successful Mayors and Chairpersons*, San Francisco: Jossey-Bass.

Syrett, M. and Lammiman, J. (2002) *Successful Innovation*, London: Profile Books.

Taleb, N.N. (2007) *Black Swan: The Impact of the Highly Improbable*, London: Allen Lane.

Taylor, M. (2009) 'Reflections on the Crunch', *Prospect,* 23 July, issue 161.

Teague, B. et al. (2010) *Final Report 2009 Victorian Bushfires Royal Commission*, Victoria, July.

Thaler, R. and Sunstein, C. (2008) *Nudge: Improving Decisions about Health, Wealth and Happiness*, Boston: Yale University Press.

Thomas, K. (2000) *Intrinsic Motivation at Work*, San Francisco: Berrett-Koehler.

Tomasselo, M. (2009) *Why We Cooperate*, Boston: Massachusetts Institute of Technology.

Trivers, R. (1985) *Social Evolution*, Menlow Park, CA: Benjamin/Cummings.

Trivers, R. (2002) *Natural Selection and Social Theory*, Oxford: Oxford University Press.

United Nations (2008) *World Population Prospects*, The 2008 revision medium forecast.

Utterbuck, J. (1994) *Mastering the Dynamics of Innovation*, Boston, MA: HBS Press.

Von Hippel, E. (2003) *Democratizing Innovation*, Cambridge, MA: MIT Press.

Weber, M. (1922) *Economy and Society*, Berkeley: University of California Press.

Westen, D. (2007) *The Political Brain*, New York: Public Affairs.

White, J. (2007) *London in the Nineteenth Century*, London: Jonathon Cape.

Wilson, J.Q. (1993) *The Moral Sense*, New York: Free Press.

Womack, J. and Jones, D. (2003) *Lean Thinking*, London: Simon & Schuster.

Womack, J. et al. (2007) *The Machine that Changed the World*, London: Simon & Schuster.

Woodward, B. (2010) *The Obama Wars*, New York: Simon & Schuster.

Work Foundation (2006) *Deliberative Democracy and the Role of Public Managers*, London: Work Foundation.

World Bank (2010) *Poverty Reduction and Equity*, worldbank.org.

Yates, D. (1977) The *Ungovernable City: The Politics of Urban Problems and Policy-making*, Cambridge, MA: MIT Press.

Young Foundation and Office for Public Management (2010) *The Capital Ambition Guide to Behaviour Change*, London: available at www.youngfoundation.org.uk.

Zajonc, D. (2004) *The Politics of Hope*, Austin: Synergy Books.

Zakaria, F. (2007) *The Future of Freedom*, New York: WW Norton & Co.

Zimmer, R. et al. (2010) *Report of the New Jersey Privatisation Task Force*, State of New Jersey.

Zohar, D. and Marshall, I. (2004) *Spiritual Capital*, San Francisco: Berrett-Koehler.

Zurn, M. and Leibfried, S. (2005) 'Reconfiguring the National Constellation', in S. Leibfried and M. Zurn, *Transformations of the State*, Cambridge: Cambridge UP.

Index